MW00779419

Pablo Abeita

The Young Pablo Abeita, 1903, DeLancey W. Gill, photographer. Courtesy of the National Anthropological Archives, Smithsonian Institution, Negative no. BAE GN 01994A 06337800

PABLO ABEITA

The Life and Times of a Native
Statesman of Isleta Pueblo, 1871–1940

MALCOLM EBRIGHT

AND

RICK HENDRICKS

UNIVERSITY OF NEW MEXICO PRESS

ALBUQUERQUE

Library of Congress Cataloging-in-Publication Data
Names: Ebright, Malcolm, author. | Hendricks, Rick, 1956- author.
Title: Pablo Abeita : the life and times of a native statesman of Isleta Pueblo,
1871-1940 / Malcolm Ebright and Rick Hendricks.
Description: Albuquerque: University of New Mexico Press, 2023. | Includes
bibliographical references and index.
Identifiers: LCCN 2022037854 (print) | LCCN 2022037855 (e-book) |
ISBN 9780826364876 (cloth) | ISBN 9780826364883 (e-book)
Subjects: LCSH: Abeita, Pablo, 1871-1940. | Statesmen—New Mexico—
Isleta Pueblo—Biography. | Isleta Pueblo (N.M.)—History—20th
century—Biography.
Classification: LCC E99.I8 E37 2023 (print) | LCC E99.I8 (e-book) | DDC
970.00497497—dc23/eng/20220823
LC record available at https://lccn.loc.gov/2022037854
LC e-book record available at https://lccn.loc.gov/2022037855

Founded in 1889, the University of New Mexico sits on the traditional homelands of the Pueblo of Sandia. The original peoples of New Mexico—Pueblo,
Navajo, and Apache—since time immemorial have deep connections to the land
and have made significant contributions to the broader community statewide.
We honor the land itself and those who remain stewards of this land throughout
the generations and also acknowledge our committed relationship to Indigenous
peoples. We gratefully recognize our history.

Cover image adapted from *The Young Pablo Abeita, 1903,* DeLancey W. Gill,
photographer. Courtesy of the National Anthropological Archives, Smithsonian
Institution, Negative no. BAE GN 01994A 06337800
Designed by Isaac Morris
Composed in Copperplate, Corundum, and Toppan

Dedicated to Randy Jiron, former Isletan lieutenant governor and war captain, and to his cousin Frank Jiron. Their help has been invaluable.

CONTENTS

Acknowledgments

This book began on the day in the fall of 2017 that Randy Jiron, former lieutenant governor and war captain of Isleta Pueblo, and his cousin, Frank Jiron, invited us to search for documents at Pablo Abeita's old residence in the ruins of the Abeita family compound. After many years, during which no one had entered the rooms, Frank Jiron, an indirect descendant of Pablo's, started to gather up various papers he found scattered about. Now we, Malcolm Ebright and Rick Hendricks, were visiting the almost untouched room to search for more documents. What we found was a historian's fondest dream, a trove of Pablo Abeita's correspondence that covered the two-decade period starting around 1900. These papers comprise the Frank Jiron Collection of Pablo Abeita's Papers. Both Randy and Frank gave us unlimited access to these papers and encouraged our project to write the story of Pablo Abeita's life. We are deeply grateful and indebted to Randy and Frank Jiron for this opportunity.

The leadership of Isleta Pueblo has also supported this project from the beginning. We are grateful to former governor, Max Zuni, current governor, Vernon Abeita, and current lieutenant governors, Virgil Lucero and Blaine Sanchez.

Randy Jiron has been a continual source of Isletan knowledge and lore. He read the entire manuscript and suggested many important changes. He welcomed us into his home on numerous occasions and facilitated our interviews of many Isletans, including James Abeita, William Abeita, Mary Abeita, Valentino Jaramillo, Ernest Jaramillo, Norman Jojola, former Isleta governor Verna Teller, Richard "Dikki" Garcia, and former Laguna governor Richard Luarkie. We wish to express our heartfelt gratitude to them all.

Isletan genealogist Richard "Dikki" Garcia deserves special thanks for his unstinting help with matters of Isleta history and genealogy. Leonard Abeita, a direct descendant of Pablo Abeita, gave us access to another treasure: the leather trunk Pablo used to store his most precious keepsakes. Besides many more documents and photographs, the trunk contained the rifle said to have been given to Pablo by President Theodore Roosevelt. We offer our sincere thanks to Leonard Abeita for sharing the contents of Pablo Abeita's trunk with us.

We also received expert help beyond the call of duty at the New Mexico State Library from Laura Calderone and Amy Schaefer, as well as from Matthew Benbennick, Katie Montoya, Nico Montoya, and James Phelps. Thanks also to Alison Colburne, Laboratory of Anthropology librarian. The following photo archivists have searched out and provided the photographs that appear in the book: Hannah Abelbeck and Catie Carl, Palace of the Governors Photo Archives; Jillian R. Hartke, digital archivist, Albuquerque Museum; Cassandra Smith, archivist, Pueblo of Isleta; Liza Posas, head of research and archives; Marilyn Van Winkle, rights and reproduction coordinator, Autry Museum of the American West; Daisy Njoku, archivist, National Anthropological Archives, Smithsonian Institution; Nathan Sowry, reference archivist, National Museum of the American Indian, Smithsonian Institution; Cindy Morris, pictorial archivist, Center for Southwest Research, University of New Mexico Libraries; and Richard Tritt, photo curator, Cumberland County Historical Society. Thanks also to Jonna Paden, archivist and librarian, and Patricia Maez, librarian, Indian Pueblo Cultural Center.

Special thanks go to Henry Walt, historic preservation officer for Isleta Pueblo. State Records Center and Archives director Felicia Lujan, Bureau Chief Elena Perez-Lizano, Gail Packard, Margarita Romero, and Senior Archivist Dena Hunt have been helpful over the long haul. Patricia Hewitt, former archivist, and Heather McChere, librarian, at the Fray Angélico Chávez History Library rendered valuable help as well. We also express our appreciation to Maya Shakur for her map of Isleta Pueblo.

We wish to acknowledge the invaluable help rendered by Suzanne Stamatov as Malcolm's research assistant, and Margaret McGee, his research and word-processing assistant. Suzanne read, researched, and commented on the entire manuscript, and Meg typed and helped research what is now a book. *Mil gracias.*

Finally, the authors extend their gratitude to University of New Mexico Press director Stephen Hull, to Senior Acquisitions Editor Michael Millman, Copyeditor Bridget Manzella, and the peer review readers, all of whom helped make this book a reality. Both readers—the anonymous reader and Isletan Theodore "Ted" Jojola—offered valuable suggestions that greatly improved this book.

Figure 1. *Randy Jiron holding rifle given to Pablo Abeita by President Theodore Roosevelt*, November 2018, Malcom Ebright, photographer.

A Note on Usage

We capitalize "Pueblo" when referring to the Pueblo people and when using the name of a specific pueblo, as in Isleta Pueblo, but not when making a general reference to an Indian village. This has been a standard convention among scholars writing about Pueblo Indians for many years. In the case of this book, however, the situation is more complicated. Most of Pablo Abeita's contemporaries, particularly government officials, referred to Pueblos (uppercase) and pueblos (lowercase) without distinguishing between people and place. Moreover, Abeita himself used both Pueblo and village to refer to Native communities. Therefore, the reader will find examples of all these forms. When quoting, we have taken care to preserve the word the way it was used in the original. Most Pueblo people today (and many scholars), especially younger ones, refer to these Native communities as villages. There are at least two reasons for this. First, knowledge and use of Spanish among Natives in New Mexico has declined as English has come to predominate. Pueblo is the Spanish word for village, and the latter English word has displaced the former. Second, the use of village represents a measure of decolonization and expression of Pueblo sovereignty and self-determination. In a similar vein, Isleta people do not use written accents on their names of Spanish origin, hence we write Jiron rather than Jirón, and so forth.

When Theodore Roosevelt became president in 1901, the Indian agents that remained in federal government employ were replaced by Indian school superintendents who absorbed the duties of the Indian agents. Nimrod S. Walpole was the last Indian agent with whom Pablo Abeita worked. Nevertheless, in New Mexico the men who held the positions of school superintendents and figure in Abeita's story were and still often are referred to as Indian agents.

Introduction

*You never gave us any land. The land that we have was always ours. You
gave us the papers only, you never gave us any money, nor do now, never
any cattle or sheep, not even a wagon . . . We did not kill any white man,
but instead, fed them and protected them when they were in need, and
now that we are in need, the Government wants to take away . . . what
land we have left, and turn us into the wrath of our neighbors.*
Pablo Abeita, Statement to the Senate Committee on
Indian Affairs, 1923

Pablo Abeita was well known in his day as a Pueblo statesman and later as "the grand
old man of Isleta." Pablo was born in 1871, during a time of major change in US
policy towards Indians when forced assimilation was just beginning to be implemented.
He lived through a period of reform of those harsh and unwelcome policies, and largely
through his efforts, was able to witness the first steps toward modernity and constitutional government for Isleta. His advocacy helped Isleta move forward into the twentieth
century.

Isleta oral history tells of a time when Isleta was part of Tiwa-speaking Taos Pueblo
living in the Blue Lake area. Isleta split from the Taos community, moving to the area
south of Sandia, another Tiwa-speaking pueblo. The future Isletans occupied and abandoned at least seven sites before they settled at present-day Isleta.[1] One of those places,
known as the Water Basin Village, was situated atop the Mesa de los Padillas near the
north boundary of Isleta Pueblo. The fortified village commanded a strategic view of the
whole valley so that inhabitants could be warned of an impending attack. Pottery shards
found at the site date its occupation from AD 1550 to AD 1650. The Water Basin Village
is still recollected in an Isletan folktale, "The Town of the Snake Girl," that recounts the
exploits of two enchanted sisters whose treachery against an unresponsive suitor led to
their being turned into rattlesnakes. This tale is regarded as portending the abandonment
of this mesa village.[2]

Two other ancient villages that were precursors of today's Isleta Pueblo were White
Earth Village and Yellow Earth Village, whose locations were said to be near today's
Isleta on the east side of the Rio Grande. These villages were rivals, and their violent
encounter is retold in another Isletan folktale. A foot race was proposed between the
villages as a way to settle the ill-feeling between them. Antelope Boy from White Earth
Village was pitted against a runner named Deer-foot from Yellow Earth Village. They
took the race to the four corners of the earth where Deer-foot shape shifted into a swift
hawk. However, Antelope Boy, with the help of a mole, won the race. Now his people
could settle the score with the Yellow Earth Village. They burned all the witches because
that had been the main issue between the villages, and the rest of the Yellow Earth

Village merged with the White Earth Village.[3] The fate of Yellow Earth Village and the slaying of all its witches are examples of the violent beginnings of Isleta Pueblo. The conflict in the ancient villages was a portent of future factionalism within Isleta.[4]

Finally, ruins of another ancient village known as Whib-stick Place, or simply *tu-ai* (village), are still found in the northwest corner of the existing Isleta plaza. Pottery shards found in a 2021 sewer line excavation date this ruin as between 1540 and 1650.[5] The village of Isleta was and is located near the Rio Grande on the west and was encircled by the old riverbed before the river changed its course. With the spring runoff, the Rio Grande overflowed and would completely encircle the village, leading the Spaniards who came with Juan de Oñate in 1598 to name the pueblo Isleta (little island). Isleta was ideally situated on a fertile floodplain near the Rio Grande, a perfect place for irrigated agriculture.

The Spanish colonizers quickly realized that the village of Isleta occupied a strategic location at the junction of two heavily traveled, pre-Columbian bison trails, one leading south toward the Piro pueblos and Socorro, the other leading east toward the other Tiwa pueblos and the Great Plains. Given its important location, Isleta was one of the first pueblos to be missionized. As early as September 1598, Fray Juan Claros was sent to begin conversion at Isleta and surrounding villages.[6] The Franciscans also started building missions among the Piro pueblos in the Salinas Basin about this time, but by 1671, famine and Apache raids had caused them to be abandoned. First to close was Los Humanos. According to Isleta oral tradition, by 1679 many of the Piro refugees from these pueblos, and Tiwa refugees from villages like Chilili and Tajique, settled opposite the village of Isleta on the east bank of the Rio Grande.[7]

Isleta did not participate in the Pueblo Revolt of August 1680 because the village was headquarters to the Hispanic lieutenant governor Alonso García and a military garrison of about fifty soldiers. During the early days of the rebellion, García gathered about a thousand Hispano settlers from the surrounding area and decided to head south to the El Paso area, not knowing the fate of Governor Antonio de Otermín in Santa Fe. García took many of the local Isletans with him. According to Isletan oral history, the Piros went voluntarily while the Isletan Tiwas were forced to carry the Spaniards' baggage.[8] But not all Isletans went to El Paso with either García or Governor Otermín. Those who stayed, living in nearby pueblos, later formed the nucleus of the resettled Isleta. The inhabitants of the newly founded Isleta would have the stories of past migrations embedded in their bones.

THE RESETTLEMENT OF ISLETA

Even before the formal resettlement of Isleta in 1710, Governor Diego de Vargas had broached the idea of repopulating the abandoned pueblo, but nothing came of it. Then a decade-and-a-half later, Franciscan Juan de la Peña reconstituted Isleta with some Tiwas he brought back from Ysleta de Sur, as well as other former Isletans who had not gone south in 1680. An alcalde of Taos also arranged for any Tiwas with Isletan roots to move to the resettled Isleta Pueblo.[9]

The Pueblo of Isleta grew in population between 1750 and 1809 from 428 to 487. At the same time, however, the Spanish government started making land grants south of the village that began to encroach on Isleta land. Chief among these were the combined

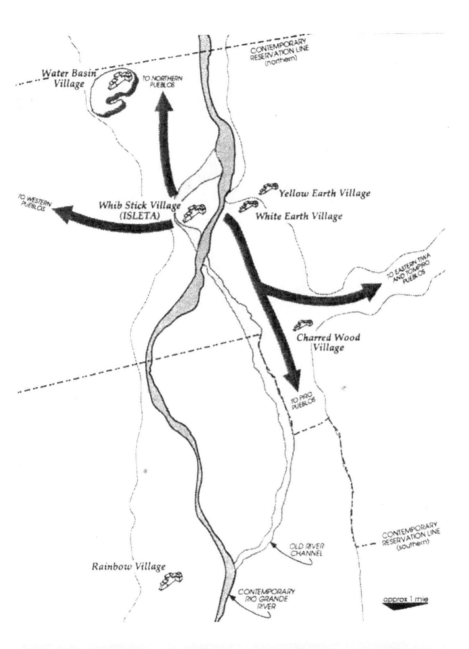

Figure 2. *Water Basin Village and surrounding villages*, map by Theodore "Ted" Jojola

Gutiérrez (1716) and Sedillo (1734) grants and the Lo de Padilla (1718) grant. The Spaniards had not measured Isleta's southern boundary because the pueblo did not have clearly established limits like those spelled out in the 1748 Sandia grant or the grant to San Felipe whose pueblo league had been partially measured. Yet, Isletans knew perfectly well that their lands extended from the Rio Puerco in the west to the crest of the Manzano Mountains in the east.[10]

Isletans forcefully resisted the increasing encroachment on their southern boundary, which was a unique response among the Pueblos at the time. When Diego Padilla, owner of the Lo de Padilla grant, began allowing his livestock to graze on Isleta lands, trampling its fields and damaging its acequias, the pueblo filed a protest with Governor Gervasio Cruzat y Góngora. When the governor ruled in Isleta's favor, Padilla resisted vociferously. But then Isleta hired an advocate to present its case, and Padilla backed down. Isleta had won, but Padilla's animals continued to trespass on the pueblo's land. Finally, Isleta showed how much it had adopted the ways of its aggressive Hispano neighbors: it purchased both the Lo de Padilla grant and the Gutiérrez-Sedillo grant, thus solving the encroachment problem and substantially increasing its land base.

Isleta Pueblo showed a great deal of sophistication and political know-how in acquiring the two grants on its southern border. Nevertheless, Hispano settlers continued to encroach on Isleta's recently purchased grants.[11] For example, when Hispano settlers moved onto the Lo de Padilla grant and started the community of Peralta, Isleta Pueblo sold them the land they were occupying, apparently taking the view that if the Peralta trespass on Isleta land was to become permanent, the pueblo might as well reap some benefit. Even with this loss of acreage, when Isleta Pueblo received the Isleta grant from the US Congress in 1858 after the 1846 US invasion, it was the third largest pueblo in New Mexico after Zuni and Laguna.[12] It is unclear exactly which Isleta leaders engineered the massive land acquisitions that to this day have greatly benefitted the pueblo. Although the details are sketchy, the first Isleta governor who appears to have fit the role of an Indigenous capitalist was Pablo Abeita's grandfather, Ambrosio Abeita.[13]

Ambrosio amassed a fortune running sheep on Isleta's vast pastures. Just like his wealthy *rico* neighbors in the nearby Rio Abajo communities—the Oteros, the Chávezes, and the Pereas—Ambrosio must have had flocks upward of five thousand sheep. In one claim alone, Ambrosio is said to have lost more than two thousand head in one Navajo raid. Like the Hispano ricos, Ambrosio trailed vast flocks to Chihuahua and received payment in gold and silver coins. According to Isleta lore, Ambrosio had a whole room filled with ollas, or water jars, filled to the brim with gold coins. He famously lent the US government some $18,000 in 1862 to pay back wages to Union troops defending New Mexico from invading Confederate forces from Texas.[14]

Ambrosio Abeita and his family were ricos by the standards of the day, unlike other Pueblo leaders. Their activities in acquiring land for Isleta and protecting it from encroachment greatly benefitted the village, but their business dealings and their prosperity must have caused other pueblo members to envy and resent them, another factor that led to the conflict that later beset the community. This is evidenced by the lawsuit that was filed against Ambrosio in 1847, alleging that he was using his position as governor to grant lucrative concessions to his relatives.[15]

Figure 3. *Ambrosio Abeita, 1868*, A. Z. Schindler, photographer. Courtesy of the National Anthropological Archive, Negative no. NAA GN 01923

In addition to safeguarding and expanding Isleta land, Ambrosio Abeita worked hard on behalf of Isleta and other pueblos. He testified before the surveyor general of New Mexico regarding the boundaries of the Isleta grant: a league (2.5 miles) to the north, a league to the south, the Rio Puerco on the west, and the crest, or spine, of the Manzano Mountains on the east. This comprised an ample tract of land on paper; it would take Pablo Abeita, Ambrosio's grandson, to get the US government to properly survey this land. Ambrosio Abeita also traveled to Washington, DC, with an Isleta delegation to testify against a series of laws and court decisions that restricted Pueblo sovereignty and encouraged non-Indian encroachment on Pueblo land.[16]

The mid-1800s were good years for Isleta and the Abeita family, although it was a time when the federal government was embarking on a policy of assimilation of Native Americans and eradication of their culture. The Abeita family "built a grand hacienda purportedly styled after the Palace of Governors in Santa Fe."[17] By 1880, however, the lifestyle the Isletan ricos had become accustomed to would be changed forever by two events: the Laguna Migration of 1879 and 1880, and the coming of the railroad in 1880.

THE LAGUNA MIGRATION AND THE COMING OF THE RAILROAD

In 1879 traditionalists from Laguna Pueblo had reached their limit. Laguna progressives, led by their non-Indian Protestant governor, Robert Marmon, had destroyed the kiva and forced the traditionalists to watch as they burned some of the sacred objects in the plaza. A group of the leading traditionalists decided to move to another pueblo, taking with them the remaining sacred objects along with the ancient ceremonies. The Keres-speaking Lagunas ended up in Tiwa-speaking Isleta where they were offered a home and land at a place called Old Oraibi south of the main pueblo. By 1880 over one hundred Lagunas had made the journey to Isleta and were adopted by the pueblo. The Laguna migration was a continuation of the pattern of relocation that led to the reconstitution of Isleta Pueblo; it also created a new fissure between Isletans and Laguna descendants that added to the existing fault lines within Isleta.[18]

The other event that changed Isleta forever and created new fissures of conflict was the coming of the Atchison, Topeka, and Santa Fe (AT&SF) railroad in 1880. The spur of the railroad, which was the only major junction of the western and southern routes, was located at Isleta Pueblo. Trains waited at regular intervals at the Isleta depot to gain clearance to proceed. Isletans used this waiting time to peddle items such as fruit, vegetables, bread, pottery, and other Indian crafts. The "exotic appearance of Isleta Pueblo dress . . . added appreciably to the festival atmosphere of the stop."[19] Railway officials encouraged this type of passenger interaction and hired distinguished writers, artists, and entrepreneurs like Fred Harvey to create a romantic image of the Pueblo Indian. The railroad, with the help of former Isleta resident Charles Lummis, even brought Isletan vendors to Los Angeles to sell their wares and perform dances at the Los Angeles festival. "Eventually jealousies emerged among [Isletans] competing for the chance to travel to Los Angeles," and the trips were canceled. The trips brought the outside world to Isleta and created another major conflict between those who took advantage of this new visibility and those who resisted it.[20]

In the mid-1870s, another split occurred between the religious leaders and the pueblo council. This led to the formation of the so-called progressive and conservative factions that would continue for several decades.[21]

This was the community of Isleta Pueblo into which Pablo Abeita was born. Several of these momentous changes, like the Laguna migration and the arrival of the railroad, took place while Pablo was attending school in Albuquerque and Santa Fe. He was such an accomplished scholar and a member of such a leading progressive family that it soon became apparent that he was destined to be an important Pueblo leader. As early as 1892, Abeita was chosen to be a member of the village council. It would become Abeita's life work to advocate on behalf of all pueblos, and to navigate the schisms and factions at Isleta to bring the pueblo into the modern world of the twentieth century.[22]

The Abeita family had always taken advantage of economic opportunities brought by the arrival of the Americans in 1846 and the coming of the railroad in 1880. Soon after the arrival of the railroad, the family constructed an imposing two-story hotel and general store on the plaza next to the church. Not all Isletans, however, were in favor of such an open-door policy toward outsiders.[23]

Many Isletans feared that bringing outsiders into their midst would lead to an erosion of cultural values and a loss of Pueblo sovereignty and would breach the strict policy of secrecy regarding ceremonies and dances. Pablo Abeita would face criticism on each

Figure 4. *View of Isleta Pueblo, 1904*, Frank Churchill, photographer. Courtesy of the National Museum of the American Indian, Negative no. N26964

of these fronts. Perhaps the most serious charge involved the Abeita family welcoming the photographer, author, and newspaperman Charles Fletcher Lummis into the village. Lummis rented a room from and became friends with the family of Juan Rey Abeita. Even though he was still in his teens and early twenties during the four years beginning in 1888 when Lummis lived at Isleta, many blamed Pablo Abeita for Lummis's activities. Not only was Lummis taking numerous photographs of activities within the pueblo, but he was also learning many secret stories from the disaffected Carlisle Indian Industrial School graduate, Henry Kendall. Kendall had come to accept the assimilationist's rhetoric about "kill the Indian, save the man" and was willing to take payment from Lummis in return for his divulging of tribal secrets.[24]

This conflict over the preservation of Isleta cultural traditions was one that Pablo Abeita negotiated by refusing to be fully defined by either the progressive or conservative category. Abeita was conservative in his lifelong devotion to Isletan traditional values and his participation in its clan society. Yet he was progressive in his attempts to bring Isleta into the twentieth century through reforms in agriculture, education, and pueblo politics, often with the help of the Indian agent or school superintendent. He saw no contradiction between bringing modern plows and other efficient farm equipment to Isleta and maintaining a vibrant ceremonial calendar of dances independent of outside scrutiny. Pablo Abeita defied categories, just as Isleta does to this day.[25]

Another conflict that almost tore the pueblo apart was between those who wanted no contact with the federal government and those like Abeita who saw the benefits Isleta could accrue by working with the Indian agent or school superintendent. Pablo Abeita became adept at navigating the bureaucracy through letter writing, filing petitions, and even testifying before Congress. As early as 1899, he began his quest for a resurvey of the crest of the Manzano Mountains as Isleta's eastern boundary. On behalf of the pueblo, he wrote the recently appointed special attorney for the Pueblo Indians that this was one of Isleta's highest priorities and asked for help. Abeita persisted for over three decades in pressuring the government to accomplish that goal. His high visibility in working with the government created suspicion and even hostility among many Isletans.[26] This conflict came to a head in November 1915, during the annual feast day, at a time of celebration and performance of traditional dances. Superintendent Philip T. Lonergan, an invited guest, soon became the center of a major battle. During one of the dances, Lonergan noticed several intoxicated individuals and feeling the impropriety of the situation, took the ceremonial drum in order to stop the dance. Former governor Juan P. Lente defiantly took the drum back so the dance could continue. When Lonergan persisted and seized the drum again, former governor Lente urged his followers to get clubs and attack the superintendent. Lonergan warded off several blows before order was restored. He sued Lente in the Court of Indian Offenses presided over by none other than Judge Pablo Abeita. After a contentious trial, Judge Abeita found Lente guilty and sentenced him to forty days in jail. Lente's appeals were denied, and from that time on Lente and his conservative followers became more radical in their opposition to anything Abeita tried to do, even when it stood to benefit the entire pueblo.[27]

This new rift had no ideological basis but was solely a reaction to Pablo himself and his growing power and influence. Joining the anti-Pablo Abeita faction were litigants who lost cases heard by Judge Abeita. Nevertheless, Abeita continued administering

Figure 5. *Pablo Abeita and Family, n.d.*, Sumner Matteson, photographer. Courtesy of the Milwaukee Public Museum, Negative no. 44451

justice as Court of Indian Offenses judge for another nine years. He strengthened his alliances outside the pueblo with prominent lawyers, judges, and government officials. Above all, Abeita negotiated this hostility toward him with a wry sense of humor, devotion to his family, and a love of the pueblo of Isleta and its people.

During the decade after the Lente trial, Abeita followed events on the national scene, such as the 1913 Supreme Court Sandoval decision on federal wardship of the pueblos and the 1923 Bursum Bill regarding non-Indian encroachments on pueblo lands. He took a leadership role on both issues, testifying before Congress about the dangers posed if the pueblos did not have federal protection and if they were subject to state taxation. He helped mobilize the protest against the Bursum Bill and educated pueblo leaders about its threat to their lands. In these efforts Pablo Abeita became the spokesperson for the Pueblos of New Mexico at the same time as he was fighting these battles at home, navigating the fault lines of Isleta's various factions.[28]

Despite its conflicts, Isleta Pueblo, like all the other eighteen New Mexico pueblos, has persisted and thrived. As Edward Dozier points out, factionalism exists in all the pueblos. And when we substitute the word *conflict* for *factionalism*, we see that it exists in all communities. In the past, groups who disagreed with the majority could simply leave as did the Laguna colony in 1879–1880. Isleta's oral history and its stories of the early pre-Isletan villages are replete with migrations, many due to similar conflicts. As Dozier points out, citing Alfred L. Kroeber, the Pueblos have persisted, conflict notwithstanding, because the various factions crosscut one another. "By countering each other they . . . produce an almost marvelous complexity [that] can never break the . . . entity apart."[29]

Others have pointed out, using Jemez as an example, that conflict and factionalism have existed in most pueblos, even before European contact "as a legitimate form of argumentation" or discussion. Using the model of a case in a judicial setting, the process begins with each side or faction presenting its case and ends with a judicial decision and the possibility of resolution of the conflict and healing.[30]

At Isleta, whether healing and resolution occurred depended on the importance of the issue and the polarization of the factions. In *Isleta v. Lente* the issue was important, and the factions polarized. It has taken many generations for healing to occur as descendants of both sides gradually forget and make peace. In a more recent example, Laguna Pueblo, led by Governor Richard Luarkie, sponsored a symposium around 2013 about the Laguna migration with the goal of healing old wounds and providing historical information about the Laguna migration and what led up to it. The symposium, which many Isletans attended, did provide healing, but as ex-Governor Luarkie recently said, "there is a need to continually cultivate [the connection between] Laguna and Isleta. There is no end to the migration."[31]

Pablo Abeita, as judge of the Court of Indian Offenses, made many decisions that resulted in reconciliation and healing. From enforcing a promise to marry to resolving a conflict over farm equipment, he always tried to bring about an amicable settlement whenever possible. In many cases, he accomplished this with the help of tribal policemen like Louis Abeita, who was trusted and liked throughout the pueblo. In domestic cases, Judge Abeita usually tried to bring a disputing couple back together and achieve reconciliation. The judicial process provided a means for the two sides in a conflict to present their arguments and have a definitive decision. In many instances this led to reconciliation and healing.[32]

Another way in which Pablo Abeita was able to rise above the conflicts within Isleta was by forging alliances with those outside the pueblo who could assist Isleta in achieving its goals, as well as with other Native leaders who were able to unite the pueblos in their resistance to legislative attacks. Two of the most prominent of those leaders were Sotero Ortiz of San Juan (Ohkay Owingeh) and José Alcario Montoya of Cochiti. Sotero Ortiz learned about litigation and history in the library of Thomas B. Catron, for whom he worked. Ironically, Sotero became adept at fighting for Pueblo land and water rights by befriending the enemy. Ortiz began working closely with Pablo Abeita when the All

Figure 6. *All Pueblo Council Bursum Bill Protest Delegation, 1923*, photographer unknown. Courtesy of the National Anthropological Archives, Negative no. BAE GN 02860q
Sitting, left to right: Santiago Naranjo (Santa Clara), Martín Vigil (Tesuque), Sotero Ortiz (San Juan [Ohkay Owingeh]), Santiago Peña (Santo Domingo), Juan Pablo García (Acoma), Wushusiwa (Zuni). Standing, left to right: Charles Seonia (Laguna), José Alcario Montoya (Cochiti), Antonio Abeita (Isleta), Frank Paisano (Laguna), Charlie Kie (Laguna), ?, Jesús Baca (Jemez), James H. Miller (Acoma), Juan Avila (Sandia)

Pueblo Council appointed him president and Pablo as its secretary at its reorganization meeting at Santo Domingo in November of 1922. When Sotero was reluctant to speak in public when he went to New York and Washington, DC, as part of the anti-Bursum Bill delegation, Pablo Abeita told him, "Don't be afraid. Just look over their heads. . . . What you don't cover, I'll tell them." Ortiz became an accomplished advocate and public speaker, serving as president of the All Pueblo Council for almost two decades, until 1940.[33]

José Alcario Montoya also served the All Pueblo Council from 1922 to 1940. Montoya, like Pablo Abeita, became proficient in several languages, becoming the council's official interpreter. At a typical council meeting in its early days, Montoya would interpret first in Spanish, then in his native Keres, and finally in English for any guests. He also worked

Figure 7. *Father Anton Docher with medals, left medal is Knight of the Order of Leopold presented by King Albert of Belgium, right medal is the French Colonial Medal, c. 1919–1928*, Cobb's Studio Albuquerque, Cobb Memorial Photography Collection. Courtesy of the Center for Southwest Research, University of New Mexico Libraries, Negative no. 000-119-0268

closely with Abeita and the All Pueblo Council in explaining the dangers of pending legislation and organizing the pueblos to take their cause to the American people.[34] By partnering with other Pueblo leaders, several of whom came from pueblos with similar factional divisions as Isleta, Pablo Abeita received support as he became the leading Native statesman, known throughout the Southwest and beyond.[35]

Abeita also became friends with writers and photographers like Charles Lummis, lawyers like Richard Hanna, school superintendents such as Philip T. Lonergan and Leo Crane, religious leaders like Father Anton Docher and William H. Ketcham, and even US presidents such as Theodore Roosevelt. He always spoke his truth with his unique blend of down-to-earth eloquence, wit, and humor—coupled with biting sarcasm—endearing him to most of these allies.

Abeita was particularly drawn to lawyers and even judges as allies. He was especially close with Francis Wilson and Richard Hanna, both of whom served as special attorney for the Pueblo Indians. Wilson sued many of the non-Indian encroachers on Isleta land and helped educate Abeita by giving him cases and judicial opinions to read. As judge of the Court of Indian Offenses, Abeita was as knowledgeable as any member of the New Mexico legal bar, as the transcript of the Juan P. Lente case demonstrates.[36] Hanna advocated for Isleta in the late 1920s and early 1930s in the aftermath of the Pueblo Lands Board. Even though the pueblos successfully defeated the Bursum Bill, which would have recognized almost all non-Indian claims to Pueblo land, the subsequent Pueblo Lands Board's decisions still resulted in an overall loss of Pueblo land of about thirty-six thousand acres. Hanna was instrumental in obtaining compensation for Isleta resulting from legislative hearings in the early 1930s. Abeita and Hanna made a good team as they both testified at the hearings. Pablo spoke about the history on the ground of the claims of unfairness against the Pueblo Lands Board, and Hanna testified about the legal basis for the claims. As a result, Isleta received substantial monetary compensation under separate legislation. Richard Hanna was one of Isleta's strongest advocates in a long tradition of advocates who obtained a degree of justice for Isleta.[37] Hanna was the leading advocate for the pueblo's cause during the Pueblo Lands Board era. In his career he always intervened to defend the rights of the underdog.[38]

Abeita also partnered with Indian agents and school superintendents to bring needed programs to Isleta, such as the one providing farm equipment like wagons and plows on convenient terms. Philip T. Lonergan, who served from 1911 to 1919, did not always agree with him, but supported Abeita's decisions as judge of the Court of Indian Offenses and called him his friend. Pablo Abeita was definitely Lonergan's "go-to man" whenever the superintendent had a problem or questions involving Isleta. Another of Abeita's strong supporters was Superintendent Leo Crane who followed Lonergan, serving from 1920 to 1922. Crane said of Abeita's testimony before Congress in 1923, "He was not without a certain trenchant wit. [When he spoke], it was like throwing the harpoon with unerring accuracy and then twisting it around."[39]

Finally, Abeita found powerful allies in Father Anton Docher, the Catholic priest from 1891 to 1923 at Isleta's church of San Agustín, and from Father William Ketcham of the Bureau of Catholic Indian Missions in Washington, DC. Both priests worked closely with Abeita on projects that benefitted Isleta.

Father Docher was born in a small village in France. After being ordained in Santa

Fe, Father Docher served for a year at Taos Pueblo before coming to Isleta. He was well liked throughout the village, where the people called him Tamithá, or Little Helper. He had a certain moral authority at Isleta, which he wielded on the night of June 11, 1905, when he stopped a large group of Isletans with picks and shovels intent on destroying a portion of the train tracks due to the flooding caused by the railroad's embankment. Pablo Abeita worked closely with Father Docher on projects that benefitted the church. In 1905, when Bautista Lucero was governor and Abeita's mother, Marcelina, was church warden, or *mayordoma*, Pablo seems to have been instrumental in facilitating a gift to the church of a statue of the Virgin of Guadalupe by the rico merchant Felipe Chávez.[40] The most extravagant event coordinated by Pablo Abeita and Father Docher was the visit to Isleta on October 19, 1919, by the king of Belgium. Abeita convened the Isleta council, which agreed to support the event and provide entertainment. Thousands of people attended, many brought by a special train from Albuquerque. Father Docher provided a sermon in French and was presented with a Belgian medal as a knight of the Order of Leopold. After the entertainment, at the king's request, Pablo Abeita gave him a tour of his home in the family compound. The visit of the king that day certainly put Isleta on the map where many in the pueblo would rather be off the map.[41]

Father William Ketcham was a Catholic priest who worked for the pro-Native lobbying group, the Bureau of Catholic Indian Missions. Father Ketcham visited Pablo Abeita at Isleta in the early 1900s, and the two carried on a lengthy correspondence until Ketcham's death in 1921. Ketcham and Abeita became friends, a relationship reflected in their letters. Perhaps their greatest accomplishment was to obtain Congressional funding for two bridges, one built at Isleta, the other at San Felipe. Prior to this, Isletans had to cross the Rio Grande by barge, or *barco*, as all the bridges built by Isletans soon washed out by floods. Father Ketcham and his office also provided Abeita with copies of legislation and books. Their close relationship was one of many that Pablo Abeita forged to provide a network of supporters to help realize Abeita's vision of a modern Isleta.[42]

One of the recurring themes in Pablo Abeita's letters to Father Ketcham was the unfairness of many of Isleta's elections. In times of acute polarization, a conservative governor might use improper means to stay in power. Depending on which superintendent was in office, the Bureau of Indian Affairs (BIA) was often reluctant to intervene. The resulting stalemate sometimes meant that the pueblo was unable to conduct its business. Many other pueblos faced similar problems caused by factionalism. At Santa Clara Pueblo, for instance, two governors claimed to be legitimately elected.[43] Until John Collier began addressing this problem of tribal self-government in 1932 when he became Commissioner of Indian Affairs, there seemed to be no solution. Pablo Abeita worked closely with Collier, starting with the movement against the Bursum Bill. Collier's 1934 Indian Reorganization Act (IRA) provided that tribes could adopt constitutions drafted pursuant to the IRA, which provided for election of tribal officials. Here was a new non-traditional method of managing factionalism while preserving tribal self-government. Tribes were required to vote by referendum on whether or not they accepted the IRA. The pueblos could then adopt a constitution when they were prepared for the new form of elections. Pablo Abeita did not live to see the adoption of a constitution by Isleta

Pueblo in 1947.[44] Nevertheless, he would undoubtedly have supported the pro-constitution group because it finally provided a means of managing the conflicts in tribal elections that he had complained about. His progressive policies had led his people to accept this new form of self-government. Pablo Abeita had prepared the way, built the bridge, for Isletans to enter the twentieth century and beyond while maintaining its traditional values.[45]

"Through all the changes in the civil life of the Pueblo and all the changes in the world outside the one thing that did not change," wrote Pueblo historian Joe Sando, "was Pablo's feeling for his native religion." Pablo Abeita realized that Isleta's cultural values would hold it together in the modern world.[46]

Figure 8. *Governor Juan Felipe Jojola and His Lt. Governors (Pablo Abeita second from left), 1894*, Charles F. Lummis, photographer. Courtesy of the Pueblo of Isleta Tribal Archive, Yonan Cultural Center, Negative no. YACC00741.2008. Original print housed at the Autry Museum of the American West, Negative no. P8296

CHAPTER ONE

Pablo Abeita

An Overview of His Life and Times

Pablo Abeita has worked in [Isleta's] interest, both here and at
Washington and has largely kept this pueblo alive.
Superintendent Leo Crane, general meeting, Dec. 15, 1921, IPCC

Pablo Abeita was an Isleta Pueblo Indian born into a prominent family in 1871, two decades before the Indian Wars ended and most Native Americans had been moved from their homelands and settled onto reservations. Isleta Pueblo, about fifteen miles south of Albuquerque, is one of the largest pueblos, with a population of about three thousand. The village is situated along the often-flooding Rio Grande at an altitude of five thousand feet at a place called *tshia-hui-pa*, or where the water gathers. Isleta was ideally located at the crossroads of several trade routes, in the shadow of the towering Manzano Mountains, in the middle of the bosque, one of the largest cottonwood forests in North America.

The first three decades of Pablo Abeita's life were among the darkest for Isleta and the other pueblos as the federal government pursued its policy of assimilation of Native Americans into mainstream society. Despite these challenges, Abeita was able to rise above the assaults on Pueblo Indians: he got a superior education in a private school in Santa Fe, maintained mostly good relations with Indian agents and school superintendents, and spent much of his career fighting for legislation that protected Indian land. And he helped secure title for the pueblo to the over-21,000-acre Isleta mountain tract after a three-decades-long struggle. In 1890 Abeita began serving on the Isleta Pueblo council before he was twenty years old, a position that he retained for decades off and on for the rest of his life. He served as lieutenant governor five times, the first time in 1899 and again in 1900, 1925, 1929, and 1935.[1] From 1914 to 1924 Pablo Abeita was the judge on Isleta's Court of Indian Offenses. In addition to these achievements, he simultaneously operated a mercantile business in the pueblo, served as postmaster several times, took the 1910 Isleta census, raised a family, and farmed throughout his adult life.

Pablo Abeita's ancestors were well known in the pueblo. His grandfather, Ambrosio Abeita, served as governor and represented Isleta before the surveyor general when Isleta claimed its pueblo grant. As previously mentioned, Ambrosio was famous for lending the US government $18,000 in gold in 1862 to pay the Union troops who had successfully rebuffed the Texas Confederate army that invaded New Mexico.[2] Pablo's mother, Marcelina, also came from a well-to-do family that controlled a large mercantile business in the pueblo.

The future leader of Isleta Pueblo was born on February 10, 1871, to Jose Prospero

Abeita and Marcelina Lucero and baptized Juan Pablo on February 18, with Juan Baptista Lucero and Marcelina Abeita serving as godparents (*padrinos*).[3] Raised in the traditions of Isleta Pueblo, Pablo also received more than nine years of formal education. The ability to thrive in two worlds—that of Isleta and the wider New Mexico and national communities—characterized Abeita from an early age. For his first few years of schooling, he studied at the Jesuit school called the Holy Family Select School for Boys in the home of Ambrosio Armijo in Albuquerque.[4] The Jesuits established the school in 1872 with the dignified title of *collegium inchoatum* (elementary college). However, it differed little from a public grammar school. The Jesuits, an order known for its high scholastic and teaching standards, taught Spanish, English, and the ABCs. Pablo Abeita was one of the few Native Americans in the student body.[5] After studying under the Jesuits, he attended the Sisters of Charity school in Albuquerque. Following that, he was a member of the first class to enter the Presbyterian mission school—Albuquerque Indian School (AIS)—when it opened in 1881 when he would have been ten years old. His stay at the school lasted only eight months, however.[6] He continued his studies at Santa Fe's St. Michael's College, which Bishop Jean-Baptiste Lamy had founded in 1859.[7] As early as 1879, St. Michael's had begun to offer special classes for Pueblo Indian boys, which were similar to the ones Abeita joined a few years later. Rev. James H. Defouri described the classes as follows:

In the year 1879 there were twenty-two Pueblo Indians attending school in a separate department of the college in charge of Bros. Filiberto and Jude Michael . . . I have examined them myself, and like many others who visited them, was astonished at their remarkable proficiency in reading and writing English and Spanish. Their progress in arithmetic was no less surprising.[8]

St. Michael's provided the young Pablo a classical education, quite different from the day schools and the all-Indian boarding schools at Carlisle and Hampton, which emphasized vocational training and attempted to supplant traditional native knowledge with a practical education. Abeita, however, had some opportunities for vocational study, noting in 1916 that his educational experience included training in bookkeeping, printing, carpentry, and "a little blacksmith[ing]."[9] With the exception of his time at AIS, his father paid for his schooling.[10] Among the all-male student population at St. Michael's were the sons of prominent New Mexico families. The friends and contacts Pablo Abeita made at St. Michael's stood him in good stead for the rest of his life. In addition to speaking his mother tongue, Tiwa, when he completed his studies, Abeita was fluent in Spanish and English, as well as the other Pueblo languages spoken in New Mexico: Northern Tiwa, Keres, Towa, and Zuni.[11] Abeita later noted that "even as a young fellow, I had the urge to be well educated so that eventually I could return to my people and help them climb the ladder toward a better life."[12]

Two years before completing his studies in Santa Fe at age seventeen, Abeita participated in a tradition that Isletans had followed since acquiring the horse: the buffalo hunt. As he related the story, the 1886 hunt was the last one where men from Isleta took part. Abeita lassoed a two-year-old buffalo after another hunter roped the animal. It is said that

Figure 9. *Maria Dolores Abeita, Wife of Pablo Abeita, 1900*, photographer unknown. Courtesy of the National Museum of the American Indian, Negative no. P18421

Pablo killed the animal by severing its spine. After the disappearance of the buffalo, there were still inter-village antelope and rabbit hunts. The last antelope hunt involving men from Isleta, Jemez, Santo Domingo, San Felipe, and Santa Ana took place around 1896.[13]

Less than two weeks before his eighteenth birthday on February 7, 1889, Pablo married twelve-year-old Maria de los Dolores Abeita in the mission church of San Agustín de la Isleta.[14] His bride was the daughter of Juan Rey Abeita and Maria de los Reyes Zuni to whom she had been born on May 19, 1876.[15] Rumor had it that the young couple were first cousins, and their local priest could not have granted them a dispensation from that impediment to marriage. However, although not first cousins, the couple was closely related by consanguinity in a prohibited degree on the Zuni line; Pablo's great-grandmother, Juana de la Cruz Francisca Zuni, was the sister of Dolores's great-grandfather, Vicente Zuni, making them related in the second degree of consanguinity. Pablo and Maria Dolores also shared a common great-great grandfather, a third-degree relationship. However, Father Andre Antoine Echallier, the French priest serving in Isleta, granted the couple a dispensation and performed the marriage ceremony.[16] Father Echallier recorded the marriage, noting the impediment to their union as *tertii gradus secundum attigente*, meaning that they were related by third-degree consanguinity on the second line.[17] In other words, the great-grandparent of one party was a sibling to the grandparent of the other party. The witnesses to the marriage were Juan Domingo Abeita and Guadalupe Lucero. Even though they were not actually first cousins, there was still considerable envious talk about the union within the pueblo. Some speculated that the marriage was engineered to keep the considerable Abeita wealth within the family.[18]

Pablo Abeita became involved in Isleta politics in 1890 when he began serving on the Isleta tribal council. In addition to his early entry into the Isleta government, Abeita worked at various jobs, availing himself of the skills he had learned in school. After leaving St. Michael's, he found employment with Whitney Co. Wholesale Hardware in Santa Fe at a salary of $90.00 per month, a well-paid job in those days.[19] Then, in 1900, when he was twenty-nine years old, Abeita took a job as a typesetter for the *Albuquerque Morning Democrat*, now the *Albuquerque Journal*; two years later he became a commercial clerk for the newspaper.[20] This position kept him abreast of the news of the day both from New Mexico, then still a US territory, and from Washington, DC. Abeita maintained a lifelong connection with the newspaper, publishing many letters to the editor in the 1930s. These positions, together with the contacts he made during his schooling, would benefit him greatly as he began his career as advocate for the Pueblos.

In 1905 Abeita started working for the Indian Service. Tasked with providing information on modern farming methods—including seeds and farming tools—as a farmer himself, he was much more aware of Isletan farming practices and how new methods could be introduced than the outsiders who usually held this position. In 1905 Abeita took the first complete census of the pueblos of Sandia, Santa Ana, and San Felipe.[21] Then in 1907, he left his post with the Indian Service and returned to Isleta to run the family's general store, which he would do for the rest of his life. He also served as postmaster at Isleta off and on for several years.[22]

As an advocate, Abeita traveled to Washington, DC, numerous times to advance Pueblo interests and to try to obtain government protection from encroachment on

Pueblo land. When in 1911 the Isletans were considering a delegation, Abeita stated that he had already been to the nation's capital twice. On one of those occasions, eleven Pueblo Indians from different pueblos accompanied him; three of them understood some English, but the other eight spoke only Indian languages.[23] In 1913 he participated in a fifteen-man delegation to DC. En route, when the train stopped in Chicago, locals tried to patronize the Pueblos, most of whom were wearing blankets and moccasins. The Ashland, Illinois, newspaper reported the following incident: "Heap big Injun on warpath," laughed a station porter, coming up to the group. "Here, boy, take this bag to the smoking room. I'll be there in a minute," ordered one of the Indians. Of course, the Indian with the quick riposte was Pablo Abeita.[24] When the delegation arrived in Washington, Abeita testified before Congress regarding the effect of the 1913 Sandoval decision, raising the possibility that it would lead to the taxation of Pueblo lands. He told the legislators in a not-so-subtle barb that when it came to taxation, "we ought to tax the white people for the land they took away from us instead of the white people taxing us for what land they never gave, because what land we have at present is only what the white people did not appropriate."[25] This would be small compensation for the damages Native Americans suffered since the coming of the Europeans.

In 1914 the Indian Service appointed Abeita as judge of the Court of Indian Offenses at Isleta, and he served in that position until 1924. The cases that Abeita judged ran from petty personal altercations to issues of inheritance to mediating the return of Indian-owned animals that had wandered onto a non-Indian's property. One of the most sensitive cases Judge Abeita had to deal with, as noted earlier, was the charge of assault that his political rival, Juan Pomecino Lente, perpetrated against Superintendent Philip T. Lonergan. After Lente urged his followers to attack Lonergan, Abeita sentenced him to forty days in the Isleta jail. According to one scholar, "Abeita dealt with problems in a dignified and informed manner . . . efficiently [dispensing] justice, usually with wisdom, mercy, and a dash of dry humor."[26]

Known in Indian Country and beyond as "the most colorful and prominent resident of Isleta Indian Pueblo," Pablo Abeita had a "wry sense of humor. Even when criticizing his political foes, he made his points with quaint sarcasm rather than malicious barbs."[27]

In May 1940 the Coronado Cuarto Centennial Committee, marking roughly four-hundred years since Francisco Vázquez de Coronado and his troops arrived in New Mexico, invited Abeita to speak. He reportedly surprised some of his audience by saying:

> I am afraid I will have to contradict some of the things you gentlemen have said. Coronado came by Isleta, and as you who have read his chronicles know, was given food and royally received. He came up the valley, and what did he do? Well, we had better say no more about it, for his record isn't good and you know it. I don't know why you invited me here, because I am not particularly proud to be here to observe this quatrocentennial. After all, you people are honoring those who brought diseases to my country and my people, thereby reducing the Indian population. We have very little land left, but you continue to encroach upon our villages. You strip our trees from the watersheds to

Figure 10. *Abeita store interior with Pablo standing in background, n.d.*, photographer unknown. Courtesy of the Leonard Abeita Collection, Isleta Pueblo

produce lumber and floods; you plow up the earth to raise grain crops and sandstorms; and you have turned a large section of land that used to be fertile enough for at least a subsistence economy for Indians, into outright desert.

It is also reported that when Abeita spoke "the crowd broke into the heartiest applause of the afternoon and did so at every pause as the respected Isletan continued a short and cutting debunking of white man's history."[28]

As it happened, the address at the Coronado Cuarto Centennial commemoration was his last. Pablo Abeita died suddenly the night of Tuesday, December 17, 1940, at age seventy. His body was wrapped in the burial blanket he had chosen long ago, placed on the floor in his home in a room from which the furniture had been removed and surrounded by lighted tapers. Sobbing women mourners from the pueblo huddled against the walls of the room, replacing the candles that burned out. During the following day, non-Isletans came to pay their respects to his family. Bearers placed the body on a canvas litter and carried it to the church. There, Father Michael Dumarest conducted a brief service, but he did not celebrate a requiem mass. The priest then led a procession to the cemetery south of the pueblo. As the people walked through the streets of the village, a single voice chanted an *alabado* (hymn) in Spanish, and other marchers joined their voices in reciting the chorus. At the graveside, Father Dumarest said Latin prayers and sprinkled the grave and body with Holy Water. Then family members touched the body for a final time.[29]

Two men jumped into the grave and other men lowered the body by the corners of the blanket, while Father Dumarest intoned "requiescat in pace." He tossed in the first handful of dirt, and close friends and relatives followed, each adding a handful of dirt to the grave. When the grave was partially filled, a young man jumped in and smoothed and tamped down the dirt with a well-worn wooden block. Six women then each poured an olla of water over the covered face of Pablo Abeita. The shoveling resumed only to be interrupted again for the smoothing and tamping. Finally, when the grave was completely filled, Juan Abeita, Pablo's eldest son, and other men laid stones in the form of a cross on the grave.

Only a few mourners remained at the graveside when Jose Jojola, the aged leader of the Abeita extended family, tearfully said words over the grave in Tiwa, sobbing in grief. Of Pablo's five sons, Juan, Ambrosio, Jose, and Andy attended the funeral. Remijio, who lived in Washington State, unable to make flight connections, missed the services. Pablo's widow did not attend, in accordance with Isleta custom. This was a fitting end to a life well lived, as both the Catholic and Isleta traditions came together to lay Pablo Abeita to rest.

The blending of Roman Catholic and Isleta Pueblo customs was typical of Isleta life at the time. Writing in 1922 to introduce himself to Father William Hughes, the director of the Bureau of Catholic Indian Missions following the death of Father William H. Ketcham, Abeita related that "I am called a pagan Indian but I hope to die as I live 'a catholic.'"[30] Years earlier, in 1912, when Abeita was advocating for the appointment of Francis C. Wilson as special attorney for the Pueblo Indians, Abeita had noted that the lawyer was "not a Catholic which he ought to be."[31] When his beloved mother died in 1914, Abeita commented to Father Ketcham that he was "glad to say that she was a good Catholic. . . . Please pray for her."[32]

Other observers pointed to Abeita's embrace of Native traditions. Joe Sando of Jemez Pueblo sums up his profile of Pablo Abeita, "through all the changes in . . . the pueblo . . . and . . . in the world outside the one thing that did not change was Abeita's feeling for his native religion. Every morning with his corn pollen sack in his hand, he would address the Great Spirit, thank Him for the many blessings," and pray "for peace and prosperity for all mankind."[33] So it was that Pablo Abeita began every morning in the traditional Isleta way, and he always fully participated in the ceremonial life of his village. In 1940, near the end of his life, Abeita told a writer for *Desert Magazine*, "[A] factor that has helped us is that our main occupation is farming. Living close to the earth does something beneficial to men's nature."[34]

Pablo Abeita's long life spanned some of the most cataclysmic events of the late nineteenth and early twentieth centuries: the end of the Indian Wars and the government's attempt to break up tribal nations, widespread droughts and insect infestations leading to crop failures, the First World War and the global influenza pandemic of 1918, the Great Depression of the 1930s, and the beginning of Indian reform with John Collier and the Indian New Deal. Through it all, he persisted in advocating for Isleta (and all the Pueblos) to recover lost land, to stop encroachment on Pueblo land, and to improve conditions within the village with better health care, better education, and better farming and cattle-raising practices. Largely through his efforts, Isleta became one of the most progressive and prosperous of all the New Mexico pueblos.[35]

Pablo Abeita was at the forefront of the movement for reform of federal and state policies, focusing particularly on protection of Pueblo lands, education, and improved relations with Indian agents and school superintendents. He traveled to Washington on numerous Pueblo delegations, testified before Congressional committees on several occasions, and asserted that he had met every president in the period between 1890 and 1940 except Calvin Coolidge.[36] Theodore Roosevelt befriended Abeita when visiting Albuquerque, gave him a rifle that became one of Pablo's most prized possessions, and may even have spent time in Isleta. Another of Abeita's keepsakes was signed photos of very young Franklin and Eleanor Roosevelt.[37]

People gravitated to Pablo Abeita because of his charm, biting sense of humor, and wit. He became friends with almost everyone he dealt with, from lawyers to judges to federal officials, even to the president of the United States. He took every opportunity to speak in public or write letters to editors to elucidate his viewpoints and to publicize the plight of the Pueblo Indians. He was well known locally and throughout New Mexico as "the Grand Old Man of Isleta." However, as one of the leaders of the progressive faction within Isleta, Abeita made enemies among the group of conservatives who distrusted the government and wanted to maintain the status quo. During his term as judge in Isleta's Court of Indian Offenses, Abeita often delivered quite strict rulings, sometimes handing down sentences censuring sitting governors and their families, which did not make him any friends. While these conservatives often made things difficult for Abeita, sometimes hindering his advocacy work in Washington, DC, he persevered, remaining in Isleta Pueblo and working for the good of his people until the day of his death. One of his greatest triumphs may have been the part he played in the defeat of the Bursum Bill in the early 1920s. He pressured government officials and rallied allies in both the Indian and greater New Mexican communities. His leadership and advocacy did not stop the unfair adjudication of Pueblo land titles, but it did awaken the entire country to the plight of the Indians. According to one scholar, "it made the 1920s a seedbed for reform in Indian affairs."[38]

Figure 11. *Juan Rey Abeita, 1890,* Charles Lummis, photographer. Courtesy of the Pueblo of Isleta Tribal Archive, Yonan Cultural Center, Negative no. YACC01535.2008. Original print housed at the Autry Museum of the American West, Negative no. P8045

Pablo Abeita and Charles F. Lummis

These men [the friends of Indians] are supposed to be interested in Indians . . . everybody is interested in Indians, except the Indian himself, who is never consulted.
Pablo Abeita to William Hughes, Isleta, June 11, 1923, Roll 113, fr. 92–3, BCIM

Pablo Abeita was only seventeen when Charles Lummis arrived at Isleta Pueblo. Lummis stayed at Isleta for four years, from 1888 to 1892, during most of which Pablo was in school in Santa Fe. Although Juan Rey Abeita, who rented Lummis a room, was better acquainted with him during this period, Pablo Abeita and Lummis later became friends and carried on a correspondence until Lummis's death in 1928. From the time he arrived at Isleta, Lummis made his living through writing. Between 1891 and 1900 he wrote no fewer than eight books and numerous articles dealing with the Southwest; most of his books went through extensive reprintings.[1] Lummis was beginning to publicize and romanticize the Southwest and Isleta Pueblo in his writings, and Abeita realized he would be a tremendous asset in the quest for justice, especially regarding the pueblo's land rights. Lummis also employed numerous Isletans to help build his house in Los Angeles, El Alisal, and to work for him as caregivers and groundskeepers. Lummis, in turn, enabled Isletans to sell their pottery, clothing, and silver jewelry at local festivals.[2] Above all, Lummis was a fighter who battled for causes such as Native American land rights, a characteristic the two men shared. Yet, Abeita learned to stand aside from the intense controversies Lummis generated and focus on his family's interests and those of Isleta and the wider Pueblo world.[3]

Lummis was said to have been short of stature—he was 5′ 7″—but tall in character, with "bold ideas, ample ego, huge passions, and an outsized personality." Isletan scholar and teacher Ted Jojola characterized him as "maniacal at times . . . a womanizer, braggart . . . [whose] arrogance undercut his relationships . . . [and] almost cost him his life in several situations."[4] Lummis characterized himself as a popularizer, not an academic, so "he felt no compulsion to display either scholarly detachment or consistency in his work.[5] Yet he was quick to criticize other writers for their lack of precision or factual errors."[6] His work sought to promote both Hispano and Native American cultures in the Southwest, which sometimes led him into inconsistencies, prompting the California historian Kevin Starr to call him "the bantam cock of paradox."[7] Abeita, on the other hand, was much more diplomatic, exhibiting flexibility and a wry sense of humor; he searched for common ground and attempted to work with his adversary, be it the Indian agent, a school superintendent, or a member of the opposition party in his own pueblo.

Lummis tended to polarize a conflict, often demonizing his opponent. While Abeita was a peacemaker, Lummis was a pugilist who loved a fight, especially if he got a good story out of it. "At times his proclivity for jaunty journalism and the easy joke superseded consideration" and respect for Pueblo religion. Nevertheless, he was a tireless promoter of the New Mexico Pueblos and their rich traditions.[8]

Born in Lynch, Massachusetts, on March 1, 1859, Lummis studied the classics at home, taught by his father, a Methodist minister and educator. As a young boy he read Greek, Latin, and Hebrew. In 1878 he entered Harvard College but left Cambridge in 1881 following his marriage to Dorothea Rhoads, a young woman studying medicine in Boston, whom he later divorced. He then went to work for his father-in-law in Chillicothe, Ohio, where he managed a large farm for a year before accepting a position as editor of the *Scotia Gazette*, a local newspaper.[9] Lummis first encountered Indians during his epic walk in 1884, from Chillicothe to Los Angeles—a distance of 3,500 miles—where he had been promised a job with the *Los Angeles Times*. He wrote travel letters that were published in the *Times* and, in somewhat more accurate versions, in the Chillicothe paper that had employed him to make the journey.

Lummis arrived at Isleta on December 5, 1888, partially paralyzed from overwork at the *Los Angeles Times*. When he hobbled into the pueblo, he frightened many residents who believed if they touched a paralytic, they would come down with the same malady. Others wondered if there was a mystical kinship between Lummis and their paralyzed cacique.[10] Less than a month after he had arrived, Lummis had a room on the outskirts of the village on the main road leading into the church courtyard. He supported himself by turning out books and articles about Isleta and the Southwest.[11] He also took on a tutor named Henry Kendall to teach him Tiwa, the language spoken at Isleta, and paid him twenty-five cents to fifty cents per session. Kendall, whose given name was Domingo Jiron, revealed many sacred pueblo stories and ceremonies to Lummis.[12] Kendall will be discussed in chapter 7.

Lummis often visited the family of Archibald Rea, a local merchant with a store in the community. There he began a relationship with Eve Douglas, a teacher at the day school and sister of Rea's wife, Alice. At first welcomed at Isleta, pueblo officials later asked Lummis to leave, but his generosity to pueblo members and the protection the Abeita family provided him earned Lummis a place in the pueblo. His acceptance in Isleta was secured when he joined the fight against the government's policy of coercing Indian children to attend boarding schools such as the AIS and not letting them go home during vacations.[13]

THE "CAPTIVE ISLETAN STUDENTS" AT AIS

In 1891 the Isleta council of elders asked Lummis to assist parents with children at AIS who were kept almost as captives not being allowed to leave even during summer vacation. Juan Rey Abeita had eagerly enrolled two of his sons at AIS, but three years earlier, Antonio, his third and youngest son, had been carried off to the school. When Juan Rey went to Albuquerque to visit his children, professional bouncers threw him off the campus, threatening him with prison if he returned. He and the parents of the other thirty-six Isletan students at AIS were deep in grief, not knowing anything about their children.

Figure 12. *Henry Kendall, aka Domingo Jiron, in His Carlisle Institute Uniform.* Courtesy Cumberland County Historical Society, Carlisle, PA, Negative no. BS-CH-032

At the behest of the elders, Lummis gathered sworn affidavits from parents alleging that Superintendent William B. Creager was holding their children at AIS against their will. In 1891 he wrote to Commissioner of Indian Affairs Thomas Jefferson Morgan seeking permission for all Isleta students to be allowed to return home for summer vacation. Lummis was keenly aware of Morgan's views on Indian education, particularly his belief that Native Americans should be forcibly separated from their families and their culture. Morgan believed in taking whatever steps were necessary to keep Indian children in school.[14] Lummis noted that Superintendent Creager obtained the children by promising that they could spend summer vacations at home because their parents needed their help. However, "the promise had not been kept." Lummis wrote specifically on behalf of Vicente, Louis, and Antonio Abeita, the sons of Juan Rey Abeita "[who had] been forcibly detained for two years."[15] He also mentioned Remijio Chaves, Marcelino Jojola, and Antonio Jojola, whom he asked to be released. Lummis promised that the students would return to school at the end of summer vacation.[16] A week later Commissioner Morgan wrote to Creager, advising that "it would be well, probably to allow the children to go home for the summer, unless there are special considerations."[17]

Superintendent Creager, however, would only allow three students to return home that summer, one at a time. Then, in 1892, he flatly rejected the request of the Isleta parents that their children be allowed to return for summer vacation.

Lummis responded to this challenge by hiring Albuquerque lawyer Owen Marron of the firm Collier and Marron to petition the state district court for a writ of habeas corpus to force the children's release. The night before the July 6 hearing, Creager and two assistants, including Henry Kendall, Lummis's former tutor, came to Isleta and tried unsuccessfully to waylay Juan Rey Abeita to prevent him from attending the hearing. The next day, as Lummis and Abeita prepared for the hearing in Marron's office, a courier arrived from Creager, saying that he capitulated and would release Abeita's boys.

Figure 13. *Charles Fletcher Lummis with his wife Eve Douglas, daughter Turbesé, and Louis Abeita, one of the "captives" from the Albuquerque Indian School, c. 1892–1893,* photographer unknown. Courtesy of the Pueblo of Isleta Tribal Archive, Yonan Cultural Center, Negative no. YACC01800.2022. Original print housed at the Autry Museum of the American West, Negative no. P.33473B.

With the hearing cancelled, Lummis picked up the boys in his wagon by 11:00 a.m., to be delivered to Isleta that evening. All the villagers turned out in the plaza in front of the church for a celebration of the students' homecoming. Juan Rey Abeita and his wife were especially pleased to begin getting reacquainted with their youngest son, Antonio (Tuyo), whom they hardly knew. It would take another week before Creager released the girls because they were away at summer camp in the mountains. Lummis had to make many trips to AIS to force Creager to free all the children.[18]

Lummis was a fearless advocate for the Isleta children kept at AIS against their will. He scored a major victory by standing up to Creager, but in doing so he earned the ire of Commissioner of Indian Affairs Thomas J. Morgan who charged the arrogant newspaperman with "a slanderous attack upon the entire government system of schools."[19] Yet Lummis was undaunted. Throughout his career he kept up his criticism of Creager and Indian education, gaining powerful allies, including President Theodore Roosevelt. This led to important reforms in government-sponsored Indian education. Those reforms included the prohibition of forcible removal of Indian children from their families and a reversal of the policy favoring the break-up of family ties between parent and child. During the tenure of Commissioner Daniel M. Browning, Morgan's replacement, Congress enacted a law requiring parental consent before sending Indian children to eastern boarding schools.[20] A gradual easing of Superintendent Creager's strict, repressive policies led to a more humane approach to Indian education.[21] As Lummis's son Keith recalled in his biography of his father, "he had many things in his life to regret, but against them he set the day he took those three boys [sons of Juan Rey Abeita] back to Isleta."[22]

Figure 14. *El Alisal, Back View*, 2017, Dennis Harbach, photographer. Courtesy of Dennis Harbach, Negative no. Lummis HDR

Soon after the victory over Creager in 1892, Lummis and his new wife Eve became parents of a daughter, christened Turbesé (Sun Halo) by the child's godmother, Marcelina Abeita. In the iconic photograph (fig. 13), Lummis stands proudly next to Eve on his left, with Turbesé on her lap, and the young, recently rescued Louis Abeita on his right.

Always looking for a new adventure, Lummis left Isleta later in 1892 to begin a career in Los Angeles where he resided for the rest of his life. During the next thirty-six years, Charles Lummis raised a family, built his home, published a magazine, established a museum, headed a library, founded a Native American rights advocacy group, wrote several books, and took numerous photographs of Isletans, among other things. He maintained his connection with Isleta Pueblo through his photographs and visits, his correspondence with Pablo Abeita, and the building of his house, El Alisal.

EL ALISAL

Charles Lummis retained a close connection to Isleta, visiting the pueblo frequently to hire Isletan children to help construct his stone house in Los Angeles; he also hired Isletans to operate his household, helping in the kitchen, taking care of his children, and engaging in general housework. It is fair to say that without these Isletans, Lummis would not have been able to build and operate his house, outbuildings, and landscaping at El Alisal. It took him more than seventeen years to build it, although the finishing details took even longer; one might say that during Lummis's lifetime he never fully completed El Alisal.

Lummis named his house after the alder trees growing in the Arroyo Seco adjacent to his property. The compound eventually consisted of the main house, the second story of which served as his office, several outbuildings that housed the workers and guests, and extensive landscaping. El Alisal is now a historic site, maintained by the Los Angeles Department of Recreation and Parks.[23]

Pablo Abeita and Charles F. Lummis   **29**

Lummis paid his Isletan workers, although their parents often received the money. Sometimes payments were late, as Lummis was always struggling to make ends meet, as his wife Eve could testify. The usual arrangement with the workers involved Lummis purchasing train tickets and making advances to buy them clothes, expenses that were deducted from their salaries, which ranged from six to fifteen dollars per month.

When Lummis visited the pueblo to engage a new group of workers and make payments to their parents and guardians, he also renewed acquaintances and deepened friendships. In September 1900 Lummis traveled by train to Isleta, bringing his daughter Turbesé along with three workers: Marcelina, Marcelino, and Faustin. Only Marcelino returned to Los Angeles, along with two new workers, Felicita and Antonio (Tuyo).[24] Lummis's closest friend in the village was Juan Rey Abeita, father of the boys Lummis rescued from AIS in 1892, two of whom, Antonio (Tuyo) and Louis (Luis), worked for Lummis at El Alisal. When Lummis arrived in Isleta on September 7, 1900, he visited Juan Rey before anyone else.[25] Lummis packed a huge amount of socializing into his twelve-day September visit to Isleta. On the day of his arrival, he visited ten people, two of whom were related to his workers. Jose Felipe Abeita was Felipe's father, and Simon Zuni was Marcelina's grandfather.[26] Lummis spent much of his time visiting Juan Rey Abeita and Simon Zuni whose wives had similar nicknames. Juan Rey's wife was Fita (Josefita), and Simon Zuni's was Pita.[27] On the fifth day of his sojourn, Lummis borrowed Juan Rey's horse and visited several ranches of Isletans along the Rio Grande, including that of Pablo Abeita, whom Lummis called "compadre Pablo."[28] Juan Rey Abeita was the last person Lummis saw the day he left, September 28. His final entry in the diary of the trip says it all: "We gather at Juan Rey's after dinner. I buy a bottle of wine. We are at the depot at 9:45."[29] Lummis did not consider Pablo Abeita one of the "important men" of the village at this point. Nevertheless, the two carried on an extensive correspondence in the following decades as Abeita rose in prominence in the pueblo.[30]

Juan Rey's son Antonio (Tuyo) Abeita also admired Lummis and considered him a friend. They carried on a voluminous correspondence until Lummis's death in 1928.[31] In 1900 Tuyo first went to work for Lummis after he negotiated with Juan Rey for his son to go to Los Angeles. Tuyo befriended Lummis, and they often went hunting together. Tuyo managed the kitchen at El Alisal during the winter of 1900 and was working there on Christmas Day when Lummis's son, Amado, named after the respected politician Amado Chavez, died.[32] Tuyo returned to Isleta and in 1902 wrote to Lummis asking him to find him another job in Los Angeles. Lummis agreed to try but was unsuccessful. Then later in 1902, Tuyo asked for Lummis's support in applying to the Hampton Institute in Virginia, a boarding school similar to Carlisle in Pennsylvania. Lummis apparently agreed and sent a letter of recommendation even though he had been railing against Indian boarding schools in print for years.

Tuyo attended Hampton for several years, writing Lummis in 1905, "I . . . like this place very much. I was working on a farm in Sheffield, Mass. [where] Mr. and Mrs. Brown . . . often invite me to their cabin to sing Indian songs." After leaving Hampton, Tuyo returned to New Mexico, living at the village for a while, then moving to Silver City where he worked for his uncle doing carpentry work. Tuyo kept up his correspondence with Lummis during the nineteen teens, sending him specimens of local wildlife for the Southwest Museum, which Lummis founded while he was raising his family. Antonio lived outside the pueblo in Albuquerque for a while, returning to open a store in competition with Pablo Abeita's mercantile establishment.[33] Tuyo briefly entered the political life of the pueblo as treasurer, only to challenge and defy Pablo Abeita at every turn. In 1926 Antonio wrote Lummis, "We have moved to Albuquerque on a fruit ranch in Old Town, not far from the old San Felipe Church." He became involved in pueblo affairs in the early 1920s, charting a course similar but often opposed to that of Pablo Abeita.[34] In October 1922 Antonio Abeita told Lummis, "Collier was here a few days ago bringing your letter of introduction. Collier and I got busy the evening he was here and had the governor Remijio Lucero call a meeting of the principals. Collier explained to us the danger we were in should the outrageous Bursum bill become a law. It was decided to send a delegation to the general Pueblo Indian junta in Santo Domingo on Nov. 3. Collier told us it was you (Lummis) who started the movement in fighting for the Indian's rights."[35] (See chapter 9 for the fight against the Bursum Bill.)

Pablo Abeita started acting as an intermediary between Lummis and the pueblo, sometimes asking Lummis about Isletans working for him in Los Angeles and sometimes inquiring about payment of their salaries. In 1906 Pablo wrote Lummis, asking about a boy named Felipe who had worked for Lummis for a year and wanted to go home to Isleta to visit. Lummis responded that he could not let Felipe go until Abeita sent him another boy because Eve had no one to help her. It is not clear when Felipe received permission to leave, but just a few months after Lummis's June 12 letter, he wrote Abeita about a tragedy that befell another Isletan worker named Procopio Montoya. Lummis's servant, Francisco Amate, a Hispano folksinger who entertained guests at dinner, killed Procopio because of some petty argument over a watering hose. Procopio chased Amate with a rock after the singer had sprayed him with the hose. Amate shot him, claiming self-defense. Amate had obviously overreacted, and Isletans blamed Lummis for later defending Procopio's killer who was not charged.[36] Understandably, that incident ended the employment of Isletans at El Alisal and led to an estrangement between Lummis and Isleta that endured for more than a decade. Adding to the rift was Lummis's divorce from Eve who had helped negotiate his relationship with Isleta. Universally liked within the pueblo, she smoothed the rough spots in Lummis's character. Among the few Isletans who communicated with Lummis during this period were Antonio "Tuyo" Abeita and Pablo Abeita.[37]

LUMMIS IN LOS ANGELES

While building El Alisal with Isleta laborers, Lummis began his career as publisher of *Land of Sunshine* magazine—later *Out West*—and advocated for Native American causes, especially the California Mission Indians.[38] In November 1901 some fifty people gathered at Lummis's home and formed the Sequoya League, named after the famous Cherokee leader credited with inventing the Cherokee alphabet.[39] Lummis and the Sequoya League began to lobby President Theodore Roosevelt and Commissioner of Indian Affairs William A. Jones, focusing at first on the Cupeño Indians northeast of San Diego, threatened with eviction from their land. The Cupeños' homeland was located near Agua Caliente, or Hot Springs, walled off from the desert by a narrow mountain range. This band of Indians, consisting of 154 men, women, and children under a leader or captain, lived in a village of some forty houses, a small adobe chapel, and a new schoolhouse. They were called Cupeños because *cupa'*, in their language, meant hot springs. The springs fed a reservoir that in turn provided water to a system of acequias irrigating several hundred acres of farmland.[40] The Cupeños earned a substantial income from the hot springs, attracting tourists and health-seekers. They had survived various European onslaughts for over eight centuries, developing an independent and vibrant culture until the 1890s. Beginning in 1893 a claimant to a Mexican land grant that overlapped the Cupeño homeland began litigation to obtain title to the land in the Superior Court of San Diego County. The court ruled that the Cupeños must leave their homeland, basing its decision on the tribe's failure to submit a claim to the California land commission. Lummis testified in the Indians' favor in those proceedings, but the Cupeños lost their appeal, first to the California Supreme Court and then to the Supreme Court of the United States. The Cupeños were doomed to eviction.[41]

In December Lummis recommended to President Roosevelt that he establish a commission consisting of Lummis and other Sequoya League members to relocate the Cupeño Indians.[42] Lummis secured appointment to the commission, which recommended the so-called Pala tract over the government's choice of land for the Cupeños' new home.[43] Lummis wanted to supervise the removal of the Indians himself and suggested that federal troops forcibly remove the Cupeños to the Pala tract.[44] In the end, the government overruled Lummis and decided on a peaceful removal without government troops. Lummis had overplayed his hand, after boasting that only he and his Sequoya League friends could solve the Cupeño Indians' problem.

The Cupeño Indians resisted the move from their homelands. When the removal took place successfully without federal troops, the *Los Angeles Times* reporter noted that if Lummis "had appeared in [the Cupeños'] camp, it might have gone hard with them." The *Times* article lead read, "Lummis was superseded [*sic*]" and was titled "Indians Bundled Away Like Cattle to Pala." Lummis's influence on Indian affairs through the Sequoyah League waned after the Cupeño Indian debacle.[45]

LUMMIS'S LEGACY AND HIS CONNECTION WITH PABLO ABEITA

Pablo Abeita and Lummis communicated frequently during the first three decades of the 1900s about personal matters and business such as the promotion of Pueblo arts and crafts. Abeita arranged for selected ceramic artists, jewelry makers, and others to travel to Los Angeles at Lummis's expense to participate in the annual celebration of the city's founding, selling their wares and demonstrating their crafts. This event proved so popular in the village that it attracted many more craftspeople than there was space available; also, jealousy among competing participants led to cancellation of the event.[46]

An examination of the trajectories of the professional lives of Pablo Abeita and Charles Lummis reveals that the two men took markedly different paths. Both were passionate about the cause of Indian rights, but while Lummis engaged in grand gestures and epic battles with the federal bureaucracy, Abeita favored cooperation and focused on business close to home. By the early 1890s Abeita was starting a family, preparing to run the family business, and participating in the political and ceremonial life of the pueblo.

Lummis's acquaintance with the young Pablo Abeita turned into a friendship that lasted several decades until Lummis's death in 1928. In their correspondence, Abeita, as *padrino* (godfather) to Lummis's children, addressed Lummis as compadre; Lummis reciprocated.[47] The early relationship between the two men illustrates an important aspect of Abeita's character: his flexibility in negotiating polarized situations coupled with his firm adherence to his core principles. Lummis, by contrast, often antagonized officials with whom he disagreed, even alienating colleagues with whom he basically agreed. Unlike Abeita, Lummis sought major confrontations, as with AIS superintendent William Creager, which made for a good story at the time but often failed to accomplish lasting

Figure 15. *The Young Pablo Abeita, 1903,* DeLancey W. Gill, photographer. Courtesy of the National Anthropological Archives, Smithsonian Institution, Negative no. BAE GN 01994A 06337800

Pablo Abeita and Charles F. Lummis   **33**

change. Abeita on the other hand had the ability to find common cause with officials with whom he disagreed, thus achieving more long-term results. Lummis, for example, began his career as a political commentator, throwing down gauntlets and completely alienating opponents. There was no compromise or negotiation with Lummis, no middle ground.

As Pablo Abeita began to assert himself on behalf of Isleta, both with lawyers for the pueblo and with US government representatives, he evolved his core principles: 1) Isleta Pueblo was and is a sovereign nation with the right to govern itself and conduct its traditional religious ceremonies; 2) pueblo members could freely engage in economic pursuits (farming and ranching, mercantile businesses) to better their economic and social positions; 3) the US government should promote these individual efforts toward self-sufficiency without imposing restrictions on Isletans' self-government; and 4) because of the historical legacy of conquest and injustice imposed by the United States, the government should protect the pueblo from encroachment on pueblo land and water by non-Indians. Abeita took strong stands, but he remained open to compromise to achieve enduring results.

LUMMIS AND ISLETA PUEBLO

Charles Lummis exerted a powerful influence over Isleta Pueblo, some of it positive, some of it negative, and much of it decidedly mixed. Today, Isletans have mostly positive views about him, thankful for his photos of their ancestors. Lummis entered the village in 1888 at the invitation of the Juan Rey Abeita family and with the support of Amado Chavez but without formal permission from the pueblo. Isleta's war chief even asked Lummis to leave the village soon after his arrival. However, he gained some acceptance from the pueblo when he married the popular Tiwa-speaking teacher at the day school, Eve Douglas. Then, in 1892, Lummis became a hero when he forced AIS to release Isleta students who had not been allowed to go home during summer vacation. From 1892 when he left Isleta to move to Los Angeles until 1907, most pueblo members accepted Lummis as an important contact with the outside, non-Indian society. Isletans sent their children to work for him as household servants and construction workers to help build his house, El Alisal. Lummis also assisted Isletans in getting jobs in Los Angeles. But, when Lummis's favorite employee, singer, and repository of folklore, Amate, killed the Isletan Procopio Montoya over a minor disagreement, the murder put an end to most exchanges between Lummis and Isleta. Lummis did, however, continue to communicate with some Isletans, including Pablo Abeita, and frequently returned to the pueblo to visit and take more photographs.

Lummis's tenure in the village seems to have exacerbated the split between so-called conservatives and progressives. The conservatives objected to Lummis's photographs and his published writings revealing secret ceremonies, rituals, and dances. In 1902 the pueblo adopted a rule prohibiting the rental of property in the village to outsiders; violators were subject to fines and imprisonment. Although Juan Rey Abeita successfully challenged the rule in court, it reveals the depth of feeling in Isleta against what was seen by some as an unwelcome intrusion.[48] Lummis's mixed reputation in the pueblo is mirrored by a split among scholars. Some are embarrassingly laudatory, believing that Lummis could do no wrong, while others are more critical. Sherry Smith pointed out that Lummis's admiration for and support of Indigenous tribes, particularly in New Mexico and California, clashed with his publicity in favor of the Spanish settlers who conquered and subjugated the Indigenous peoples. When these two ideas came into conflict, something had to give.[49] That happened when he took sides after the killing of Procopio Montoya, protecting his Hispanic friend Amate from criminal prosecution.[50]

Lummis's reputation today rests primarily on the trove of photographs he took of the Pueblo Indians, most of them at Isleta. Many of these images are at the Autry Museum of the American West (formerly the Southwest Museum), in other photo archives, and in an exhibit called "Time Exposures: Picturing Isleta Pueblo in the 19th Century," organized by Henry Walt and sponsored by Isleta Pueblo.

Figure 16. *Before: Pupils and Teacher, Miss Turner of the Isleta Day School, 1904*, Frank Churchill, photographer. Courtesy of the National Museum of the American Indian, Negative no. N26974

Figure 17. *After: Children Scrambling After Candy, 1904*, Frank Churchill, photographer. Courtesy of the National Museum of the American Indian, Negative no. N26980

CHAPTER THREE

Photography at Isleta Pueblo

The 1912 D. W. Griffith Movie and the Wanamaker Expedition of 1913

Gentlemen of the expedition: The Indians of the pueblo of Isleta are very glad to see you and shake hands with you. . . . [However] I feel person- ally that I cannot sign this allegiance, because . . . my people have not been treated right by the United States Government. When such men as you gentlemen come and talk friendship to us, it reminds us of the tricks that were played upon us. . . . When all is settled as above said, you can get me to walk clear to New York to sign the name of Pablo Abeita.
Pablo Abeita, Statement to the Wanamaker Expedition regarding the Declaration of Allegiance to the US, June 27, 1913

When photographers and cameras first fanned across the country, Isletans and other Native Americans believed that anything that captured their likeness, such as a drawing or photograph, made them vulnerable and weakened their protection from harm. In that sense it was like witchcraft. "Parsons noted a tradition at Isleta against having one's picture taken; it was corroborated after a woman fell dead after seeing a photo of her deceased daughter. Perhaps the woman died of fright, but one might say she died of the photograph."[1] Over time the fear diminished, but Pueblos would go on to protect their cultural practices against the intrusive lenses of photographers' cameras.

Photography in the 1880s and 1890s was based on the wet-plate method requiring a wooden box camera, a tripod, and other accessories, including a lightproof tent for devel- oping the glass plates while they were still wet. James K. Hillers was one of the first expert Pueblo photographers in New Mexico. He joined the Bureau of American Ethnology's expedition that James Stevenson led to Zuni in 1879. Stevenson's wife, Matilda Coxe Stevenson, took her own photographer to Zia Pueblo where she offended the village leaders by photographing a four-day-long curing ceremony. Subsequently Zia ejected her from the village.[2] As the number of tourists and other visitors to the annual pueblo feast days grew—there were more than a thousand cars at Santo Domingo for their feast day in August 1925—the Pueblo Indians' response to unwanted picture-taking became more direct. Santo Domingo enacted a ban on photography in 1908 after an encounter with Superintendent Clinton J. Crandall, who tried to get permission for Ralph Emerson Twitchell to photograph the corn dance for the Santa Fe Railway. The governor and tribal council turned them down, apparently irritated by Crandall's implied threat, "if the Indians refuse to grant permission the chances are that they . . . will take pictures anyway." In this instance, unlike other cases to be discussed, "Twitchell took 'no' for an answer."[3] As most New Mexicans are now aware, today all pueblos prohibit photography and drawing in their communities or from the Rail Runner train, which passes through several villages.

Charles Lummis realized that "we have been very ill-mannered many times . . . and pictured many people against their will. . . . Enthusiasts are always liable to place their own zeal ahead of the rights of others."[4] Other photographers used such forms of persuasion as giving children candy after they posed for the camera.

It is said that this strategy worked better at Isleta than it did at Acoma.[5]

While taking pictures of dances and other similar ceremonies is now universally banned in the pueblos, there were some occasions in the past when photographs were not only accepted but actually embraced. Early examples were the use of photographs of Pueblo children sent away from home to boarding schools like Carlisle. When parents from San Felipe, Laguna, and Cochiti Pueblos asked Indian Agent Benjamin Thomas about the welfare of their children in the boarding schools, he showed them photographs of the boys, thus pleasing the parents greatly.[6] In 1882 when Isleta parents worried about their children at Carlisle, Thomas obtained photos of them in their uniforms, which he sent to the parents, "who never tired of looking at them."[7]

Pablo Abeita expressed gratitude for the photos Lummis took of him and of his family, usually at the pueblo. He frequently wrote Lummis inquiring about existing photos and asking him to come to Isleta to take his picture. Abeita posed for other photographers as well along with his wife and children, often in casual attire as if he just stepped outside his house with no ceremony or preparation. But even he had his limits, as the stories of D. W. Griffith's 1912 movie and of the Wanamaker Expedition demonstrate.

THE 1912 D. W. GRIFFITH MOVIE, *A PUEBLO LEGEND*, AND THE ATTEMPTED FILMING BY THE ST. LOUIS MOTION PICTURE COMPANY

The intrusive nature of the camera—especially the motion picture camera—was demonstrated with the making of the D. W. Griffith movie, *A Pueblo Legend*, at Isleta Pueblo, often under protest, in late May and early June 1912. Also, in September, the St. Louis Motion Picture Company attempted to make another film at Isleta, an effort that Pueblo leaders, especially Pablo Abeita, thwarted to the great displeasure of Superintendent Lonergan. Just as the photograph had a duality—helping Pueblo parents who celebrated photos of their boarding school children and hurting the spiritual life of the pueblo that depended on secrecy—so did the movies, which caused major conflicts within the pueblo.[8]

Although *A Pueblo Legend*, which Griffith shot in Isleta in just four days, from May 30 to June 4, 1912, was the first full-length movie filmed in New Mexico, it was not the first movie made in the village. The Edison Company earned that distinction when it filmed *Indian Day School* in 1897. Released in 1898 and lasting only fifty seconds, the film showed eight Isleta students and their teacher parading in and out of the school.[9]

During a brief stop in Albuquerque on New Year's Day 1911, D. W. Griffith announced that he would return the following year to shoot a film in places like Isleta.[10] In April 1912 he sent his advance man, Wilfred Lucas, to secure permission from Isleta and to make preparations for filming. Arriving at the pueblo in late April, Isleta's priest, Father Anton Docher, and the lieutenant governor received him because the governor was away. It is not clear how fully Lucas described the proposed movie, but Griffith claimed that Isleta leaders

Figure 18. *Still from* A Pueblo Legend, *1912*, D. W. Griffith, cinematographer. Courtesy of the State Archives of New Mexico, New Mexico Movie Stills Collection, Image no. 39465

had agreed "to permit the motion picture people to take practically complete possession of the village and assist . . . in making the film a complete success."[11] This turned out to be an overstatement.

Griffith arrived in Albuquerque in late May with forty-five crew members and actors, including Mary Pickford. He checked them into the Alvarado Hotel, "the finest, most modern facility in town."[12] Griffith claimed that he wanted to make the movie as culturally authentic as possible, using extras from Isleta Pueblo, but he failed miserably in this effort. The arrangement to hire Isletan extras fell through, as did an attempt to hire Native students from AIS. One reason for the reluctance of the Indians might have been the appearance of an article in the *Albuquerque Evening Herald* earlier in the year, claiming that Indians were falsely portrayed in the movies.[13] Thus no Isletans appeared in *A Pueblo Legend*, except briefly in background scenes. Nor were the props and costumes authentic. They were borrowed from the Harvey House Museum's extensive collection in the Alvarado Hotel. Yet the movie's credits refer to the "Museum of Indian Antiquities" as the source of the movie's props. The plot of the movie also lacked the authenticity of a true Pueblo legend promised in the title and narrative text and, in fact, did not make sense. Mary Pickford played a Hopi maiden, but she hardly resembled one. The plot involved the search for a lost talisman known as the Turquoise Sky Stone of Happiness and a battle scene between Isletans and Apaches during which Pickford's character improbably came to the Isletans aid, overpowering Apache warriors in battle. Finally, Pickford was accepted as the pueblo's heroine, falling in love with and marrying the Pueblo warrior, Big Brother. As Isleta governor Carlos Jojola charitably put it, "the movie does not make sense and is entirely made up."[14] More to the point is Professor Enrique Lamadrid's comment, "the plot is inane."[15]

Griffith's lack of preparation and cavalier attitude toward the pueblo almost led to the movie's demise in the middle of shooting. Soon after arriving at the village and loading supplies in waiting wagons, a pueblo leader stopped one of the movie crews "because he did not understand what was happening."[16] Only when he received a satisfactory explanation of the group's purpose did he release the wagon. But this early misunderstanding foreshadowed things to come. On the first day of filming, Isletan leaders suddenly halted production. Former governor Jojola believed that Isletans were offended by Griffith's failure to obtain formal permission to shoot the movie in the first place, in addition to the inaccurate and insensitive costumes that outraged Isletan leaders.[17] Mary Pickford provided more details about the costumes in an article she published in 1923:

> On our way from California to New York we stopped off at Albuquerque, New Mexico, to make this supposedly historical picture. In those days, motion-picture companies did not have research departments, and no work of this sort was done by anyone. We proceeded to the Indian village of Isleta, sixteen miles from Albuquerque, where the inhabitants were shocked when they saw us in our incomplete dress. None of them knew what motion pictures were except a few who were Carlisle graduates. A Frenchman who was cast for the part of a medicine man had been given permission to select a costume for himself from the museum in connection with the Harvey Hotel at Albuquerque. He had the ill luck to choose a very weird one with a short skirt trimmed with bells. When he came dancing into the scene with bathing trunks underneath his short skirt the Indians were furious; they thought we were trying to make fun of them. It seems that this was a sacred skirt, and they insisted that he take it off or that we all leave the village.
>
> The Indian Chief [the pueblo governor] . . . demanded that our chief, Mr. Griffith, come to their kiva, . . . which was in the middle of the village. A long ladder led up to it and there was but one entrance. Mr. Griffith was detained there all afternoon, and the rest of us did not know what to do. He told us afterwards that through the long session his hair stood on end several times. There was only one Indian who spoke English [Pablo Abeita], and Mr. Griffith had no idea whether he was translating his speeches fairly or not. He could not tell from the Indians' faces, as they were quite expressionless. He offered them two thousand dollars if they would allow us to stay the rest of the afternoon; but the council decided that no matter how much money we had, we must leave the village.[18]

According to Isleta oral history as expressed by former governor Carlos Jojola, Griffith was fined $2,000 after the council finally decided to allow the filming to continue for that day. Pablo Abeita, as a member of the tribal council, is likely to have played a major role, both in stopping the filming and allowing it to resume. The council members realized that Griffith's purpose was serious and undoubtedly saw the economic benefits that would accrue because of the national exposure the movie would provide. Abeita and the rest of the tribal council would not be so lenient the next time a film crew arrived at the village, however.

In September 1912 the St. Louis Motion Picture Company appeared at the pueblo to film the sacred Harvest Dance. The film crew arrived in the company of Superintendent Lonergan who thought he had obtained permission, but he was sorely mistaken. Isletans "forced them [the film crew] to take down the machine and cease their efforts to film" the dance.[19] Thoroughly miffed at Isletans' unwillingness to "dance for the motion pictures," Lonergan wrote Abeita a vitriolic letter quite inappropriate for official business of the Indian Service, saying that after all he had done for Isleta, "I will continue to do my duty, but it will not be so pleasant to aid people who refused the first favor I ever asked of them." Lonergan added that he did not think he had requested a huge favor, saying, "had I asked anything that would be difficult to grant or if this dance was a secret one I could readily overlook it."[20] Apparently he did not realize that all Pueblo dances are sacred as part of the annual round of ceremonies and as such are subject to the ban on photographs, whether single shots or multiple ones making up a movie.[21] Lonergan soon recovered from his fit of pique, but Pablo Abeita, who played a major role in Isleta's refusal "to dance for the movies" would continue to protest further intrusions into Isleta Pueblo's ceremonial life.

THE 1913 WANAMAKER EXPEDITION

Pablo Abeita adeptly turned potential intrusions into beneficial exchanges whereby Isleta received helpful publicity or government benefits, but he drew a line at exploitative interactions that yielded little benefit to the pueblo. Such was the case with the 1913 Wanamaker Expedition. Abeita experienced his share of patronizing admiration, but he soon developed an ability to deflect that attitude in his dealings with a broad spectrum of society and to find ways to turn the interaction in his favor. His contacts with the ill-fated Wanamaker Expeditions of 1913 and 1914 are good examples. It is difficult to overstate how misguided the Wanamaker Expedition for American Citizenship was, especially during its visit to Isleta in June 1913. Russell Barsh described the expedition and subsequent Wanamaker projects as involving "the entire Indian people in a melodramatic charade from which Indians gained nothing but empty promises."[22]

Abeita first connected with Wanamaker's aide, Joseph K. Dixon, who promoted and executed all of Wanamaker's historical projects. Dixon, a self-styled expert on Native Americans, created his credentials out of thin air, including his PhD; when Dixon contacted Abeita, he called himself Dr. Joseph K. Dixon. Dixon had attached himself to the merchandising magnate Rodman Wanamaker, whose high-end department store in Philadelphia successfully marketed the latest Paris fashions and luxury goods. Wanamaker became extremely wealthy, with homes in New York, Philadelphia, Newport, Atlantic City, London, and Paris among other places, which he filled with fine art. He "actively backed the Taft presidency, socialized with the 'Robber Barons' and

Photography at Isleta Pueblo   41

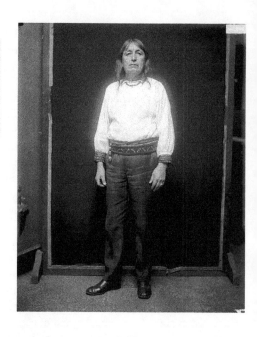

Figure 19. *Pablo Abeita, 1923,* DeLancey W. Gill, photographer. Courtesy of the National Anthropological Archives, Negative no. BAE GN 01997A 06338400

[was] intimate with the British royal family."[23] At Dixon's urging Wanamaker funded a series of projects aimed at making himself a renowned "Friend of the Indian." The first two projects were photographic expeditions that took Dixon, a would-be professional photographer, to numerous Indian reservations (not including the pueblos), where he collected 34,000 feet of motion picture film and 4,200 stills. At the Crow Agency in Montana in 1908, Dixon made a silent film of Longfellow's *Hiawatha*, using Crow Indians in the leading roles even though Hiawatha was Ojibwe; all with the blessings of the Indian Office. Wanamaker was so pleased with the results that he arranged for Dixon to deliver illustrated lectures in Philadelphia and New York where an estimated 400,000 people heard him speak.[24]

As popular as it was to the general public, compared to the work of the Bureau of American Ethnology and pioneering anthropologists of the day, "Dixon's work was maudlin, romanticized, and commercial." He learned his trade from Buffalo Bill Cody, an admired friend. Flushed with success, Dixon conceived of two more projects that were even more sensational and misguided: The American Indian Memorial and the 1913 Expedition for American Citizenship. Dixon envisaged the memorial as "a monumental statue of an Indian in New York harbor, as large as the Statue of Liberty, welcoming everyone to this shore." The memorial never came to fruition.[25]

Pablo Abeita had not heard of Wanamaker or Dixon until Lonergan notified him that the 1913 Expedition of American Indian Citizenship would soon arrive at Isleta Pueblo. The 1913 expedition grew out of the groundbreaking for the American Indian Memorial, which had been accompanied by much fanfare and publicity. President William Howard Taft turned over the first shovelful of dirt with a silver spade in the presence of hundreds of invited guests. Dixon described the only Indians present as a council of "thirty of the most famous chiefs, sensationalized as 'warriors' who have participated in hundreds of battles."[26] After raising the flag, the Indian Council signed a document the Indian Office had approved and President Taft had signed, called the Declaration of Allegiance to the Government of the United States by the North American Indian. It was this document, hand-lettered on vellum, that Isleta Pueblo and Pablo Abeita received four months later.

By the time the 1913 expedition arrived at Isleta, the romance of Dixon's projects had begun to give way to the reality of Indian life. Inspector James McLaughlin, appointed to supervise the journey, told Dixon, "it would be difficult to overcome the inherent distrust of the average Indian to sign any paper, fearing that it represents the cession of land or the relinquishment of . . . other rights."[27] That turned out to be an understatement. Dixon and McLaughlin found that resistance was wider than anticipated and strongest among the Pueblo Indians, including Isletans.

When the expedition arrived at Isleta, Dixon gathered leaders from Isleta, as well as from Acoma, Laguna, and Sandia, to raise the flag together and sign the Declaration of Allegiance. As these leaders were about to raise the flag and sign the document, Pablo Abeita, representing Isleta, balked. He notified Dixon and the gathered assembly,

> I feel personally that I cannot sign this allegiance, because I feel that my people have not been treated right by the United States Government's people. . . . When such men as you gentlemen come and talk friendship to us, it reminds us of the tricks that were played on us. I do not mean to say that this is another of the tricks, but until our rights are settled to the satisfaction of the Indians. . . . I dare not sign. When all is settled as above said, you can get me to walk clear to New York to sign the name of Pablo Abeita.[28]

Taken aback, Dixon called upon his power of persuasion and offered another empty promise: "whatever the other people may have done in the way of tricks, this is no trick . . . The new spirit in the White House is going to bring about just what you want: true justice and fair play." Dixon's empty assurances did not fool Abeita, and he held firm, saying, "Fair play and justice is all we ask. We have always been under the American flag, and have honored and respected it . . . and it seems to me that my heart is not in signing this." Faced with Abeita's two refusals Dixon resorted to a veiled threat wrapped in a vague assurance, "If you sign this allegiance today, what is the government going to say? They are going to say, 'Pueblos are loyal to the flag and we are going to help them.'" Abeita responded, "When I consider myself and my people,—my people come first, and then the flag."[29]

Abeita was asserting Pueblo sovereignty, something he would reiterate over and over in his oratory. The declaration's language did not recognize Pueblo sovereignty. On the contrary, it spoke of the Indian as "a conquered race, fast losing his identity in the face of the great waves of Caucasian civilization."[30] How could anyone expect Pablo Abeita to sign a document such as this? The Declaration of Allegiance was an admission of defeat, an end to Pueblo sovereignty, almost an informal treaty of surrender. Dixon saw it this way and had tried to cloak the document with authority by having President Taft sign it and by having Taft, as well as Commissioner of Indian Affairs Frederick H. Abbott and Secretary of the Interior Franklin Knight Lane, record messages to be played at each stop. President Taft's communiqué noted that the record of Indian affairs "was stained with the greed and avarice of those who have thought only of their own profit," but he whitewashed that record, saying that "the purposes and motives of this great Government . . . toward the red man have been wise, just, and beneficent."[31] This sounded like business as usual rather than a new spirit in the White House, and Abeita clearly saw through the entire charade.

Abeita knew that the Indian Office supported the expedition, so as Dixon continued pressing him to sign, he interrupted him, turned to Superintendent Lonergan and said, "What do you advise, Mr. Lonergan?" Without hesitation, Lonergan responded, "Sign." So, having made his point, Abeita signed.[32] Inspector McLaughlin chimed in, encouraging all the Pueblo representatives to sign, adding, "Pablo, your speech was fine." Then all the representatives signed the so-called Declaration of Allegiance.[33] After raising the flag, the expedition packed up and left, never to be heard from again. Arthur C. Parker, the Society of American Indians's secretary, provided an accurate if understated assessment of the entire Wanamaker project when he said, "The expedition had been marked by sensationalism, personal exaltation and even fakery . . . Mr. Dixon has overestimated the value of his labors."[34]

Abeita stayed in touch with Dixon, however, and engaged with him in two other projects involving Wanamaker. He realized that Dixon's promises and veiled threats were without substance but saw an opportunity to humor Dixon and the superintendent in a masterful piece of theater. In characteristic fashion, Abeita would press them to make good on their promises, as he had been doing all along. Thankfully, the American Indian Memorial never came to be, and the signed Declaration of Allegiance disappeared into private hands.

In spite of his bad reviews and his benefactor's waning interest, Dixon persisted with new Wanamaker-financed projects, some more harebrained than ever. A more sensible Wanamaker-sponsored project, however, paid for the education of two boys from the southwestern tribes to study at a prestigious eastern prep school with the ultimate goal of admission to Wanamaker's alma mater, Princeton University. Wanamaker's educational project was superior in its simplicity to most of the projects overseen by Dixon, who was apparently not involved in this one. In July 1914 Pablo's son, Jose, received a letter from Wilson Irvine, PhD, LLD, headmaster of the Mercersburg Academy in Pennsylvania, notifying him that he had been recommended (probably by Pablo) as being a boy "worthy of our selection."[35] This must have raised Abeita's hopes of having one of his sons graduate from an Ivy League university. Two months later, however, Pablo and Jose learned that headmaster Irvine and Wanamaker had selected a Choctaw named Gibson and a Pima named McGilberry as the first beneficiaries of this project. Headmaster Irvine told Jose that when those two boys had completed their studies at the Mercersburg Academy, Wanamaker would consider Jose for the next round.[36]

Abeita soon heard from Dixon again about a new project, just as ill-considered as the Indian Memorial and the 1913 expedition. The City of New York was celebrating the 300th anniversary of the so-called "purchase" of Manhattan Island from the Indians. Dixon proposed to lecture and exhibit his photographs for the occasion and wanted

Abeita "to put up a miniature adobe house, as an educational feature . . . for the schools of New York will attend in a body." Wanamaker would pay all his expenses as well as those of "some Indian woman who makes good pottery." Although Abeita was not interested in celebrating the anniversary of the Dutch conquest of the Onondaga Indians, he accepted the invitation and found ways to use the trip for his own benefit.[37] Dixon first contacted Abeita in mid-October 1914, requesting his presence in New York from the 7th to the 21st of November to construct a typical pueblo house "to show how the Pueblo Indians live." Abeita could either build a miniature house and bring it with him or build a full-scale adobe house at the exhibition. He chose the former option since Dixon did not have any adobe bricks and expected Abeita to bring them, an impossible task.[38] Besides the expenses for himself, Abeita requested more funding; in a wire to Dixon a few days before he was due to embark for New York he telegraphed, "Impossible to get Pueblo pottery-maker to go unless her husband is permitted to go with her."[39] Wanamaker eventually covered all these additional expenses, and Abeita negotiated extensions of the initially planned trip so he could stop in Washington, DC.

The miniature house was a great success. Abeita told Superintendent Reuben Perry about it, and the agent responded, "I am glad to know . . . that your house has been a revelation to the people of New York." But Abeita had other things to accomplish on the trip and told Dixon that he wanted to return to Isleta by way of Washington, DC, to meet with the commissioner of Indian affairs to discuss troubling matters relating to Isleta as well as other issues that Superintendent Lonergan had outlined in a five-page letter to Abeita.[40] Lonergan wanted Abeita to persuade Commissioner Cato Sells to visit Isleta and the other pueblos to see conditions for himself. It seems that Lonergan was under fire from conservatives at Isleta Pueblo, such as Juan Nepomuceno Lente, who had filed a petition for his removal.[41] Whether Abeita had any success, or even met with Commissioner Sells, is unknown, but it is likely that he was able to use this side trip on his Wanamaker-funded journey to put in a good word for Lonergan, who served another five years until Leo Crane replaced him in 1920.

It seems that Abeita did not know exactly what to make of Wanamaker when all was said and done. Writing to Father William H. Ketcham a year after the event in New York, Abeita seemed to think that Wanamaker might be able to use his influence in Washington, DC, to help Isleta with such matters as the eastern boundary question. Yet, he was wary that Wanamaker would want to do things on such a large scale in trying to help the Indians that it might end up hurting their cause. Abeita reckoned that cooperation and a good understanding between Wanamaker and the Indians, and among the Indians themselves, should be the first step before seeking his assistance.[42]

The Wanamaker projects began with photography, and those images are its most enduring legacy. It appears that Dixon's son, who never received any credit, took most of the photographs. As with Lummis's photographs, their quality varies, but some are excellent. Finally, D. W. Griffith's insensitive intrusion, like the Wanamaker Expedition, was exploitative of the Isletans, yet Pablo Abeita found ways to make it a more positive experience. Abeita managed to shift the focus of both events and give them a meaning that had greater relevance for the people of Isleta.[43]

Figure 20. *Bridge over the Rio Grande 1.* Courtesy of the Leonard Abeita Collection, Isleta Pueblo

Figure 21. *Bridge over the Rio Grande 2.* Courtesy of the Leonard Abeita Collection, Isleta Pueblo

CHAPTER FOUR

Abeita and Father Ketcham

The Bridges over the Rio Grande

*The white man . . . want[s] us to be left without a home, without a
country, without a place where to lay our head.*
Senate, Committee on Indian Affairs, Pueblo Indians of New
Mexico. Pablo Abeita, Statement to the Senate Committee on
Indian Affairs hearing, February 13, 1913, Washington, DC. *Pueblo
Indians of New Mexico*, 62nd Congress, third session, Washington,
DC, 1913

Although Isleta and other pueblos were blessed with ample lands irrigated by the
Rio Grande, the river often flooded, causing damage to fields and destroying make-
shift bridges. The 1886 flood was especially severe, wiping out much of Santo Domingo
Pueblo, including its church, and damaging Isleta's wheat and cornfields, and its vineyards. Most existing bridges were destroyed, including the one at Isleta that connected
the village west of the river to its fields to the east and to the main north-south highway.
Pablo Abeita had seen this devastation in his youth, and after the severe deluge of 1905
that flooded the community, he began his campaign to get the government to pay for
permanent bridges across the Rio Grande at Isleta and San Felipe.[1]

Abeita's contact in Washington, DC, was Rev. William H. Ketcham, director of the
Bureau of Catholic Indian Missions, an influential advocacy society founded in 1872
and one of the funders of the Sisters of Loretto's Indian Industrial School in Bernalillo.[2]
When his father moved from Texas to Oklahoma City, Ketcham attended the Sacred
Heart Monastery there. In 1892 the vicar apostolic of Indian Territory ordained Ketcham,
making him the first priest to be ordained in that jurisdiction. He became interested in
Indian work when he served for eight years as a missionary, first with the Muskogee and
then with the Choctaw Nations.[3] This experience set Ketcham apart from other so-called
"friends of the Indians," who had never worked with Natives.

During a visit to New Mexico in early 1910, Ketcham became acquainted with Pablo
Abeita and Isleta Pueblo, at which time he inquired what the community could use to
improve the lives of its inhabitants. Abeita explained the culture and the needs of the
pueblo, and a friendship began to grow between the unlikely pair. Isleta's most pressing
need was a bridge. Ketcham wrote to Abeita, "to my mind the bridge you desire over the
river at Isleta, is one of the things of foremost importance, and I talked about the matter . . .
with the Commissioner [of Indian Affairs]." Ketcham asked Abeita to draft a letter to the
commissioner "giving your reasons for the bridge and some idea of its length, cost, etc."[4]

As a result, Abeita conveyed the information to Superintendent Reuben Perry who, in turn, wrote the commissioner of Indian affairs pointing out that the Rio Grande separated San Felipe and Isleta from their farms. Perry noted that at San Felipe the village was on the west side of the river, and its farmland and the railroad were on the east side, which meant that the villagers had difficulty "getting their products [produce] to their homes . . . [and were] not even able to maintain a footbridge by which they can cross the stream." Even more compelling was Isleta's situation where the homes and railroad station were on the west side of the river, but the residents cultivated some four thousand acres of land east of the river. There they raised alfalfa, corn, wheat, oats, melons, and other crops in large quantities, all of which the Isletans had to transport across the river to the village. It was very difficult for them to get their agricultural products across the river where they needed them and for them to get back and forth when the Rio Grande was running high, as it did in April, May, June, July, and occasionally in August and September. Perry estimated the cost of the bridge at $15,000.[5]

Abeita and Ketcham did some lobbying during the remainder of 1910, and by February 1911 the New Mexico Territory congressional delegate William Henry "Bull" Andrews of Albuquerque notified Abeita, "I got the bridges in . . . the bill passed the house and is now in the senate . . . I am sure it will get through." By March the bill had passed the Senate and was signed into law.[6] Abeita would have his bridges. The contracts to build them were negotiated in October with the Patterson-Burghardt Construction Company of Denver, which specialized in the design and building of bridges. Abeita was able to get work mixing and placing concrete and laying the wood plank floor of the original bridge for several Isletan men. The bridges still stand with modifications, monuments to Pablo Abeita's foresight and perseverance.[7] Soon after completion of the bridges, Abeita wrote Ketcham, expressing his gratitude on behalf of the entire pueblo for his help. He told Ketcham, "it is a fine Bridge. We are proud of it." When it was finished, Isleta priest Father Docher and two other priests blessed it. Then the Isletans walked "in procession from the Church to the Bridge and back." As Abeita exclaimed, "it was a sight I'll never forget."[8]

Unlike other projects for which Abeita advocated, this one moved remarkably fast. It was less than two years from initial discussions of the bridges until their completion in December 1911. Father Ketcham told Abeita in April 1912, "I am delighted indeed that the [Isletans] have a bridge, and proud of the fact that I was instrumental in getting it for them. I appreciate their gratitude."[9]

Initially, Isleta considered the bridge as its bridge. Non-Isletans had to get permission to cross it from Abeita or from the pueblo.[10] Within a couple of years after its construction, when it was opened to everyone, the bridge created a problem. Abeita wrote to Ketcham in June 1913, "the bridge is worth to us Isleta Indians more than a million dollars, but it is worth more than two million to our neighbors . . . who cross . . . between three to twenty thousand head of sheep a week." He complained that the sheep owners used the Isleta bridge even though they had access to closer bridges at Albuquerque or Los Lunas "so they can pasture or graze their sheep on our lands for a week or two before and after crossing the bridge."[11] Ketcham sent Abeita's letter to the assistant to the commissioner of Indian affairs, Edgar B. Merritt, who responded by passing it along to Superintendent Lonergan. Yet, nothing was done to correct this trespass.[12] At one point

Abeita took the idea that the bridge was Isleta's bridge one step further, suggesting to Ketcham that Isleta charge tolls to be applied to maintenance.[13] The bridge over the Rio Grande was a similar story to the coming of the AT&SF: a mixed blessing. The railroad brought tourists to Isleta to buy Pueblo arts and crafts and transported Pablo Abeita and other Isletans all over the country, but it also caused flooding and injured livestock and people. Initial boons to Isleta, both the railroad and the bridge also became thorny problems.[14]

PABLO ABEITA AND WILLIAM H. KETCHAM

The successful completion of the Rio Grande bridges, one at Isleta, the other at San Felipe, was a huge victory for Abeita's on-the-ground advocacy and Father Ketcham's lobbying skills. Throughout the nineteen teens until Ketcham's death in 1921, the two continued a voluminous correspondence and scored many more successes. After Ketcham's death, Abeita continued writing to other representatives of the Washington-based Bureau of Catholic Indian Missions, particularly Secretary Charles S. Lusk and Father William M. Hughes.[15]

During the negotiations for the bridge in 1911, Ketcham told Abeita that after talking to the commissioner of Indian affairs, he thought it would be a good time to send a delegation from Isleta to testify before Congress about Pueblo government and customs.[16] Abeita replied that he would very much like to be part of the delegation and asked Ketcham to use his influence "so that the pueblos would send me as one of the delegates." Abeita explained that he had been to Washington twice before and had been elected president of the delegation. However, on those occasions he did not speak for the delegation and "[Commissioner Francis E.] Leupp got a very bad idea of what the pueblos are." Abeita wanted to be part of this new delegation so that such a thing would not happen again.[17] Ketcham convinced school Superintendent Reuben Perry to write a letter of support, noting that "Pablo Abeita [is] the best posted of all the Pueblo Indians," but in the end Isleta did not send a delegation.[18] Abeita wrote Ketcham in February 1911, "as regards the . . . delegation to see . . . [Commissioner] Valentine,[19] the Indians have given it up . . . until sometime during [the] fall. As soon as I have a little time I will write a long letter about our customs and rules for governing our people and just what we need in the way of authority."[20] In April Abeita followed through, telling Ketcham, "I sometimes cannot but feel sorry for my people, they are my people, I love them and will stick by them to the end." What was needed he said was "one who understands the Indians and one who the Indians understand and respect . . . this man, that should be appointed by our commissioner, need not meddle with the Gov. and Council except when invited for an explanation." Here Abeita and Ketcham were laying the groundwork for Abeita's appointment in 1914 as judge of the Court of Indian Offenses, to be discussed hereafter.[21]

Abeita and Ketcham worked well together because the Isletan saw the priest as a man of principle who understood Indians and could get things done. Abeita displayed a keen interest in Isleta farming in 1913 when he wrote Ketcham about the current situation with the agency farmer. After an Isletan had resigned the position, the Indian Service appointed a non-Indian named Stevenson as agency farmer. Abeita noted, "we have to teach Stevenson what he will have to . . . teach us. . . . I would like to see an Indian given a place . . . [as agency] farmer."²² Abeita was eventually appointed agency farmer at Isleta, which is discussed in more detail hereafter. Throughout their correspondence, he regularly advised Ketcham of farming conditions at Isleta. "One thing I can assure you father," he wrote in December 1913, "we will not starve so long as there is water in the Rio Grande."²³ The next spring Abeita reported, "the year promises fine, the wheat looks fine, alfalfa . . . ready to be cut, the corn coming up and vegetables all in fine shape and lots of fruit too."²⁴ These reports show that Pablo Abeita was always connected to the agricultural cycle at Isleta, both for himself and for the community as a whole.

Father Ketcham also proved instrumental in helping Abeita stay informed about the happenings in Washington, DC, that affected Indian Country. He obtained copies of legislation and books for Abeita that were hard to get at Isleta. One of those books, edited by Frederick Webb Hodge and published by the Smithsonian's Bureau of American Ethnology, was the *Handbook of American Indians North of Mexico*. It was first published around 1906 and reprinted in 1975 in two volumes covering every Indian tribe in North America, including Isleta.²⁵ Abeita requested a copy of the book in January 1911, and Ketcham sent it a month later. Abeita was pleased to receive it but was critical of the entry on Isleta, which Charles F. Lummis contributed. "Lummis says a lot [about] us Isletas and [I] can only say that his guesses are wrong . . . not until I finish my book . . . [will] those living then . . . know the real and true tradition of the Pueblo Indians of New Mexico." If Abeita finished his manuscript, no part of it has surfaced to date.²⁶ In addition to books, Ketcham and his staff dispatched copies of pending legislation for Abeita and explained the important provisions.²⁷

All in all, Father Ketcham was an indispensable part of Pablo Abeita's project to improve conditions at Isleta. Ketcham and his successors at the Bureau of Catholic Indian Missions lobbied Congress to pass legislation favorable to Isleta, like the bridge bill, and to defeat harmful legislation like the Bursum Bill.

CHAPTER FIVE

Pablo Abeita in the Pueblo

*The taxation question; I could put an argument 2 miles long, and in the
end I would conclude by saying that we ought to tax the white people for
the land they took away from us instead of the white people taxing us for
what land they never gave, because what land we have at present is only
what the white people did not appropriate.*

Pablo Abeita, Statement to the Senate Committee on Indian Affairs
hearing, February 13, 1913, Washington, DC

After completing his formal education and working for the Albuquerque newspapers,
Pablo Abeita returned to Isleta and began a life-long involvement in the governance
of the pueblo. He served in Isleta's government on numerous occasions as secretary,
councilman, and lieutenant governor. In addition, the Indian Office employed him as an
agency farmer with duties such as managing the sale of Isleta alfalfa. As agency farmer,
Pablo utilized the censuses for various purposes such as determining school enrollment,
making him uniquely suited for taking the federal census of 1910. Later he assumed the
judgeship of the Court of Indian Offenses in Isleta (see chapter 8). Finally, he served as
the postmaster of the pueblo and on the Isleta Cattle Trust in his later years. In each
post he gained experience that provided him a firm foundation for subsequent positions
and informed his role as an advocate for Isleta and New Mexico pueblos more generally.
Besides his official positions, Abeita entered into the life of the pueblo in many other
ways—through his participation in all the ceremonial rituals, and his involvement in
traditional and modern games, like baseball.

By the time Abeita entered political service, Isleta had had a long history of self-
governance. "We have a form of government that we inherited from our ancient forefa-
thers long before the birth of the U.S. Gov't. in North America," he said. The government
consisted of a governor, a first lieutenant governor, and a second lieutenant governor. A
council, with six men (later, women as well) appointed by the governor and six by the superintendent, worked in tandem with the governor. The governor appointed a secretary, and
the council designated the treasurer. The council controlled the community funds. It also
consented to any new land given to an Isletan, land the member had to use within a year,
otherwise it reverted to the community. Other positions in the government consisted of a
mayordomo (who supervised the ditch work), elected by the community, and guards, elected
or appointed, who watched for stray animals. The pueblo also elected a war captain for
internal affairs who, with the help of assistants, was in charge of the lands used for grazing.[1]

Pablo Abeita's years of service began as early as 1894, when at the age of twenty-four,
he served as lieutenant governor, a post he would go on to hold four more times. While
serving as lieutenant governor in 1904, the governor appointed him secretary. Older

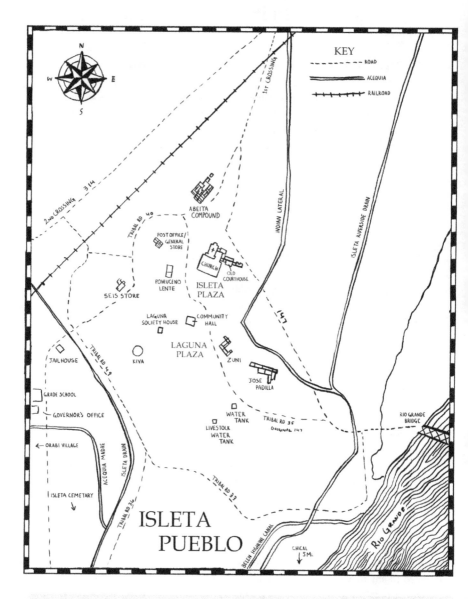

KEY

- - - - ROAD
═══ ACEQUIA
+++++ RAILROAD

N
W E
S

1ST CROSSING

INDIAN LATERAL

ISLETA RIVERSIDE DRAIN

2ND CROSSING 314

TRIBAL RD 40

ABEITA COMPOUND

POST OFFICE / GENERAL STORE

CHURCH

OLD COURTHOUSE

POMUCENO LENTE

ISLETA PLAZA

SEIS STORE

147

LAGUNA SOCIETY HOUSE

COMMUNITY HALL

JAILHOUSE

TRIBAL RD 49

KIVA

LAGUNA PLAZA

ZUNI

JOSE PADILLA

GRADE SCHOOL

GOVERNOR'S OFFICE

WATER TANK

TRIBAL RD 36

RIO GRANDE BRIDGE

LIVESTOCK WATER TANK

ORIGINAL 147

ORABI VILLAGE

ACEQUIA MADRE

ISLETA DRAIN

TRIBAL RD 23

ISLETA CEMETARY

TRIBAL RD 36

ISLETA
PUEBLO

BELEN HIGHLINE CANAL

RIO GRANDE

CHICAL 5 Mi.

Figure 22. *Map of Isleta Pueblo, after Stanley Stubbs, Bird's Eye View of the Pueblos,* map by Maya Shakur, 2022

governors often turned to younger men who were able to read and write in Spanish and English, enabling the governors to communicate with the superintendents and the territorial—later state—and federal officials. As a representative of his pueblo's government, Abeita looked to the BIA for help on various issues, including encroachment, but he also ably defended the pueblo's culture and sovereignty from US government overreach.

PABLO ABEITA AS CENSUS ENUMERATOR

Pablo Abeita was well prepared to be the enumerator or census-taker for the 1910 Federal Census of Isleta Pueblo. As Superintendent Reuben Perry said in his letter of recommendation, "he is well known to all the Pueblo Indians and speaks English, Spanish, and the various pueblo languages."[2] Also, in July 1905, Abeita helped Superintendent James K. Allen prepare his annual report by providing him with the data regarding "the people who have died and . . . the children who have been born in the past year (1904)." To do this he had to familiarize himself with the 1900 Federal Census of Isleta. Abeita knew everyone in the village from his experience running the store in the family compound.[3]

After receiving Superintendent Perry's letter of recommendation, census official Paul A. F. Walter notified Abeita on April 20, 1910, of his appointment as enumerator. Thus began a long correspondence with Walter culminating in Abeita's completion of the detailed, fifty-one-page census on May 17, 1910. From the outset Abeita peppered Walter with questions, revealing how conscientious he was and how silly some of the questions in the census were. For example, one question was, "language spoken." Abeita correctly listed "Tiwa," but Walter somewhat patronizingly told him to change his response to "Isleta" because "that is the way Uncle Sam wants it."[4]

One of Abeita's first questions, even before he received the appointment, was whether he might serve as enumerator for other pueblos besides Isleta. He pointed out that he was quite familiar with nearby pueblos such as Laguna and San Felipe and that those communities might not have a resident as well educated and with such good penmanship as he. Walter responded somewhat curtly that each pueblo would have a separate enumerator and that Abeita would be assigned to Isleta.[5] So much for his hopes of full employment in the spring of 1910. Abeita continued to pose questions to Walter after he received the blank census forms. For instance, the simple question of a person's age was complicated when Abeita knew people's ages better than they did. What was he to do if the known age differed from the reported age? "If you know a man's age better than he does himself . . . it is your duty to put down what you believe to be the facts," instructed Walter. In other areas, such as agricultural production, Walter noted, "it must be mostly guesswork, but get your guesses as near to the facts as you can."[6] Abeita apparently questioned the propriety of some of the census queries, including those in the agricultural census. The reluctance of tribal elders made him testy about answering detailed questions regarding the quantity and value of crops and fruit produced on every tract of land when that value exceeded $250 per year. Abeita was charged with reporting on the animals that every Indian owned and responded that individual Isletans only produced enough livestock, crops, and fruit for their subsistence and did not know their market value because they did not sell them.[7]

When Abeita objected to these and other similar questions, Walter turned the matter over to Special Agent Elmer W. Marsh, an official sent to New Mexico specifically "to wrestle with the census of the Indians."[8] Marsh was a troubleshooter tasked with making sure that the census of the pueblos went smoothly. He had to deal with villages such as Sandia and San Felipe that had been assigned non-Indian census takers and whose members were reluctant to communicate with them.[9] Pablo Abeita was the least of Marsh's problems. He knew Abeita would provide a complete census once he was convinced that all the questions were necessary and that the answers would not be used against the Indians. Special Agent Marsh was persistent in requiring answers to all the census questions, asking Abeita for his best estimate in response to these detailed questions, telling him, "I note what you say regarding the suspicions of some of the older Indians, and you must endeavor to allay these as much as possible; telling them that the information which you are trying to obtain will not be used to hurt them in any way; on the contrary, it will be a benefit to them inasmuch as it will give the Indian Bureau a thorough understanding of the conditions of the Indian people, and thus place it in a position to help them."[10]

Presumably, Abeita provided complete and informative answers to the questions in the agricultural census, but unfortunately, we will never know. After being housed at the census bureau for ten years, the government deemed them to have "very little or no probable value," and, backed with authority from Congress, the bureau sent all the agricultural schedules, weighing approximately a hundred tons, to the Government Printing Office where they were "mutilated and sold as waste paper." Unlike the New Mexico archives that met a similar fate under the administration of Governor William A. Pile (1869–1871), but were later retrieved, none of the mutilated agricultural censuses for the year 1910 survived, although the rest of the census did.[11]

Other dubious and intrusive questions were found in the section titled "Special Inquiries Relating to Indians." The questions included: "proportion of Indian and other blood" and "whether living in polygamy [and] if living in polygamy whether the wives are sisters," and "[whether] living in a civilized or aboriginal dwelling."[12] In most instances, Abeita duly entered the answers, but he left the polygamy question blank for every household. Responding to the question about whether the people lived in civilized or aboriginal dwellings, he wrote "civ" in each blank. As to the question about blood quantum, Abeita responded "full" in all but twenty-five cases. Doubtless Pablo Abeita found these questions offensive, but he did his best to answer them.

Another census question that generated inquiries from Abeita was section 42, "Graduated from what educational institution." Unlike the agricultural census questions, which he was reluctant to answer, Abeita was eager to provide all the information he had about Isletans who had studied at recognized schools and colleges, as he himself had done. Abeita attended prestigious schools in New Mexico and actively encouraged his own children to take advantage of every educational opportunity. Special Agent Marsh, however, was not interested in the details of Isletans who had attended—but had not graduated—from an educational institution. Instead, he instructed Abeita that "unless an Indian is a graduate from some school no entry should be made [in column 42]." Abeita, however, refused to follow this instruction, listing 102 entries of Isletans who had both attended and graduated from various schools. This information was clearly a source of pride for Abeita and the students themselves, and Marsh was not going to prevent them from providing it.[13] With a population of 963, Isleta Pueblo could boast a 10 percent rate of students who attended off-reservation schools, mostly in New Mexico, near the pueblo. By contrast, Laguna, with a total population of 1,472, reported only ten such students (less than 1 percent), and all but two of them attended either Carlisle or Haskell Institute.[14] This was undoubtedly an undercount because the Laguna census-taker was not as aggressive as Pablo Abeita. Census figures for the year 2000 show Laguna with about 79 percent having attended high school and higher, while Isleta's figure is about 73 percent.[15]

The three most popular schools among Isletans were AIS, St. Catherine's, and the Sisters of Loretto's school in Bernalillo. The information Abeita provided showed that more than half of those who attended off-reservation schools went either to St. Catherine's Indian School in Santa Fe (thirty attendees) or the Sisters of Loretto's school in Bernalillo (thirty-eight attendees); most of the others attended AIS (twenty-four attendees). Catholic religious orders operated the schools, and both earned good reputations at Isleta Pueblo. What sets Isleta apart from other pueblos was not only the enrollment at these schools but also how the parents chose local schools over the eastern boarding schools, such as Carlisle, Haskell, and Hampton. This was due in part to the example set by Pablo Abeita and his brother Marcelino, both of whom attended the prestigious St. Michael's College in Santa Fe.[16] These schools are discussed in more detail in chapter 7, "Pablo Abeita and Indian Education."

At the outset of his work, Abeita was told that his pay would be $6.00 per day, the maximum he could bill. He tried several times to no avail to get his compensation increased because of the additional work he was required to perform. His final invoice totaled $156, but because of bureaucratic red tape, and lost checks, he did not receive compensation until July 2, 1911.[17]

Figure 23. *Superintendent James K. Allen with Jar on Head in Front of Day School, 1904,* Frank Churchill, photographer. Courtesy of the National Museum of the American Indian, Negative no. N26973

Figure 24. *Student and Teacher in Classroom at St. Catherine's Indian School, Santa Fe, n.d.*, Tyler Dingee, photographer. Courtesy of the Palace of the Governors Photo Archives, Negative no. 120412

Abeita had many other jobs and activities to occupy his time, including judge of the Court of Indian Offenses and agency farmer, so when the 1920 census was due to be taken at Isleta Pueblo, he did not offer his services. Instead, Donaciano D. Romero became the census-taker. His handwriting was impeccable, but he elicited less information than had Abeita in 1910. This was due in part to a simplified form that did not contain the section, "Special Inquiries Relating to Indians."[18] Abeita appeared in household 164 in the 1920 census, occupation: farmer, with his wife, Maria D. [Dolores], and their four sons, ranging in ages from twenty-two to three: Juan Rey, Jose S., Remijio, and Ambrosio.[19] The 1910 census to which Pablo Abeita devoted so much time now stands as perhaps the most detailed and informative of all the Isleta Pueblo censuses.

Pablo Abeita as Agency Farmer

In addition to monitoring internal affairs, Isleta's government had ongoing interactions with the Indian Office. Indian agencies employed a variety of personnel besides agents or superintendents, including teachers, stockmen, farmers, and laborers. The duties of an agency farmer were to oversee farming activities, which included the teaching of modern farming methods to Native farmers. The responsibilities of the farm laborers were similar, but they received a reduced salary. Pablo Abeita served in both positions off and on between 1905 and 1916. During the time that he did not fill one of these positions, he often performed tasks similar to those of agency farmer or farm laborer, and was the superintendent's "go-to man" in Isleta. In 1905, Pablo Abeita was employed as a farm laborer at an annual salary of $720. In that year there were 280 farms at Isleta, with an average of seven acres each under cultivation and irrigation. There were about eight thousand acres of irrigable land and forty thousand acres of grazing land at Isleta.[20] The jobs he undertook ranged from ascertaining which farmers had alfalfa to sell to helping Isletan farmers acquire modern farm equipment. For instance, Superintendent Lonergan wrote Abeita in August 1912, asking for the names of those who wished to sell alfalfa and the price for which they would deliver it on board railroad cars at Isleta.[21] Then in June, Lonergan wrote to ask Abeita if a Mr. Yessler of Nara Visa, New Mexico, could obtain a carload of mares, weighing eight hundred pounds.[22] In both instances, Abeita had to inquire whether anyone in the village wanted to sell horses or alfalfa. In addition to facilitating the sale of the grain and livestock for Isletan farmers and stock raisers, the agency farmer helped them to acquire needed farm equipment. Farmers informed Abeita of their needs, and he, in turn, let the superintendent know. For example, in July 1914, Lonergan wrote him about a harness for Bautista Montoya. The superintendent agreed to find a harness, see if there were funds available to pay for it, and if not, give it to Bautista on credit, allowing him four years to make full payment.[23]

In 1916 Abeita wrote Father Ketcham that he had asked to be named agency farmer for Isleta. He may also have served in this capacity before. In 1916 he believed he would be able to continue to help the Indian Office and his people. He got the job.[24]

The superintendent also depended on Pablo Abeita to assist him in the functioning of the school system. Upon completion of primary school at the Isleta Day School, the students made the trek to AIS or began schooling in Bernalillo or Santa Fe, usually at the Sisters of Loretto's school, SFIS, or St. Catherine's. Lonergan told Abeita on October 9, 1912, "I am enclosing herewith a list of pupils between the ages of 7 and 14 not included in Miss Watson's [the day-school teacher] school roll. We have no way of knowing which of these are attending the Albuquerque school and the Sisters' [of Loretto] school." Lonergan asked Abeita to get a copy of the census so he could track down the parents.[25] Finally, Superintendent Perry of AIS gave notice in September 1912 that he would be sending two teams to Isleta to gather up children for the school. He sent a memo to Abeita as well and added a handwritten note: "Pablo: Please help us this time all you can."[26]

On other occasions the superintendent tasked Abeita with cleaning out the school coal shed, and in the same letter, depended on him "to run things at Isleta during my absence."[27] The superintendents also turned to Abeita for help in matters regarding Isleta's eastern boundary, state taxation, and the bridges (see chapters 8, 9, and 10). In one letter, Lonergan informed him that he was going to Santa Fe to meet with Special Attorney Wilson "to discuss our work" on the eastern boundary.[28] Superintendent Lonergan relied on Abeita for a wide variety of matters beyond the traditional duties of the agency farmer.

The position of agency farmer kept Abeita well informed about what was happening within the pueblo and the outside world. He was able to meet the people with influence and power who could help further his hopes for Isleta. Abeita was a farmer himself, raising produce he sold in his store.

Pablo Abeita worked hard, like most Isleta farmers, but he also enjoyed leisure activities. Although few documents exist about them, photographs and pueblo lore reveal that he actively participated in Isleta's games. Visitors to Native American communities, like Charles Lummis, were struck by the number and variety of games and the ubiquitous gambling on the outcomes. Most men, especially leaders in both civil and religious realms, came to the games to mark a feast day or to celebrate the completion of the hard labor of a communal task like cleaning the acequia. Year after year, community members and Pablo Abeita gathered to have fun, offer prayers, and compete.

ISLETAN BASEBALL TEAMS

In the early 1900s, Pablo Abeita organized and coached the first pueblo baseball team at Isleta. John T. Jojola led the team in defeating the Los Lunas Tigers 24 to 4 in one legendary game in July 1911. He hit two home runs and "carried off the fielding honors by making a sensational one-handed catch over second base." Thus began a long tradition of great Isleta baseball teams for the next four decades. The Pueblos embraced the team sport of baseball since they had traditionally played shinny (like field hockey), a popular game marking the end of irrigation ditch cleaning.

Abeita undoubtedly read about the great Native American baseball players in the major leagues while working as a typesetter at the *Albuquerque Journal* in 1905. Indian players of the time included Louis Sockalexis, Penobscot, who played for the Cleveland Indians in 1897; Charles Albert Bender, Ojibwe, who played for the Philadelphia Athletics in 1903; and Moses Yellowhorse, Pawnee, who played for the Pittsburgh Pirates a few decades later. Then there was the incomparable Jim Thorpe, a Sac and Fox Indian, who excelled at all sports and led Carlisle's team to a national collegiate football championship in 1911. Inspired by their example, Pablo Abeita became a lifelong baseball fan. Two of his sons, Andres "Andy" Abeita and Ambrosio "Buster" Abeita, became stars in the 1930s and 1940s.

The first Isleta baseball team included Felipe Padilla, Domingo Jojola, Paul Shattuck, Frank Anzara, Tony Abeita, Lazaro Abeita, John T. Jojola, Marcelino Abeita, and Juan Rey Abeita. Marcelino was Pablo's brother, Juan Rey was his oldest son; none of the other Abeitas, however, were related to Pablo. After that famous game in 1911 when Isleta trounced Los Lunas, coach Pablo Abeita told a reporter that he was "well pleased with the showing." After this typical understatement, the team received very little press coverage until the 1930s and 1940s. But in the waning years of his life, Abeita would have every reason to be well pleased with the showing of the Isleta team—first called the Isleta Indians and then the Isleta Braves—and with the performance of his sons, Andy and Buster Abeita.

When Abeita led a delegation of seventeen Pueblos to Washington, DC, to consult with Commissioner John Collier in 1936, he reportedly asked upon arrival in the nation's capital what team the Washington Nationals were playing that night. When he learned it was the Boston Red Sox, Abeita expressed his hope that Lefty Grove would pitch. He noted that he had not seen a baseball game in Washington since Walter Johnson was playing. Johnson played twenty-one seasons for Washington from 1907 to 1927.[29]

By the 1930s, the Isleta baseball team had reached its pinnacle; some of its stars were Mariano Jojola, Sam Jojola, and Joe M. Abeita. Joe Abeita was a catcher until a ball struck him in the head and he moved to another position. He was a silversmith and a cultural leader at Isleta all his life. He played against some of the best teams in the Albuquerque

Figure 25. *Isleta baseball team, c. 1911*, photographer unknown. Standing, left to right: Felipe Padilla, Doming Jojola, Manager Pablo Abeita, Paul Shattuck, and Frank Anzara. Seated, left to right: Tony Abeita, Lazaro Abeita, John T. Jojola, Marcelino Abeita, and Juan Rey Abeita. Courtesy of the Leonard Abeita Collection, Isleta Pueblo

area; he even played against future US senator Pete Domenici. In 1935 Laguna Pueblo hosted the first All-Indian baseball tournament in the United States. It coincided with their annual September Feast Day honoring its patron saint, San José. The tournament started with only three teams, including Isleta and Laguna, but grew into an enormous southwestern tradition, bringing teams from as far away as California. The Isleta Indians, as they were then called, won consecutive championships in 1935 and 1936. By 1936 Isleta's star, Joe M. Abeita, focused exclusively on pitching while Buster Abeita took over as manager. Buster led the Isleta Braves to their second All-Indian championship when they defeated Laguna. In 1937 Isleta again won the championship, winning fourteen of their nineteen games with Buster Abeita even pinch hitting in the sixth inning of one game with the bases loaded. Buster followed in Pablo's footsteps when he founded a new team, bought their uniforms, and hired Native semi-pro players from the East.[30]

Sam Jojola became manager of the Isleta team when Buster quit to form a new semi-pro team, the Albuquerque Indian All-Stars, playing in the Central New Mexico League. The All-Stars included Marcell Littlehorse, a Potawatomie Indian who had played at Haskell, and Nelson Hendrix, a Cherokee who also attended Haskell. By the end of July, Andy Abeita led the All-Stars with a .438 batting average. By the end of August, the All-Stars were battling Santa Fe for second place behind the first-place Madrid Miners, even though Joe M. Abeita was out with a broken rib. Buster Abeita returned to Isleta to coach the Isleta Braves to a third consecutive championship in the annual Laguna tournament.

When the Central New Mexico league folded after the 1939 season, Sam Jojola, Joe M. Abeita, and Andy Abeita returned to play for the Isleta Braves. In April 1940 the Isleta team entered the Coronado league, made up of diverse teams—Hispano, Anglo, and Native. In 1940 Isleta and Laguna made it to the semi-finals in the Coronado league, where dancers from Laguna performed the haunting Eagle Dance before the game.

According to Jimmy Abeita, a former ballplayer, Isletans felt they were born to play baseball and believed they were more skilled at it than any other pueblo. But Laguna played equally well if not better in some years, which heated up the intensity, often leading to fisticuffs. Isleta developed a reputation for having the orneriest players around, and they were notorious for fighting. On one occasion the Laguna tournament banned the Isleta team for starting a fight. Nevertheless, Isletan ballplayers compared playing in the Laguna tournament to participating in the World Series and to win the tournament was the crowning glory of every baseball team's dreams.

RELAY RACES: THE CHASE OF THE *CHONGO*

On Palm Sunday, the week before Easter, there are footraces for the boys of Isleta. The races are an initiation for boys between six and eight years old. They are taken to the kiva, divided into teams, and painted with the designs of their team (antelopes and turtles) on their bodies. The racecourse, about one hundred yards long, is marked from the southwest corner to the northeast corner of the plaza. The plaza is swept clean of stones, glass, and nails, making it as smooth as possible. The race starts at about 3:00 p.m.

The chase of the *chongo* is held the next week, on Easter, and this time the men compete. The course is from the kiva to the east end of the village, a distance of about 350 yards. Traditionally, the runners competed barefoot or in moccasins. In the 1960s, some runners wore sneakers, but many mocked them. Today runners can wear what they like. This has much to do with the state of the ground in the plaza. In the old days, people better prepared the plaza, removing stones and sharp objects; today it is very rocky.

The relay runners start out evenly, passing the baton to their teammate at the end of the course. Usually, one team is faster than the other, and soon the swiftest runner is getting to the end of the track while the slower one is just starting. Gradually, the faster team closes the gap between the two runners. As the quick runner overtakes the slower one, he reaches out and grabs the knot of long hair at the back of the slow runner's head, his chongo, and pulls it, sometimes flipping his adversary backward, and then continues on to the finish line. The chase of the chongo is over, but all is not lost for the losers. On the evening of the race, the relatives of the winners lavish gifts on the losers as a consolation. The Easter relay races are perhaps the most hotly contested of all the games, usually accompanied by heavy betting. It is said that Pablo Abeita bet a house with his archrival Juan P. Lente and lost.

PATOL

Isletans enjoyed playing patol, a game that could last for hours. The field of play was a circle of stones broken on the north, south, east, and west by four gaps or "rivers." In the center was a flat striking stone, three-to-four inches square. There were usually three or four players, each of whom had their own carved horse (a carved piece about two or three inches tall) and three patol sticks. The patol sticks, after which the game was named, were three-to-four inches long, about an inch in diameter and often made from a

Figure 26. *Runners During Footraces at Isleta, 1896,* Charles Lummis, photographer. Courtesy of the Pueblo of Isleta Tribal Archive, Yonan Cultural Center, Negative no. YACC01787.2008. Original print housed at the Autry Museum of the American West, Negative no. P.39894

Figure 27. *Isletans Playing Patol, c. 1890,* Charles F. Lummis, photographer. Courtesy of the Library of Congress, Negative no. LC-USZ62-8250

Figure 28. *Isletans Playing Shinny, c. 1930–1940*, Fred K. Hinchman, photographer. Courtesy of the Pueblo of Isleta Tribal Archive, Yonan Cultural Center, Negative no. YACC01701.2008. Original print housed at the Autry Museum of the American West, Negative no. P.8143

broom handle. If you were to cut a three-inch cylinder piece from a handle, and then split that piece in half, you would have two sticks. Then you would make another because you needed three patol sticks to play.

The game began when the first player threw his three patol sticks at the striking stone. If all sticks fell with the flat side down and the round side up, that player received a score of ten, which corresponded to the ten stones between each gap or river. Starting at the east river and moving counterclockwise, the first player moved his horse ten stones to the river on the north. It is said that he had come to the northern river to "water his horse." Then the next player threw his patol sticks, moving his horse according to his score. If the second player's horse landed on the horse of the first player, it is said that he "killed the first player," who then had to go back to the last river he had crossed. The first player who arrived at the river where he started—the east river—won. Although it might have lasted hours, the game usually generated a lot of interest, betting, and excitement.

SHINNY

Shinny was a popular game at Isleta in which both boys and girls participated but not against each other. Most pueblos and many other tribal nations across the country played shinny. Isletan men played annually after the spring cleaning of the acequia. If the ditch work took several days, then the laborers played after finishing the day's work. There may have been close to eighty players as that many Isletans cleaned the ditch. Before the game women often threw water at the men as they passed by their houses on the way to the plaza. This may have had some connection to the opening of the acequias, letting the water flow for the first time after the ditch cleaning. The players divided into sides or teams such as the North side against the South. Each player had his own shinny stick usually made of willow. Both the outer cover and the interior of the shinny ball was made of deer skin. In Taos, they stuffed the ball with seeds and played with it until it burst. At Isleta during the 1930s and 1940s, Bautista Benavides made the best shinny balls. He would bring the ball to the beginning of the game, and if play got too rough and fights erupted, Bautista might get angry and take the ball home. That was the end of the game.

Shinny is similar to field hockey where the players try to hit the ball through a goal. In this case, the goal might have been the opening or road next to the church. Although Bautista Benavides frowned on overt violence, players sometimes wielded their shinny sticks as clubs. As if defeat were not bad enough, the losing team had to suffer a further indignity at the hands of the winners. This was opposite of the relay races where the losers received gifts from the winners and their families. After a game of shinny, the losers lined up to take their punishment. The victors paraded by them and flicked a forefinger on the foreheads of the losers, lightly or not so lightly. One imagines that one or two flicks probably did not cause too much pain, but after the fortieth flick, the losers' foreheads were probably aching and covered with welts. It could very well be that the losing player who had been the most aggressive with his shinny stick would have the sorest forehead.

The Rabbit Hunt

Rabbit hunts for food by individuals and small groups have always existed, but ceremonial community hunts only take place during the Evergreen Dance in February and September. These ceremonial hunts require a lot of preparation, according to a former lieutenant governor and war captain Randy Jiron: "We ask permission; we lay the rainbow out; it's an offering."[31]

The hunt begins when a large group of Isletan men and boys go to the hunting area about three miles west of the pueblo, led by the oldest and the most mature man in the pueblo—in his later years, this man would have been Pablo Abeita. Everyone follows, from the oldest to the youngest, with the youngest ages twelve to thirteen. They make a circle about a half-mile in diameter and walk inwards, trapping the rabbits inside the circle. Originally, everyone carried a carved rabbit stick called a *hoa* in Tiwa. It has a heavy knob on one end, and when a hunter sends it flying towards the rabbit, it rotates. During the 1960s, most people started using shotguns instead of hoas, with unfortunate results. On one occasion someone failed to obey and ended up wounding Ted Jojola and his father, seriously enough to send them to the hospital. Heeding this lesson, today most people carry their hoas, although a few still carry guns.

In the 1960s, Jiron remembered that the men killed up to 125 rabbits. The hunters take them back to the plaza, where, according to tradition, the women steal the rabbits for food. In exchange, they give the hunters bread or other baked goods. During the February Evergreen Dance, the hunters do not kill the rabbits; they capture them alive and put them in boxes with their paws tied. They take the live rabbits back to the plaza for the kids to chase. In both the February and September hunts, the Isletan people end up with most of the rabbits, which was a welcome source of meat in the days before supermarkets.[32]

Pablo Abeita in the Pueblo   **63**

CHAPTER SIX

Pablo Abeita and the Railroad

If we run short of water in this valley, it is all on account of you who came, and if we are flooded with alkali, it is on account of you who came. If we run short of water for irrigation, it is because . . . you who came are gobbling up the water, and if we are flooded with it, it is because you who came are dikeing and daming the river thereby causing the water under the ground to raise, thereby when we sow wheat we raise alkali; all this is done because of you who came.

Pablo Abeita, Statement inserted in the record of the House Subcommittee on Indian Affairs from the *Albuquerque Morning Journal,* May 18, 1920

Pablo Abeita was only nine years old when the AT&SF arrived at Isleta to a hostile reception. The railroad management assumed an arrogant stance toward all the pueblos, taking rights-of-way across Pueblo land without asking and without paying the Indians the market value of their land as the law of eminent domain required—without paying them anything for that matter. Moreover, the railroad often failed to pay legitimate claims when the trains caused injuries to livestock at the crossings. Abeita and his sons later suffered such damages as did other Isletans, who wrote many letters to the Indian superintendent and the railroad claims agents seeking fair compensation. Isleta even sued the railroad at one point. Some traditionalists actively opposed the railroad, even decades into the twentieth century.

As an adult, however, Pablo Abeita soon began to appreciate the benefits the railroad brought with it. As a merchant, he could order dry goods from the East Coast and receive them in a few days.[1] As a representative of the pueblo, he could travel to Washington, DC, in days rather than weeks to testify before Congress, give speeches, and meet with US presidents. As a promoter of Pueblo culture, he could travel to Los Angeles or New York with Pueblo craftspeople, displaying and selling their wares to delighted audiences. And, of course, the trains brought tourists to Isleta to photograph and publicize the village. The visitors also purchased pottery, jewelry, and other works of art. The coming of the railroad was, indeed, a mixed blessing.[2]

As the railroad approached Isleta from the north in March 1880, it caused massive damage to irrigation ditches in other pueblos. At Cochiti "the AT&SF construction workers dumped so much dirt and rocks in the pueblo's . . . *acequia madre* that it prevented the Indians from growing their crops." At San Felipe the same thing happened to their main ditch, "preventing the irrigation of their fields." In neither case did the pueblos receive the required compensation from the railroad. The AT&SF neglected to pay when it took pueblo land; it simply laid the tracks wherever it wanted.[3] Isleta governor Vicente Jiron opposed it and was against allowing the tracks to cross pueblo land. Indian Agent Benjamin Thomas, however, wrote to Jiron directing him "to resort to no means of violence." Undaunted, Isletans resisted. They "tore up rails, removed planks from the wagon road crossings, chopped or stole heavy timbers from the railroad bridge, and threatened to burn the railroad buildings at the junction."[4]

Isleta's resistance, which Governor Jiron led, had little effect on the railroad; its indifference toward the pueblo and the damages it inflicted continued for decades. In 1886 a severe flood caused by the railroad tracks' new configuration destroyed Isleta's wheat and corn fields and threatened its vineyards. The governor commissioned a group of men to assess the damage, which they estimated at $11,050. The commissioner of Indian Affairs denied the claim because the United States no longer protected the Pueblos since wardship status had ended with US v. Joseph in 1877.[5] This was a bogus argument because the railroad was not a branch of the government, but a private entity responsible for whatever damages it caused. In 1905 Isletans were outraged when the Rio Grande, which the railroad had partially dammed again, again flooded the village. For Isleta this

Figure 29. *Isleta Group at Los Angeles Railroad Station, late 1800s to early 1900s,* Charles Lummis, photographer. Courtesy of the Pueblo of Isleta Tribal Archive, Yonan Cultural Center, Negative no. YACC01786.2008. Original print housed at the Autry Museum of the American West, Negative no. P.34748

Figure 30. *Vicente Jiron, Isleta Governor, 1886*, John K. Hillers, photographer.
Courtesy of the National Anthropological Archives, Negative no. BAE GN 02002A
06339200

was the last straw. On the night of June 11, 1905, Isletans "went out after dark to dig through the roadbed and release the water, but a railroad watchman discovered them."[6] In the words of a reporter for the *Santa Fe New Mexican*, the watchman "held the mob of excited Indians at bay until reinforcements reached him." In another version, it was Father Anton Docher, the French priest at the pueblo, who calmed the crowd. Docher had served for over two decades at Isleta, and the people trusted him. At the urging of the Indian Office, Father Docher spent the night patrolling the tracks to prevent damage to them. The AT&SF accepted some responsibility, for a change, for flood damage to Isleta, and soon after the incident, Father Docher could be seen "hauling a load of $2,500 in silver in a wheelbarrow" to his house, for distribution among the Isletans damaged by the flood.[7] In fact, pueblo members were only taking the necessary steps to "save their village at any costs."[8]

As the waters receded, and the passions cooled, Isleta took a different course, suing the railroad directly. With the help of Francis C. Wilson, special attorney for the Pueblo Indians, and AIS superintendent Reuben Perry, Isleta proceeded with the lawsuit claiming damages from the flood, eventually reaching a settlement with the railroad of $2,000. The railroad's willingness to settle, however, turned out to be a rare occurrence as Pablo Abeita soon discovered. Nevertheless, bringing suit proved to be the only effective strategy for forcing the AT&SF to provide reasonable compensation for damages it caused. The *Santa Fe New Mexican* revealed its prejudice against the Indians by accusing the Isletans of being overly litigious, "mulcting railroad companies for every conceivable damage."[9]

Meanwhile, Isletans' hostility toward the railroad continued as they "got into the habit of stoning trains as they [passed] by." The *Santa Fe New Mexican*, however, reported that the railroad workers were planning to arm themselves and "shoot into any gang of suspicious Indians," a threat they never carried out.[10] In 1899 Indian Agent Nimrod S. Walpole warned Isleta's governor that some railroad engineers had been seriously hurt and that arrests would be made unless the stoning of the trains stopped.[11] As the railroad continued to ignore the pueblo's damage claims, the rock-throwing continued intermittently. On the night of September 24, 1919, broken glass injured a traveler when a stone shattered a passenger car window. Two Isleta boys were taken into custody and sent to the Santa Fe Indian School (SFIS) for reform.[12] Although the local newspapers and the railroad portrayed Isletans as the aggressors, the people of the pueblo saw themselves as resisting the railroad's violent and uncompensated intrusion onto their lands by the only means available.

Individuals also brought claims against the railroad with the help of the agency farmer and the Indian Office. Indian agents or superintendents often filed the claims and enlisted the aid of the special attorneys when necessary. In one case, Pablo Abeita wrote to Superintendent Lonergan about a fire the railroad caused, which damaged the property of Bautista and Valentin Lente. Not infrequently trains caused fires when wooden trestles ignited from flying cinders. Lonergan wrote back asking for more details, promising to provide the information to Wilson so that he might bring suit if the railroad refused to settle. It is unlikely, however, that Wilson filed a lawsuit in this case because he retired as special attorney for the Pueblo Indians a little over a month later.[13]

Figure 31. *Atchison, Topeka, and Santa Fe Railroad Station, Isleta, n.d.*, photographer unknown. Courtesy of the Albuquerque Museum, Negative no. PA 2008-20-11

By the 1920s the railroad added more opaque bureaucracy to the claims process. Claimants found themselves dealing with different claims adjusters and different claims offices, one in Los Angeles, California, and another in El Paso, Texas. The company also found more reasons for denying claims; its delaying tactics meant that it could take years to reach a settlement. Ultimately, the AT&SF denied many claims or paid only a meager amount when it could not avoid payment. Only when faced with a lawsuit, or the threat of one, did the railroad pay a reasonable sum, but, as the company knew well, lawyers' fees reduced the net settlement, making this approach impractical for most claimants.

By the summer of 1923, Pablo Abeita's authority and jurisdiction as tribal judge had ebbed, and he started to step away from Isleta politics. No longer agency farmer, rarely did he advocate for individual claimants; instead, he turned his energy to championing Isleta and other pueblos on the national stage. The next generation stepped up to defend its rights against the railroad. Armed with gumption, perseverance, evidence, and the continued aid of the Indian Office, some claimants did receive compensation from the railroad.

In September 1923 a Santa Fe Railroad train killed a cow belonging to Isletan Francisco Jaramillo when the animal wandered onto an unfenced track. Superintendent Harmon Percy Marble notified the Los Angeles claims department and was told that the matter had been referred to a claims adjuster in Winslow, Arizona.[14] The railroad then informed Marble that it was denying liability because the accident happened at the Isleta railroad station, a place where the company could not fence the right-of-way due to the necessity of passenger access. In response Marble told the Los Angeles claims office that the accident took place near mile marker $17\frac{1}{2}$, two and half miles west of the Isleta station, and that the railroad was clearly liable.[15] The claims adjuster promptly wrote Marble that he would send Jaramillo a check to settle the claim in the amount of thirty-five dollars, which was to arrive in two weeks. When the check did not arrive on time, Marble again wrote claims agent Robert Irwin asking that the check be sent to him. Whether Francisco Jaramillo ever got paid for the loss of his cow is unknown, but if he did, it is likely only because of Superintendent Marble's persistence.[16]

On December 3, 1922, Pablo's oldest son, Juan Rey, lost a valuable thoroughbred mare when a Santa Fe Railroad train struck and killed the large workhorse and the foal she was carrying. Juan Rey Abeita notified Superintendent Marble of his claim, valuing the horse and foal at $175, a relatively large sum. Marble submitted the claim to the railroad's adjuster in El Paso, Texas, but did not receive a reply until May 1923. At that time adjuster A. F. Morrissette told Marble he would settle the claim for $50 because he believed that the horse was overvalued and was not a thoroughbred as Juan Rey claimed but "just common Indian stock." He also tried to minimize the railroad's liability by asserting that the primary reason the right-of-way was not fenced was that Isleta Pueblo had not given its permission. The adjuster complained, "it is largely due to this attitude on the part of the Indian people at Isleta that we kill so much of their stock."[17] Fencing the track was impractical because it would have cut the livestock off from pastures on the other side of the track or made access more difficult. Incensed at this cavalier attempt at blaming the victim, Juan Rey (who started signing himself as John R. Abeita), wrote Morrissette himself, noting that the horse was not of Native stock but was indeed of good breed, "raised by the Mormons at Ramah," and weighing at least 1,200 pounds. The horse had been bred to a government horse (probably a thoroughbred) at the Indian School, and he had been offered $200 for a colt from this mare. Abeita offered to take the colts to Albuquerque so the superintendent could assess their value.[18]

Instead, Marble asked Isleta policeman Esquipula Jojola and the agency farmer at Acoma to appraise the horse's value. Jojola replied that the mare had indeed weighed between 1,100 and 1,200 pounds and was bred to a government Percheron stallion. Jojola valued the mare and foal at $100.[19] With the appraisal in hand, Marble wrote the adjuster, asking him to raise his offer to $100.[20] Unmoved by the two appraisals that challenged his initial assessment, Morrissette offered only $75.[21]

In August Marble forwarded Juan Rey's response to the $75 offer to Morrissette. Abeita reduced his claim to $100, telling the claims adjuster, "we poor people have a great drawback as we have no means to fight a R. R. Co." Abeita pointed out that if he were to "fight the railroad," he would likely be awarded the fair value of the horse and foal but would still have to pay his attorney.[22] Marble continued to press the matter, asking the agency farmer, Howard Smith, to investigate.[23] In September Marble notified Morrissette that Smith's appraisal exceeded $100. A month later when Morrissette had not responded, Marble notified him that Juan Rey Abeita was willing to accept $80 to settle the claim.[24] At this point Marble's term as superintendent was ending, so having written at least eight letters on Abeita's behalf, he ended his advocacy for Juan Rey.[25] Finally, on April 2, 1924, a day after he replaced Marble as supervisor, Chester E. Faris wrote Morrissette a concise letter outlining the protracted negotiation of the claim, which had begun almost a year and a half earlier, and politely asked for a favorable reply to Juan Rey's counter offer. Faris's letter finally got results: the check was delivered, and the case settled.[26] The check for $80 was less than half the value of the horse, not including the compensation for loss of use of the animal for sixteen months. It was only because of Abeita's perseverance that such a settlement was achieved. The average claimant was lucky to receive any payment, as the company was in the habit of denying liability for specious reasons.[27] Compared to other cases of far more serious accidents, Juan Rey Abeita negotiated a handsome settlement.

Although livestock accidents were the most common, trains also caused human deaths.[28] Even in such cases, the railroad company was miserly and discriminatory in paying claims; it made substantially larger settlements with Anglo and Hispano claimants. Settlements in those cases ranged from $15,000, paid for the death of a Southern Pacific engineer in Grant County, to $700 paid to the widow of a Hispano section hand. In contrast the AT&SF paid $50 in food and clothing for the death of three Santo Domingo Indians and offered only $50 for the death of another Santo Domingo man named Calabasa. His son rejected the offer, asking for $3,000, an amount the superintendent considered unreasonable. Accordingly, the railroad paid nothing in that case. As historian Richard H. Frost summarized the railroads' attitude toward Indians, "they were accustomed to treating the Indians as marginal nomads who endangered the lives of surveyors . . . or attacked railroad operations after the tracks appeared. For the railroads, the Indians were in the way."[29]

Two Isleta Indians, Juan Andres Abeita and Juan Trujillo, were killed by train accidents. Abeita died of injuries sustained as he tried to jump on a flatcar in Albuquerque to join his companions hitching a ride to Isleta. Abeita's foot was crushed as he leapt onto the train. Standing on the adjoining track, he failed to see another AT&SF train coming in the other direction. The railroad agent sent for a doctor who amputated Juan Andres's leg, but he died three days later, having received no additional medical care following the amputation. Investigators found Abeita responsible for his injuries as a "result of his own careless[ness]." Arguably, the railroad had some liability for the negligent treatment of the man's injuries, which resulted in his death. This case shows the railroad's indifference to the plight of Indians its trains injured or killed.[30] It also demonstrates that, although catching a ride on a freight car was a common practice among Isletans and other Pueblo Indians, the practice entailed huge risks because the AT&SF was a dangerous line to ride; "engines, cars, or whole trains jumped the rails, tracks and bridges washed out, trestles caught fire from flying cinders and gave way under the weight of locomotives."[31]

Indian lives were not worth much by railroad standards, as the case of Juan Trujillo demonstrates. Trujillo, an eleven-year-old boy, was herding cattle near the tracks when "the flyer" struck and killed him near the pueblo. When his parents sought compensation through Indian Agent Walpole, the railroad refused payment on the grounds that the boy was at fault.[32] Railroad claims agents used this defense repeatedly, although in this and many other cases, a court would have rejected this defense because of the AT&SF's duty to fence its tracks.[33] It is likely that had the Indian claimants had lawyers, it would have resulted in substantial jury awards, encouraging the railroad to fence the tracks sooner. The AT&SF was also tightfisted when it came to adopting safety measures such as air brakes. This resulted in a tragic toll in injuries and deaths, causing the *Santa Fe New Mexican* to engage in a vendetta against the AT&SF on account of its accidents. Editor Max Frost launched a muckraking campaign with a brief editorial titled "Death Has Been Reaping a Big Harvest in Train Wrecks," focusing on insufficiencies in the training of engineers and conductors. Rather than changing its policies the AT&SF refused to advertise in the *Santa Fe New Mexican* except for railroad schedules.[34]

Isletans and other Pueblo Indians found ways to benefit from the railroad despite the damage it caused. Silversmiths and potters sold their wares to passengers. For a while the railroad issued free passes to children attending AIS and to Pueblo governors traveling to Santa Fe on official business (tradition holds that the railroad gave all Isletans railroad passes after the standoff between the railroad and Governor Jiron in 1880).[35] Indian Agent Thomas learned, however, that railroad officials did not grant the privilege consistently when they refused his request for free passes for several years. Finally, in August 1906, the AT&SF ceased issuing free passes because the revised 1906 Act to Regulate Interstate Commerce prohibited it.[36] All told, the AT&SF proved to be a disaster for Isleta and other pueblos. Its tracks caused flooding and cut valuable pastures into unusable pieces; shepherds with their flocks crossed the tracks at their peril until the right-of-way was fenced. The trains caused injuries and deaths to Indians and their livestock, damages for which the railroad refused to pay fair compensation except when faced with litigation or the perseverance of Juan Rey Abeita. Occasionally the railroad provided some benefits, as it did in May 1891 when a train carrying sheep from California to the Chicago market derailed, killing 770 sheep. According to the *Albuquerque Journal*, "the Indians of Isleta worked all night skinning carcasses and they will have mutton for months to come."[37]

Other intrusions connected with the railroad were the Indian Detours, run by Fred Harvey, who had established restaurants and hotels in communities along the AT&SF route. Hotels such as the Alvarado in Albuquerque and the La Fonda in Santa Fe became popular tourist destinations. The famous Harvey Girls served as waitresses in the restaurants and guides or couriers on the Indian Detours. Indian Detours, conceived and implemented by Fred Harvey employee Major R. Hunter Clarkson, were designed to expand tourist interest in Southwest attractions like the ancient ruin of Puye and living pueblos like Taos. The Detours began around 1927 at La Fonda in Santa Fe, whence tourists were brought to the pueblos by touring car. They were so successful that new hubs were established in other hotels, the Alvarado in Albuquerque, La Castañeda in Las Vegas, and La Posada in Taos. The tours were led by the Harvey Girls, young, congenial, well-educated women dressed in Navajo-style blouses, skirts, and jewelry, acting as couriers. The couriers attended classes conducted by archeologists such as Edgar L. Hewett and Alfred V. Kidder to learn about Southwest history and culture. Author Erna

Fergusson organized the classes. The tours came at a price, however, as overly inquisitive and often insensitive tourists invaded the privacy of the pueblos.[38]

The railroad also provided jobs for Pueblo Indians, particularly those from Laguna and Isleta. Both pueblos resisted the arrival of the railroad. Laguna oral history tells the story of Jimmy Hiuwec, a tribal official who single-handedly "stopped the crews preparing to lay track across Laguna land," forcing the railroad to agree that it "would forever employ as many of the Lagunas . . . who wished to work." This was referred to as the "Gentlemen's Agreement of Friendship" and was reaffirmed every year from 1922 to 1980 by what the Laguna people call "watering the flower." In fact, both Isleta and Laguna benefited from their resistance to the AT&SF, as entire boxcar communities of Pueblo railroaders were established, one made up primarily of Lagunas at Richmond, California, and one composed of Isletans at Winslow, Arizona.[39]

The greatest influx of people brought to the Pueblo of Isleta by the railroad, as well as by motorcars and horse-drawn wagons, took place on October 19, 1919, when the king of Belgium and his family and royal entourage paid a visit to the village. The visit was part of King Albert's tour across the United States in a special train provided by the Pennsylvania Railroad to accommodate a royal party of over one hundred individuals.[40] The king's trip was a goodwill journey to show Belgium's gratitude for US assistance during World War I and to seek this nation's financial help in rebuilding his country—especially its railroads—after the devastation the war had caused.[41]

A committee composed of the Albuquerque Chamber of Commerce and others, including Indian Superintendent Leo Crane, arranged the king's visit. During an inspection tour of Isleta, the committee met with Father Docher and with Pablo Abeita. Abeita convened a council meeting that promised Isleta would cooperate to the fullest in the planned entertainment, with people from Isleta and Laguna "appearing in gala dress for the occasion."[42]

When the king pulled into the railroad station in Albuquerque in his special train at 2:45 on the appointed day, he, Queen Elizabeth, and Prince Leopold were greeted with a welcoming speech by Governor Octaviano Larrazolo. After the governor presented gifts to the royal party, they proceeded to Isleta in twenty-five cars. When they were within a mile of the village, the mission bells began to peal to announce their arrival and continued to ring until they entered the pueblo. Pablo Abeita, dressed in an embroidered white shirt, dark trousers, and wearing silver jewelry, greeted the royal party; Abeita would act as interpreter during the royal visit.[43] The entourage proceeded to the church of San Agustín where Father Docher, speaking in French, presented a brief history of the church and of the Pueblo of Isleta.[44]

A special train carried nine hundred passengers from Albuquerque and along with visitors in cars and horse-drawn vehicles, the total crowd was estimated in the thousands. When the royal party emerged from the church, a cowboy band began to play the national anthems of Belgium and the United States. Laguna dancers performed to the accompaniment of war drums, which had never been removed from Laguna, and an exhibition of cowboy life followed, including lassoing and trick riding. At the conclusion of the events in the plaza, the king expressed an interest in seeing the inside of an Indian house, and so it was that he visited the Pablo Abeita compound. The king presented

Pablo with the Order of Leopold II medal.[45] Earlier in the day, Father Docher presented two gifts from the people of Isleta to the king: a turquoise cross mounted in silver as a token of appreciation for his visit and a silver sword that symbolized the king's courage as a leader of his people in battle in World War I. Both items were exquisite examples of Indian craftsmanship.[46] When the whirlwind trip came to an end, the crowds dispersed and the royal party made its way back to Albuquerque, where they caught the 6:45 special train that bore them to their next destination. The railroad trains made the extravaganza of the king's visit possible.

All in all, the railroad was a major factor in popularizing and shaping the image of the Pueblo Indian. New Mexico Pueblos experienced a huge increase in the popularity of their arts, culture, and architecture due in large measure to the arrival of the railroad in 1880, the Fred Harvey Houses, and to the efforts of Charles F. Lummis; prominent archeologist and founder of the Museum of New Mexico, Edgar Lee Hewett; and John Collier. The railroad brought the Pueblos in direct contact with Americans who slowly learned to appreciate Pueblo culture. Harvey, Lummis, Hewett, and Collier publicized, promoted, and advocated for New Mexico Pueblo Indians to the point that by 1920 they were among the most interesting American Indian tribes in the popular mind. This led to a romantic inflation of Pueblo culture that did not reflect the reality of Pueblo life. Since interactions between Pueblos and outsiders were often patronizing or condescending, the Pueblos generally did not reciprocate the admiration of Anglo society.[47] As Russel Barsh put it, "the pueblos can hardly be blamed if they failed to show gratitude; the Anglos newly found uninvited appreciation of Pueblo art and ceremony was no substitute for the losses already sustained."

Figure 32. *The King of Belgium's Visit to Isleta Pueblo, n.d.*, photographer unknown. Courtesy of the Albuquerque Museum, Negative no. PA 1999-55-30

CHAPTER SEVEN

Pablo Abeita and Indian Education

Laws are made by the white man and they compel us to obey them; how
would it suit the white man if we was [sic] to make the laws and they
[were] forced to obey [them]. . . . There never was a law that was any
good for Indians, but . . . [it] is repealed at the first chance.
Pablo Abeita to William Ketcham, April 15, 1911, BCIM

Pablo Abeita took great interest in education, especially for his own children. Abeita had attended St. Michael's College, an elite Catholic school mostly for non-Indians, in the late 1880s with his brother Marcelino.[1] Pablo and his classmates excelled at St. Michael's. One priest who examined that first class of Natives marveled at their ability to read and write both English and Spanish.

Pablo apparently reveled in his education, excelling in multiple languages and absorbing history to better understand the pueblo's rights and the best way to interact with the outside world. Abeita occupied a unique period in Indian education. Over the course of his lifetime, he witnessed profound changes in government approaches to educating Natives. Not only did he participate in his own schooling as student, he also interacted with school officials as he sought an education for his own children. Many parents and grandparents were extremely loyal to schools such as St. Catherine's Indian School and sent their children and grandchildren to the school they attended, so that three or more generations were often proud graduates of the same school.

Depending on the institution and superintendent, students' overall experiences in boarding school ranged from despair, homesickness, and indoctrination to forging new friendships, adventure, and discovery. The trauma Indian students suffered at Carlisle is best described by poet and storyteller M. Scott Momaday, in his play about the school, *The Moon in Two Windows*. The main character, Luther Standing Bear, says at the end of the story, "the Indian Industrial School at Carlisle was a kind of laboratory in which our hearts were tested. . . . Some of us were destroyed and some were made stronger. . . . We were children who ventured into the unknown . . . into an alien world that I could not have imagined."[2] Ojibwe professor Brenda Child explains that although some children responded well to the boarding schools, others ran away or refused to participate in school activities.[3] Students who missed home often took off, as did three Isletan boys in 1891.[4] Some children used the boarding school experience to enrich their lives. They joined sports teams that were very successful, allowing them to experience Native pride when defeating all-white teams, such as the United States Military Academy at West Point.[5] Often they held tenaciously to elements of Native cultures, including ceremony, song, stories, and language as they gathered away from the prying eyes of school officials. The trauma of boarding schools is still felt within Indian communities and remains an important element of Native American history.[6] Currently in 2022 an investigation is underway as ordered by Secretary of the Interior Debra Haaland, a member of the Pueblo of Laguna, focused on the location of federal Indian boarding schools, their burial sites, and the names of the children who attended those institutions.[7]

Richard Henry Pratt, founder of Carlisle Indian Industrial School (1879–1918), shaped early Indian education perhaps more than any other person. Pratt began the policy of forced removal of Indian children from their homes—his motto was "kill the Indian and save the man." He and other contemporary reformers believed that Indian people had the capacity to learn and grow intellectually. To educate the children, they believed the school had to segregate them from their parents and replace their Native languages and cultures with the English language, Christian values and work ethic, and white man's civilization.[8] Upon arrival at school, the administrators took the children's traditional garb and replaced it with school uniforms and documented the exchange by taking photographs of the transformation. Pratt also forced children to relinquish their Indian names and adopt new anglicized names.[9] One boy who left Isleta as Domingo Jiron, son of Isleta governor Vicente Jiron, returned as Henry Kendall, the boy who taught Charles Lummis Tiwa and passed on to him traditional stories and knowledge.

The BIA established other industrial schools modeled after Carlisle, and by the end of the nineteenth century it had opened twenty-five off-reservation industrial boarding schools including AIS and SFIS. Some Isletans attended distant boarding schools, but most stayed close to home and enrolled in the schools in New Mexico. Those Isletans who ventured farther afield included Paul Shattuck, who attended Carlisle, and Antonio Abeita, who went to the Hampton Institute after his early attendance at AIS. In the first decades, boarding schools taught a curriculum that included some academics and vocational instruction. The schools had a military bent with children marching to and from classes and sleeping in open-air dorms. Carlisle and other institutions also had programs whereby students worked for local farmers away from school, giving them the opportunity to learn more about non-Indian culture, to see more of the country, and even to educate their employers about Native culture. When Isletan Antonio Abeita was attending Hampton, he worked on a farm in Sheffield, Massachusetts. In the summer of 1905, he wrote that his employers had become good friends who frequently invited him to their cabin to sing Indian songs.[10]

Even in the incipient stages of the BIA's Native education policy when the mandate was to erase Indianness and incorporate Native land and peoples into the dominant white society, the Pueblos were not passive. In fact, they exercised a surprising amount of power in their efforts to use the boarding school experience for their own ends.[11] In 1892 when Isletan parents felt powerless to influence Superintendent Creager at AIS, they agitated, and with the help of Charles Lummis, they won the battle to release their captive children, as discussed earlier. And by the time Pablo Abeita was a parent, he and others did not shy away from interacting with the superintendents, taking an active interest in their children's education. As historian John R. Gram put it, "the Pueblos . . . [faced] the ever present challenge of teaching each new generation of children how to navigate competing claims on their lives and their communities. . . . During this chapter of their history, the pueblos did so, brilliantly."[12]

Parents were also proactive when considering the benefits of sending their children to boarding schools. Some parents, unable to feed and care for their children properly after the death or sickness of a spouse, welcomed the possibility of sending their children to boarding schools. Others believed their children could acquire an education that would lead to a job as adults. However, Isletan farmers often needed their children to help with the crops and insisted that their enrolled students be granted permission to return home during the summer.[13] The conflict over attendance between the school administrators and Isletan farmers continued as the truancy cases discussed in chapter 8 demonstrate. Even with their boys helping, most Isletan farmers were short of labor. In August 1919, as the troops were coming home after the war, Pablo Abeita wrote to Father Ketcham, "wheat harvesting is in full swing and we need the boys very bad," hoping that Ketcham would use his influence to get Isletan soldiers discharged so they could help on the farm.[14] As wage labor increasingly replaced farming as the principle means of employment at Isleta in the 1940s, parents no longer needed their children to help with tasks on the farms. Working full time, they were glad to have their children in school, getting a free lunch and, hopefully, a good education.

EARLY INDIAN EDUCATION

Commissioner of Indian Affairs Thomas Jefferson Morgan summed up the early harsh attitude of the BIA toward Indian education in his 1889 annual report: "the Indian must conform to the White Man's ways, peaceably if they will, forcibly if they must."[15] Superintendent of Indian Schools Daniel Dorchester, a Presbyterian minister, was just as sanctimonious and racist in his pronouncements, stating that "education should seek the disintegration of the tribes."[16]

Morgan's and Dorchester's views were typical of a time when federal Indian policy favored the breaking up of Indian tribes and their land base to assimilate them into mainstream American society. The 1887 Dawes Act aimed to apportion private allotments of Indian lands and to break up tribal governments.[17] Dorchester, responsible for twenty-five major tribal groups throughout the country, nevertheless became obsessed with the Pueblos of New Mexico. He devoted fully half of his 1892 report to the "terrible state of the pueblos of the lower Rio Grande."[18] Neither Dorchester nor Morgan had much first-hand knowledge of Native Americans, and their vision for Indian assimilation and education took no account of the Indians themselves. As Francis Paul Prucha wrote, "Morgan and his fellow reformers had no appreciation of positive values in the Indian cultures, which the Indian somehow managed to preserve in spite of the crushing attack of the allotment program and the national school system."[19]

AIS UNDER WILLIAM CREAGER

The Presbyterian Home Mission Board operated AIS until 1886 when the BIA took control. William Creager, the superintendent of AIS, adopted the beliefs and attitudes of both Morgan and Dorchester about the Pueblo Indians. Creager's tenure at the school began at about the same time that Morgan and Dorchester took office in 1889. Creager immediately changed policies that had been in place since the school was founded five years earlier. In 1885 the first superintendent, William Bryan, warned about the need to guard against "the formation of a wide gulf between parent and child and to prevent the child from acquiring notions inconsistent with the proper filial respect and duty." Bryan endorsed Archbishop Jean-Baptiste Salpointe's plan to fund the opening of more day schools in the pueblos. Creager changed that policy dramatically when he let the contract for day schools expire, forcing them to close. Creager was a follower of Pratt's approach at Carlisle, emphasizing the removal of children from their home environment to speed their assimilation into white society. He also believed that the day schools were an excuse parents used not to send their children to AIS. Creager wanted more children to attend AIS because the government based the amount of money it furnished to the school in part on the number of students on its rolls. To increase enrollment, AIS administrators shipped in Apache children and even Mexican children from south of the border, after their parents signed affidavits that they were Indian. Creager took extreme measures to ensure that his enrollment numbers did not dwindle any lower due to runaways. He personally chased down students who escaped and kept students captive in the school, holding them against their will and not letting them leave even for summer vacation. As we have seen, Creager's downfall began in 1892 when Lummis challenged his forced retention of Isletan students and compelled the superintendent to release thirty-seven Isletan students.

AIS Superintendent Reuben Perry's Correspondence with Pablo Abeita

During the early 1900s, three of Pablo Abeita's sons, Jose, Remijio, and Ambrosio, were enrolled in AIS, which was under Reuben Perry's administration. Abeita chose the school partly because of its proximity to Isleta, which allowed him to visit on special occasions and enabled his children to come home frequently. He also liked it because of his close relationship with Perry, to whom he wrote frequently about matters of administration, especially as they related to his children. Perry's long administration from 1910 to 1920 was relatively liberal compared to the earlier controversial and repressive regime of Superintendent William Creager from 1889 to 1894.

In 1910 when Superintendent Perry took charge of AIS as well as the day schools at Acoma, Laguna, San Felipe, Sandia, Santa Ana, Zuni, and Isleta, he reported that AIS was full, with 330 students.[20] By 1920 enrollment was comprised mostly of students from nine pueblos—all the southern pueblos, as well as Santa Clara, and San Juan (Ohkay Owingeh)—and about one hundred Navajos, Apaches, and Zunis, split evenly. Also represented with one or two students were the Creek, Seneca, Sioux (Lakota), Hopi, and Mojave Nations. By far the largest contingents were from Laguna with 174 followed by Isleta with 78.[21] In 1920 the House Indian affairs subcommittee gave Perry high marks when, after a tour of school facilities, the committee chairman told Perry, "We are highly pleased with what we have seen."[22]

In stark contrast to the experience of Juan Rey Abeita in the early 1890s who had no contact with his children, Pablo Abeita involved himself deeply in his children's education. His correspondence with Perry in the mid-nineteen teens reveals Abeita's profound interest in the affairs of the school, and in particular, his sons' welfare. He must have appreciated having his younger sons, ages twelve, fifteen, and eighteen, closer to home. In return, Abeita assisted Perry in many matters, such as the vetting of prospective

Pablo Abeita and Indian Education   **77**

students as to their eligibility and blood quantum. For instance, Perry asked Abeita to review Patricio Castillo's request to put his children in the Albuquerque school, asking Abeita, "Are they really Isleta Indians?"[23]

Several letters from Perry in 1914 and 1915 illustrate that Abeita was teaching his young boys how to advocate for themselves. In March 1915 his youngest, twelve-year-old Ambrosio, who was named after his great-grandfather, asked for a new pair of shoes, claiming that his present pair was worn out. Abeita relayed the request to Perry who replied with a two-page letter about the shoes and clothes already furnished to Ambrosio since the prior October. He received one pair of shoes in October, another in December, and a third pair in February. The school also issued Ambrosio a suit of corduroy pants, coat, and cap in October, another pair of corduroy pants in January, as well as socks, underwear, and handkerchiefs. This was in addition to the uniform suit Ambrosio received on returning to school. As to the request for new shoes, Perry told Abeita that "there is a limit to the quantity of clothing [and shoes] allowed for each boy . . . and . . . Ambrosio has approached the limit rather closely. He is not in need of a new pair of shoes, but no doubt would like to have a new pair of red shoes, like a great many of the boys have." Apparently Perry's patience in dealing with Pablo Abeita's son had reached its limit; Ambrosio's request was denied.[24]

Perry was not always so strict regarding Abeita's requests. He sometimes made small advances of pocket money to Jose and his younger brothers with the expectation that their father would repay him. In one letter, Perry asked Abeita to send him the three or four dollars he had lent the boys over the past months. Perry, philosophical about the many appeals of Abeita's boys, noted at one point, "there is a general condition in the make-up of every young boy to get all he can from the government and all he can from his parents."[25] Although Perry tried to strike a balance between requests for special treatment and the demands of the budget, on several occasions he did make concessions.

In early January 1914, Abeita complained to Perry that the school required his fifteen-year-old son, Remijio, to do menial housework, scrubbing and cleaning the dormitory, instead of learning a trade. Perry responded, "we realize that a boy's life work will not be scrubbing or housework," but the matron needed help in keeping the dormitory clean and the grounds also needed to be kept clean by the "picking of paper and sticks." The matron assigned the smaller boys to these tasks; once they got older the school would teach them a vocation. Perry reminded Abeita that doing menial work helped the boys acquire the habit of thoroughness and that his son Juan Rey was "learning the carpenter's trade and that Jose is becoming a very good shoe and harness maker." Nevertheless, Perry relented a bit regarding Remijio: "it is probable that we will be able to make some little change in Remijo's [sic] detail in the future."[26] Abeita's complaints about requirements that students do menial work foreshadowed the findings of the 1928 Meriam Report.

In June 1914 at the beginning of summer vacation, Jose Abeita and some other students decided to stay at the school. Although they apparently received free room and board during this time, there was no arrangement to pay the students. When Abeita wrote Perry requesting that Jose and the other boys be paid during the summer months, the superintendent responded that he did not have sufficient funds to pay Jose anything like the wages he could make at a summer job in Albuquerque. However, he offered some hope that by August, when the harness leather came in, he might be able to set up a fund to pay Jose better wages.[27] Abeita's involvement with the superintendent acted as a check on Perry's administration, which was quite responsive to Abeita's complaints. Yet the problems at AIS, such as the restrictions of student vacations, cried out for reform.

THE MERIAM REPORT

In 1928, as reformers clamored for changes in federal policies towards Native Americans, the Rockefeller Foundation employed researchers from the Brookings Institution to examine the conditions in Indian Country and relevant BIA policies, including those relating to education. The study's coauthor W. Carson Ryan uncovered substantial evidence of how lack of funding significantly weakened the mandate to educate Indian children. His findings, along with those of others were compiled in *The Problem of Indian Administration*, which became known as the Meriam Report after its director, Lewis Meriam. Ryan found that because they were underfunded, the schools depended on students' labors. Children worked in the fields, the dairies, and the chicken coops. They made their clothes and laundered them when dirty. Although one might have argued that the work gave the students skills, the Meriam Report found that the boarding schools did not provide instruction at a level sufficiently advanced to enable the students to find employment.[28] Moreover, the workloads were so great that students had little time to learn in the classroom or to relax. The Meriam Report went so far as to question whether some schools were breaking child labor laws.[29]

The constant dearth of resources also led school administrators to defer maintenance of existing buildings or renovation of old ones, which resulted in fire risks, poor ventilation, and insufficient recreational facilities.[30] Overcrowding and the absence of medical care led to disease. Many students succumbed to tuberculosis and trachoma (a bacterial eye infection). Although tuberculosis is highly contagious, schools rarely isolated those infected and instead sent them home, heedless of the vulnerability of those on the reservations. The Indian death rate for tuberculosis was six and one-half times that of non-Indians.[31]

Although the BIA's primary function should have been education, inadequate funding also led to difficulty in hiring qualified teachers and personnel. Indian school salaries were below other schools' standards and resulted in high turnover.[32] Other critiques in the Meriam Report revolved around a static curriculum and lack of creativity due to the emphasis on militarization. Finally, the experts who drafted the report emphatically believed that Pratt's policy of severing children from their families and cultures was wrong; "the modern point of view in education and social work lays stress on upbringing in the natural setting of home and family life."[33]

After the harsh Meriam Report, Herbert Hoover's administration appointed Charles Rhoads as commissioner of Indian affairs, who immediately began to implement policies to alleviate overcrowding at boarding schools and provide more food and better clothing.[34] By 1930 Rhoads had hired W. Carson Ryan as education director; Ryan now had the power to make the changes he had called for in the report. To avoid more family separations, he set out to open additional community day schools to replace the boarding schools. Ryan also enacted changes in the standard curriculum to give students a more practical vocational education that respected Indian culture. SFIS sent students to their nearby pueblos to take lessons in pottery-making. Maria Martinez, the famous potter of San Ildefonso, was one of the instructors in the 1930s.[35]

When John Collier became commissioner of Indian affairs in 1932 under the Roosevelt administration, he continued with the reforms and made a decisive break with past assimilationist policies. Collier admired Indian culture and believed it should be supported in the schools. He issued a directive to all superintendents, prohibiting "interference with Indian religious life or ceremonial expression." This policy change meant that SFIS administrators, for example, gave students permission to travel home for ceremonial training.[36]

During Ryan's tenure and that of his successor, Willard Walcott Beatty, the reforms continued with the introduction of history, art, and language into the curriculum. AIS fostered a weaving program, and SFIS began a painting program under the direction of Dorothy Dunn, creator of the studio style of painting, in 1932.[37] Construction of new day schools proceeded so that by 1941 their number had increased from 132 to 226. In Collier's first year in office, he closed ten boarding schools. Beatty emphasized the replacement of inadequate industrial training with course work that served "the long-range economic purposes of each reservation."[38]

Even though Collier's leadership was strong, he encountered roadblocks in implementing these new policies. Old-guard teachers ignored certain directives. Newly hired teachers could not speak Native languages let alone teach them. And books teaching the history and culture of Native peoples were scarce, although Beatty did create the Indian Life Series books (1940–1945). By the end of the decade, forty-nine boarding schools remained open, but most had relinquished the military component. An AIS boys' advisor observed, "We find a different atmosphere throughout the entire plant, there is more home life and more student participation . . . as compared with the old military days."[39]

Many of the critiques leveled at the government-run boarding schools by the Meriam Report applied equally to religious schools. They also lacked sufficient funds and relied on student labor. The existence of the religious schools, however, provided parents with an alternative to the secular, government schools. As with AIS and SFIS, the Sisters of Loretto's school in Bernalillo and St. Catherine's in Santa Fe were geographically close to Isleta, allowing families to visit their children. Discussed in more detail below are SFIS, St Catherine's, and the Sisters of Loretto's school in Bernalillo.

THE SISTERS OF LORETTO'S INDIAN INDUSTRIAL SCHOOL IN BERNALILLO

Many Isletans sent their children to the Sisters of Loretto's school in Bernalillo, although little information exists regarding this institution.[40] Bishop Lamy initially brought directly from France members of the Sisters of Loretto, a teaching order. Between 1863 and 1885 they opened schools at Taos, Mora, Albuquerque, Las Vegas, Las Cruces, Socorro, and Bernalillo. The sisters established the Bernalillo school in December 1885 in a building the well-known Rio Abajo merchant, José Leandro Perea, donated. The Bureau of Catholic Indian Missions, which funded St. Catherine's, also financed Loretto. The school opened with eight students all from Isleta Pueblo and by January had an enrollment of thirty students from the Tiwa and Keres villages of the Rio Abajo. As the school expanded in size, it required more teachers and larger buildings. Archbishop Salpointe drew up plans for a new building that would house sixty-five girls. The Bureau of Catholic Indian Missions and Catherine Drexel, to be discussed later, provided funds for the expansion. Even though Pablo Abeita was still in his teens at the inception of the Loretto school, he would later correspond regularly with Father Ketcham of the Bureau of Catholic Indian Missions and even occasionally with Catherine Drexel.[41] The 1910 census reveals that thirty-five Isletan students had attended the Sisters of Loretto's school.[42]

SANTA FE INDIAN SCHOOL

Isletans did not favor SFIS in the early 1900s. Eventually, more Isletan parents sent their children to SFIS, although they preferred AIS because it was close to home, and St. Catherine's because of its more relaxed atmosphere, compared to the military model of AIS and SFIS. SFIS is the only educational institution of the four discussed in this chapter still in operation today.

In 1885 Antonio Joseph, New Mexico's Congressional delegate, introduced a bill to build an off-reservation Indian school in Santa Fe. Congress appropriated $25,000 for that purpose on condition that local citizens donate a hundred-acre site. Hoping to attract businessmen from the east, the Santa Fe Board of Trade, made up of merchants, lawyers, and politicians, purchased a school site on farmland about two miles south of the plaza. The land was in the same area as the State Penitentiary, the School for the Deaf, and two cemeteries. A local builder, working under the supervision of an architect in Washington, DC, completed the original school building in 1890. Designed to be built cheaply and easily enlarged, the red-brick structure had two stories and a pitched tin roof. It comprised a main building with two side wings. It was in no way related to the architectural traditions of the region. The students and employees worked, studied, and slept in this building. The boys' wing held carpentry and shoe-making shops on the first floor. The second floor of each wing had barracks-like sleeping rooms, which could only be reached by outside staircases. The school opened on November 15, 1890, with nine Pueblo students. By the end of the year there were twenty-three students, mostly Pueblos and Apaches, with a few Navajos. By 1891 the enrollment had doubled. Students ranged in age from five to early twenties. By the early 1890s the city extended water lines to the campus, making it possible to have a large, irrigated vegetable garden. By 1900 there were three hundred students, 60 percent Pueblo and the rest Navajo, Apache, Pima, Papago, and a few others. To handle the growing number of students and staff, the school built a laundry, classroom building, hospital, barn, and four employee houses, mostly with student labor. During the summer the boys (there were no girls yet) planted some three hundred shade and fruit trees and laid brick sidewalks around the main buildings. By 1910 the school had built a girls' dormitory, a domestic science building, a dining hall, and an administrative building.[43]

SFIS superintendent Clinton J. Crandall complained that he had to look to other tribes to get older students because, "pueblo parents cannot be induced to send their children to school after they get old enough to work." Also, Pueblo parents tended to send more boys than girls.[44] When schools like SFIS and AIS had to turn away students for lack of room, they often sent them to St. Catherine's.

One of the reasons the government schools initially had such a difficult time recruiting students was that the Pueblos preferred Catholic schools. In 1891 SFIS's first superintendent, Samuel M. Cart, stated that a large percentage of the students at St. Catherine's would have attended SFIS if it had opened sooner.[45] Teofilo Tafoya, who attended SFIS from 1923 to 1936, said he and his friends decided to transfer to SFIS because, "[we'd] have more freedom, more opportunity in the way of education . . . at St. Catherine's you have to be reverent."[46] It appears that school preferences depended on the individual student.

Superintendents had one clear cut legal prerogative in combating the transfer of students between schools. Once a student or their parents signed a contract, administrators could be quite adamant in enforcing it. SFIS superintendent Thomas Jones threatened to have some students who transferred to St. Catherine's without permission forcibly removed, telling one of the sisters that the students were his "by right." Students at both AIS and SFIS played football and other sports. In 1898 the superintendent of SFIS wrote his counterpart at AIS that all his football players were vaccinated against smallpox but would be unable to play AIS because they were recovering from the side effects of the vaccine.[47]

ST. CATHERINE'S SCHOOL

Catherine Drexel, heiress to a large banking fortune, founded St. Catherine's Indian School in 1894. Unlike her siblings who carried on the family business, Catherine devoted her life and fortune to service, particularly the education of African American and Native American children. Baptized Catherine Mary, Drexel took the religious name Mother Katharine when she took her vows as a Catholic nun in 1891.[48] She established a religious teaching order, the Sisters of the Blessed Sacrament. The Sisters of the Blessed Sacrament and Mother Katharine eventually supported and staffed close to sixty schools and missions for Indians in the Southwest and for African American children in the eastern and southern United States. When Mother Katharine was beatified in 1988, it was said of her, "she saw the need to make education available to [Native Americans and Blacks] because it would lead to their self-determination." The Catholic Church canonized Mother Katharine as Saint Katherine Drexel on October 1, 2000.[49]

Upon its completion in 1887, Archbishop Lamy came out of retirement to bless the main building that housed St. Catherine's Indian School (named after St. Catherine of Sienna, rather than Katharine Drexel). It opened its doors on April 26, 1887, to a class consisting mostly of Isletan boys transferred from the Sisters of Loretto's school in Bernalillo. The beginning was rocky due to a shortage of teachers. The Sisters of Loretto taught there for two years, then the Benedictine fathers from Kansas and three lay teachers continued teaching.[50] Mother Katharine then brought nine teachers from Philadelphia in the spring of 1904. The sisters were initially unprepared for life in Santa Fe, as they faced vast cultural differences between themselves and their Native students. They quickly learned Spanish, however, and started to bridge the cultural gap with their students. Almost every night nine or ten relatives of the students would arrive at the school to visit, "expecting to be fed. They brought their horses and considered provisions necessary for them too."[51] The school gained a positive reputation at Isleta, leading to the attendance of thirty-one Isletans at the school in 1910.

In 1895 Archbishop Placide-Louis Chapelle of Santa Fe deeded the land on which the school sat to the Sisters of the Blessed Sacrament. There were ten buildings on the

Figure 33. *Students Studying at the Library, St. Catherine's Indian School, Santa Fe,*
n.d., Tyler Dingee, photographer. Courtesy of the Palace of the Governors Photo
Archive, Negative no. 120235

site, including the girls' dormitory, boys' dormitory, laundry room, playroom, shoe shop,
and carpentry shop. The school then added a one-story recreation hall, additional classroom buildings, and a gymnasium. The students raised chickens and engaged in farming
activities.[52]

By 1908 the school provided instruction to 150 pupils, offering an education through
the eighth grade. Students participated in numerous construction projects over the summer in the 1920s and 1930s and received a small remuneration. They made adobes across
the arroyo from the school and carried them on their backs two at a time. They collected
rocks on the hillside and built the perimeter walls. The students gained experience and a
sense of community, although some complained of working for little or no compensation.
By the fall of 1932, the school had enrolled 275 pupils, 247 from the pueblos, 21 from the
Mescalero Apache tribe, and 7 from the Navajo reservation.[53] By 1935 six boys and two
girls enrolled in the first senior class to graduate from St. Catherine's. Eventually the
administrators eliminated the elementary school and taught only grades seven to twelve.

St. Catherine's inspired fierce loyalty in its students and graduates. Generations of
the same family often attended. Among the famous graduates are Maria Martinez, the
potter from San Ildefonso,[54] Bob Chavez, a successful artist from Cochiti, and Pablita

Velarde of Santa Clara, the well-known painter and muralist. Sports included football, basketball, baseball, and track. Discipline was firm and strict. The students marched in line from place to place. The sisters kept the girls and boys strictly apart except for classes. Most students said that the sisters inspired loyalty and dedication from their students. Some said that at the nearby SFIS, students had more freedom and better educational opportunities, but that depended on who the superintendent was at SFIS. Punishments at St. Catherine's included floor-scrubbing and loss of privileges.

Former student Patrick Toya from Jemez Pueblo noted that, "academics was number one. The nuns also stressed discipline." Regarding religion, he said, "[The nuns] stressed their Catholic religion. . . . They respected us and our religion and we respected theirs . . . that way we were in harmony in school." The students did not have a uniform, but their clothes needed to be presentable. The boys wore a necktie and jackets, and "both boys and girls repaired [their] clothing. There was also a bakery where the students learned to bake. Andres Jaramillo from Isleta was the baker and handyman. He baked all the bread for the whole student body every day. Jose Abeita from Isleta was the coach and carpentry instructor. When anything needed to be done in the maintenance department, Joe Abeita and Andy Jaramillo got together and did it, whether it was the plumbing, electrical, or something else. They took the boys with them and showed them how to fix things. After cleaning the dormitory and putting their clothes in the laundry basket, the boys walked to town until it was time to go back for supper. The nuns took the girls in groups. They also could leave campus after classes and before the first study hour."[55] Andy Jaramillo's daughter, Isletan Mary Ruth Aquino, class of 1947, recalled that after the students learned English, they had permission to speak their native languages as they grew older. She said that when Mother Katharine visited, the boys performed the eagle and hoop dances for her. Mary Ruth lived on campus with her father and her mother, Juanita Juancho Jaramillo, also Isletan, who laundered the students' clothes and the nuns' habits.[56]

Mother Katharine visited the school nearly every year. She died on March 3, 1955, having donated more than $20 million to establish and finance the schools and missions of the Sisters of the Blessed Sacrament. When she died her support of St. Catherine's ended. Within a few years the sisters could no longer afford the $500,000 budget to run the school. In early 1998, over a hundred years since its founding, the Sisters of the Blessed Sacrament announced its intention of shuttering the school. Many former students in whom the school had inspired loyalty and gratitude for lessons learned felt a keen personal loss with its closing.[57]

The three and a half-story main classroom and convent, built in 1887 and located on Rio Grande Street near Rosario Cemetery, is still standing today.[58] It is in relatively good condition and its owner, the City of Santa Fe Housing Authority, rents it out as a set for movies.

CONCLUSION

Although the boarding school experience scarred some Isletans, others flourished. Domingo Jiron, aka Henry Kendall, the son of Isleta governor Vicente Jiron (1882) found it difficult to adjust to life in Isleta when he returned to the village after six years at Carlisle. In a somewhat incoherent reply to a Carlisle survey, he wrote that he had to prove himself in order to find employment; he also believed that the Indians needed to aid returning students.[59] By standing with Superintendent Creager against Lummis and the Isletan parent in the conflict over the release of their children, it seems that Kendall chose to work against his own pueblo.[60] Had he lost his traditional Isletan roots? Did Isletans reject him? Kendall died in 1894, still a young man. There are no records explaining how he died, making one wonder about the circumstances. His situation was not unique though; other students faced challenging homecomings.

In contrast, Pablo Abeita and others adjusted to life upon return to their villages and thrived. While in Santa Fe, Abeita remained in close contact with home. On completion of school, he immediately engaged his skills to help advocate for Isleta and to interact with federal officials. Other students from the early years also pivoted upon re-entry to their villages, finding a place to make an impact. Susie Rayos Marmon from Laguna attended Carlisle for seven years. After graduation, she enrolled at Dickenson College and completed a teachers' course. Returning to New Mexico, she taught first at the Isleta day school and then at Laguna. She merged her dedication to book-learning with her determination to help her people preserve their culture and traditional ways. In addition to teaching Pueblo children to read and write, Marmon emphasized her Laguna heritage and shared stories passed down through the generations as a means for her students to develop skills to defend and protect themselves and their community. Her passion to incorporate Laguna oral traditions into her lessons inspired her students.[61]

One of those students was Isletan Agnes Shattuck Dill. Agnes's father, Paul Shattuck, had been unable to complete his studies at Carlisle because of the need for his labor on the family farm in the Laguna village of Paguate. He was determined that each of his children would have an education. After attending the day school, Agnes went to AIS, which, in later years, she remembered fondly. She even found inspiration in the military atmosphere, becoming captain of a company that won the grand prize for competitive drills. Following in the footsteps of Suzie Marmon, Agnes Dill went on to become a teacher and a community leader at Isleta.[62] She too became a mentor; one of her favorite students, whom she treated as a son, was Theodore "Ted" Jojola.

During her tenure as assistant director of the Community Affairs Program, Dill hired Ted, a young high school student at the time, as an intern. Now a professor at UNM and a former director of Native American studies there, Jojola credits Dill with changing his life: "she provided me with a tremendous opportunity that I wouldn't otherwise have been able to gain." Dill and Jojola remained close throughout her life, and she continued to inspire him. He noted that "she had a keen intellect [and] could carry on an hours-long conversation without ever repeating herself."[63] Jojola looked to Dill for guidance and inspiration, just as she had looked to Susie Marmon.

Jojola noted the socializing aspect of AIS where students met members of other pueblos, the Navajo Nation, and even some Arizona tribes, learning about other Natives and forming lasting friendships. Each generation aided those who came after, offering counsel and encouragement. Susie Marmon, Agnes Dill, and Ted Jojola are examples of the success story of post-1928 Indian education. They all believed in using their education to help their people and protect the land. Pablo Abeita would have been proud of them.

CHAPTER EIGHT

Pablo Abeita and the Court of Indian Offenses

*If you will leave us alone and just show us that your way is a better way
than the Indian way, and show us with a smile and not with a smite
we will get there someday, not by legislation . . . [but] by consent and
goodwill, which in the end will be a lot better for all of us—and if I am
not mistaken that is what you are supposed to do by that invincible thing
called justice.*

Pablo Abeita, Statement inserted in the record of the House
Subcommittee on Indian Affairs from the *Albuquerque Morning
Journal*, May 18, 1920

In 1883 Secretary of the Interior Henry Teller established the Court of Indian Offenses
to help integrate Indians into American society. Teller, formerly a senator from
Colorado with a bias against Indians, asked his commissioner of Indian affairs to for-
mulate rules to help speed the assimilation process; he was particularly concerned with
certain Plains Indian practices such as "plural marriages, the influence of medicine men,
and the destruction of property of [a] deceased person." Commissioner of Indian Affairs
Hiram Price suggested setting up courts of Indian offenses, and Teller approved rules
to this effect on April 10, 1883.[1] The rules provided that "judges should be selected from
intelligent, honest, and upright [Indians] . . . of undoubted integrity." The jurisdiction
of the court was sweeping; it could rule "upon all such questions as may be presented
to it for consideration, by the agent."[2] The courts were to have the same jurisdiction
as a justice of the peace in the state or territory where they were located. The Indian
agents and the commissioner of Indian affairs soon established Courts of Indian Offenses
where they determined them to be desirable. Initially they excluded tribes with recognized tribal governments such as the Five Civilized Tribes, the Osage, the Indians of
New York, and the Pueblos of the Southwest. By 1900 about two-thirds of the tribes in
the United States had their own courts; a little over a decade later the Court of Indian
Offenses came to the pueblos of New Mexico.[3]

Pablo Abeita perfectly fit the statutory requirement for a Court of Indian Offenses
judge: he was indeed intelligent, honest, and upright. Superintendent Leo Crane considered Abeita to be "the man best equipped for the job."[4] Although the courts were
intended to assist in assimilation by helping stamp out "all vestiges of traditional [Native
American] society," Abeita found ways to use the court to protect Pueblo traditional
practices and ceremonies.[5] Not all tribal judges were as protective of Pueblo religion,
however. At Cochiti, Judge John Dixon, a Carlisle graduate and leader of the progressive faction, mocked the conservatives as "centuries behind in habits and customs."[6]
Although Abeita was also a progressive, he defined the term differently than did Dixon.

In a 1928 speech he explained, "progressive is that a man can plow his land better with a riding plow than with a hand plow, [but] drifting away from Indian customs, I don't call that progress." Pablo Abeita did not see a contradiction in using modern tools and participating in Pueblo ceremonials.[7]

Pablo Abeita found that the position of judge of the Court of Indian Offenses carried with it "power of impressive dimensions." Operating near the center of the agency's power structure, the judge not only shared in it by virtue of his position but also acquired "a knowledge of . . . American law and custom, and established a personal relationship with those who now directed his people's destiny."[8] His role as judge, however, brought with it personal attacks by those who lost in his court and by those who coveted the power of his office. Abeita's enemies attacked his integrity and accused him of misdeeds. Standing his ground in a small community was not easy, but his tenure as judge brought a measure of stability to a divided pueblo. In the ten-year period that Abeita sat on the Court of Indian Offenses, he learned the rudiments of American jurisprudence and procedure so well that he was almost as knowledgeable as a trained lawyer.

The procedure in the court followed closely that of a state magistrate court or district court, but usually without lawyers. The plaintiffs first stated their claim, the defendants followed with their defense, and then the court heard the testimony of other witnesses. Judge Abeita then rendered his decision, which was subject to appeal to the Indian agent or superintendent and then to the commissioner of Indian affairs. In most cases prior to 1922, these officials sustained Abeita's decisions, rarely if ever reversing them. For example, Isletan Juanita Jaramillo filed an appeal with Superintendent Leo Crane in October 1919 of Judge Abeita's decision that she pay an eighteen-dollar fine or serve twenty days in jail for immoral conduct. She appeared in person, telling Crane that she was innocent and that the evidence against her was not factual. Crane told Judge Abeita, "it is not my practice to interfere in these matters, but [I] will have to consider this appeal." He asked Abeita to inform him of the "conclusive evidence [that] was given against this woman." Abeita complied, and the next day Superintendent Crane informed him that the appeal was denied, "your judgement appearing to have been made on sufficient conclusive evidence." It is not clear what Jaramillo's immoral conduct consisted of or whether she paid the fine or served the time.[9]

The rules governing the Court of Indian Offenses provided for a small monthly salary for the judges, as well as for a clerk to maintain a docket and preserve a proper record of each case. Lacking a clerk, Abeita performed both these functions himself, lamenting to Father Ketcham that he received a salary of only ten cents a day or thirty-six dollars a year.[10] Except in rare cases, Abeita's court was a one-man operation. He issued the summons that brought the parties before the court; he heard the testimony, often taking notes in shorthand; he translated that testimony (usually given in Tiwa); and he often conducted his own investigation and then rendered a decision. If the decision was appealed to the superintendent, Abeita provided a summary of the testimony or a full transcript of the proceedings.

THE TRIBAL POLICEMAN

In civil cases, Judge Abeita usually attempted to induce the parties to settle their dispute. One way he found to encourage and enforce settlements was by using the Isleta tribal police. Congress authorized the Indian police at the same time it established the Court of

Indian Offenses. Both institutions were designed to speed assimilation, although Pablo Abeita also used the police, as he did the court, to further his progressive agenda while maintaining traditional Pueblo customs.[11]

In 1911 Superintendent Lonergan asked Abeita for his recommendation regarding two candidates for the job of tribal policeman: Esquipula Jojola and Patricio (Patrick) Olguin. After consulting the teacher at the day school, Miss Rose K. Watson, Abeita recommended Jojola (a relative) as "a better boy than Patricio in every way." Jojola got the job and began working with Judge Abeita as an arm of the court as soon as the Court of Indian Offenses was established.[12] Tribal policemen played an essential role, and the job proved to be a training ground for other political offices in the pueblo. Indeed, in 1961 Jojola became governor of Isleta after serving as lieutenant governor in 1953.[13] He also took the official census of Isleta Pueblo in 1930 as enumerator. Jojola, well-liked by almost everyone in the pueblo, proved to be an effective tribal policeman and mediator.

By 1920 Superintendent Crane appointed Louis Abeita as tribal policeman; he soon gained the trust of both Pablo Abeita and Superintendent Crane. Louis Abeita's assistance was crucial in settling cases ranging from enforcing a promise to marry to dividing an inheritance by a Navajo girl attending AIS, to be discussed later. In the promise-to-marry case Louis traveled to Winslow, Arizona, in November 1920, where Isletan Jose Seferino Abeita was working on the railroad. Jose Seferino had vowed to marry Maria Lucero before he left Isleta but reneged on his promise. Louis told him to set a date or else face punishment. Succumbing to that pressure, Jose Seferino again promised to marry Maria "during the Christmas holidays." Superintendent Crane advised him, "it will be necessary for you to keep your word in this matter, and Officer Louis Abeita has been instructed to see that you do keep it."[14] Jose Seferino Abeita did marry Maria Lucero, and in 1930 they were living at Isleta in household number 195 together with their three children, Lorenzo, Maria, and Geronimo, and a stepson, Jose M. Whipi.[15]

Superintendent Crane often praised policeman Louis Abeita, saying, "his judgement could be depended on," as did another Indian service official, who said, "if this agency had four such policemen there would be very little trouble of any sort."[16] Judge Abeita was grateful to have Louis Abeita who acted as an adjunct to his court. The policeman was well liked within the village, and his presence gave the Court of Indian Offenses greater credibility.

A Sampling of Cases in Judge Abeita's Court

In a few cases where there was a conflict of interest, another Native judge—most often Judge William Paisano from Laguna—stepped in and heard the case.[17] Near the end of his term in 1923–1924, Superintendent Marble sometimes made the court's decision himself or suggested that Judge Abeita settle the case. Abeita kept a detailed record of the cases he tried, but since his docket book has not surfaced, the table of cases in appendix 7 is only a partial list.[18]

To understand Abeita's judicial philosophy and learn about the social conditions at Isleta at this time, we have prepared a table of cases arranged chronologically in appendix 7. The types of cases range from criminal to domestic, civil, property, inheritance, community work, and truancy cases.

Criminal prosecutions made up most of the cases heard by Judge Abeita's Court of Indian Offenses just as they did with other such courts. For example, at one of the first courts established in 1886 at the Kiowa Comanche Agency in Oklahoma, most cases were criminal, only one of them a major crime. Sitting on that court, the famous Comanche chief Quanah Parker gained respect for his decisions and was probably a role model for the young Pablo Abeita when he visited Oklahoma in 1905.[19] More than three decades after the establishment of Quanah Parker's court, the criminal jurisdiction of Judge Abeita's court was sharply curtailed by the Major Crimes Act, which eventually listed fourteen major crimes—such as murder, manslaughter, and armed robbery—subject to exclusive federal jurisdiction. The Major Crimes Act was a response to the 1883 United States Supreme Court decision in *Ex Parte Crow Dog*, which reversed a territorial court's decision convicting the Lakota chief Crow Dog of killing a rival chief. Under tribal law a property settlement between Crow Dog and the victim's family had resolved the situation, but the national uproar when Crow Dog walked free after the Supreme Court decision led to the limitation of a tribal court's criminal jurisdiction to minor crimes.[20] Critics of the Major Crimes Act (still in effect today) argue that there is a dearth of prosecutions in recent years because US attorneys decline to prosecute approximately 75 percent of the federal cases turned over to them by the tribes.[21]

Figure 34. *Esquipula Jojola, Isleta Pueblo, 1935*, T. Harmon Parkhurst, photographer. Courtesy of the Palace of the Governors Photo Archive, Negative no. 002685

The criminal cases Judge Abeita heard were all minor crimes such as assault, immoral conduct, and resisting arrest. In most of those cases, he found the defendants guilty and sentenced them to either a fine or jail time. These measures seem to have been a deterrent, even when the fine was appealed. Sometimes the judge reduced jail sentences when a defendant was able to pay a fine. One important case of resisting arrest required a full-scale trial.

In the 1922 case of *Isleta vs. Jose Chavez*, Chavez challenged tribal policeman Louis Abeita's authority after Chavez took his nephew out of school. When Louis Abeita attempted to remove the child from Chavez's home, the uncle resisted and told Louis to leave his property. A scuffle ensued during which Abeita struck Chavez and said he would return with a warrant for his arrest. When he did, Chavez continued to resist, at one point "holding him [Abeita] by the collar and threatening him." As the policeman handcuffed Chavez and put him in his buggy, he continued to resist, arguing "about his innocence or guilt." When Judge Abeita heard this evidence, he sentenced Chavez to fifteen days in jail "for interfering with officer Louis Abeita in [the] performance of his duty." Even though the evidence against Chavez for improperly removing his nephew from school was scanty, the evidence of resisting arrest was clear, and Judge Abeita was determined to protect Officer Louis Abeita.[22]

The proceeds of the fines assessed in these cases were turned over to the superintendent and did not augment Judge Abeita's meager salary. But the collection and disposition of fines proved to be the issue upon which his conservative enemies would gain some sympathy from Superintendent Marble, who later accused Pablo Abeita of "dishonest, or at least careless, financial practices."[23]

In another high-profile case mentioned earlier that received a full hearing, former governor Juan P. Lente was charged with leading an assault against Superintendent Lonergan on the pueblo's feast day, October 3, 1915. Lonergan testified that he took the ceremonial drum and stopped the dance because some men were intoxicated. He said Governor Lente took the drum back and returned it to the dancers and singers. When Lonergan persisted and took the drum again, Lente urged his followers to "get clubs and attack Lonergan." Lonergan warded off several blows before order was restored. Governor Lente denied the charges. After hearing all the testimony and cross-examination of witnesses, Judge Abeita announced that he was going to be lenient and sentenced Governor Lente to forty days in the Isleta jail. Lente's appeals were denied, and from that day on Juan P. Lente and his conservative followers became more entrenched in their opposition to all of Pablo Abeita's progressive policies.[24]

CIVIL CASES REGARDING PROPERTY

Civil cases regarding property were the most numerous after criminal cases. These two categories comprise the bulk of the work of the Court of Indian Offenses. Prior to the arrival of Superintendent Marble, Judge Abeita's decisions in these cases were final and helped provide a modicum of order within Isleta Pueblo. An example of a case where Marble began to override Judge Abeita's authority was a case against Pablo Abeita himself, *Lucero vs. Abeita*. In November 1923 Remijio Lucero (who served as governor in 1922) made claims against Judge Abeita before Governor Jose Padilla, concerning rooms Abeita was renting to a Hispano railroad worker. Judge Abeita admitted that he owned one room solely and three-quarters of the second room that Lucero claimed his grandson owned. Lucero argued that the grandson should be receiving his pro rata share of the rent for the one-fourth of the room. When Governor Padilla tried the case, he found in favor of Lucero and his grandson. Judge Abeita objected and in his report to Superintendent Marble admitted that he did not own the one-quarter of the second room, but he "instructed the Mexican not to use this . . . space." The judge then complained that when he told Governor Padilla this, "[he] would not listen to it, instead he acted more as an attorney for Remijio than as Judge or Gov." It seemed "that the Gov. has got it in for me, picking at me at every turn."[25] Agency Farmer Howard V. Smith talked to the unnamed Hispano renter who admitted that Abeita had told him, "this part of the room did not belong to him," although he occupied the entire room; Smith recommended someone pay Lucero's grandson one-fifth of the rent, about a dollar per month.[26] After receiving three reports, one from Abeita, one from the governor (written by Antonio Abeita), and one from Agency Farmer Smith, Superintendent Marble wrote Judge Abeita questioning the wisdom of renting "any community property to outsiders, who might later claim ownership."[27] Judge Abeita was probably correct in his assessment that the governor "had it in for him," but he exercised poor judgement in renting rooms to an outsider, especially when he did not own the whole room. As to Lucero's claim for a share of the rent, there was no decision in this politically charged case.

Other property cases were less complicated, and most were settled, as was *Jiron vs. Lucero* involving a debt of seventeen dollars that Lucero claimed to have repaid by letting Jiron board with him without charge. The parties reached a settlement with Judge Abeita's help.[28] Another case concerned farm equipment—a mower, so important to farmers raising alfalfa and hay. *Jose Jiron vs. Antonio Abeita* involved a mower that Antonio Abeita sold to Jiron for fifty dollars, two thousand *terrones* (sod building bricks), and six days' labor. Abeita repossessed the mower when Jiron was not home, claiming Jiron paid only twenty dollars, about one thousand *terrones*, and only three hours' labor. Since Jiron had made a good-faith effort to pay Abeita, he at least wanted his money back. Superintendent Marble asked Judge Abeita to settle the case, but it is unlikely that he was successful because Antonio Abeita, a partisan of the current governor, Jose Padilla, and another of Judge Abeita's nemeses, was not amenable to compromise.[29]

DOMESTIC RELATIONS

Of the four cases sampled, three involved relations between husband and wife and one was a father and son dispute. In *Remijio vs. Remijio*, Alcario Remijio, the son, claimed that his father, Antonio, ejected him from the family home. Antonio countered that he gave his son a piece of land on which to construct a house and offered to help him build it, and that in any event, Alcario also had a house in the pueblo. In this case, as in many others, the facts depended on the credibility of the witnesses, and here Judge Abeita must have believed the father for he dismissed the case.[30]

In cases husbands brought against deserting wives, Judge Abeita usually urged the wives to return to their husbands, no matter what caused the split-up. He also sought resolutions to the problems coming before him even if the solution technically lay outside his jurisdiction. In March 1918, Felipe Sangre sued Andres Olguin, complaining that Olguin would not support his wife, who was Sangre's sister. Olguin testified that "his wife always wanted to go home [to her mother with her baby]," whereupon Judge Abeita told him to "get his wife and live with her." Abeita continued to investigate, however, and when the case came up for trial a few weeks later, he decided that the wife was too sick to keep house for her husband and ordered mother and infant sent to the Laguna Sanatorium until they were cured. Sadly, the unnamed wife died, although the child survived. The 1930 Isleta census lists Andres Olguin as a widower, living with his brother and his son, Jose Lupe, the boy who probably recovered from tuberculosis.[31]

Judge Abeita achieved his goal of uniting or reuniting families whenever possible as in the case of *Lucero vs. Abeita*, the marriage promise case previously discussed. Jose Seferino Abeita kept his promise to marry Maria Lucero, for the 1930 Isleta census shows them together in household no. 26 with two daughters and an infant son.[32] Not all domestic cases ended so happily, though. In the most serious case, Candelaria Gerilla refused to reconcile with her husband Tomas, who she claimed beat her while she was pregnant, causing a miscarriage. Although this should have led to criminal charges of domestic abuse, it was considered to be a reasonable justification for the wife's refusal to reconcile.[33]

Three cases dealt directly with truancy; although few, such cases were among the most contentious. The BIA considered Pueblo youths subject to the truancy laws requiring all children to attend school until they were eighteen years old. Because Pablo Abeita believed so strongly in the importance of education, he sent three of his sons to AIS. In all the truancy cases, Judge Abeita was strict, ordering students returned to school—by force if necessary—with no excuses considered. Some of the reasons Pueblo parents took their children out of school were because they needed their help with farm work, because of their opposition to BIA schools in general, and because of the requirement, in pueblos like Taos, for some boys to leave school for as long as a year and a half to undergo religious training.[34] At Taos in 1924, pueblo leaders requested permission to take three boys out of school for eighteen months and another six boys for six months for religious instruction and tribal initiation. Commissioner Charles H. Burke denied the request, but tribal leaders took the boys out of school anyway. The confrontation was finally resolved as the All Indian Pueblo Council came to the defense of the Taos leaders based on their freedom of religion.[35]

Isletans' main reason for taking their children out of school was the need for the boys to help their parents with farm work, especially with the spring planting and the fall harvest. Parents also wanted their children home for the Christmas holidays. That was what motivated Juan Reyes Abeita to remove three students from the Sisters of Loretto's school in Bernalillo in late December 1922.[36] Although a fabrication, Juan Reyes convinced school officials that he had permission from Superintendent Harmon P. Marble to remove the students. Indignant at the deception, Marble told Judge Abeita to have the tribal police return the boys and summon the parents before his court to explain the misrepresentation. Abeita had the students returned to school but delayed bringing their fathers to court until they completed their work on the irrigation ditch.[37] Here Judge Abeita was trying to balance two competing interests: the schools' interest in keeping the students as long as possible and the parents' desire to have their children home for the holidays. In his own case, however, Abeita repeatedly lobbied Superintendent Reuben

Perry of AIS, for special treatment for his boys—Jose, Remijio, and Ambrosio—favors that included small loans, additional clothes, higher pay when they worked at the school over the summer, and a few days off to go home for Christmas.[38]

Overall, Judge Abeita was strict in enforcing school attendance but lenient in dealing with parents with whom he sympathized. One exception was the case of Jose Chavez, discussed earlier under criminal cases. When Chavez assaulted tribal policeman Louis Abeita as he attempted to remove a truant student from Chavez's home, Judge Abeita sentenced Chavez to fifteen days in jail.[39]

COMMUNITY WORK

Although few, these cases are important because failure to perform community work was an offense particular to the Pueblos. In general, community work consisted of labor on the acequias, maintenance of roads, and participation in religious ceremonies. Since there was no way to enforce ceremonial participation, all the cases discussed here related to failure to work on the acequia. There is a connection between the two, however, as a case in Cochiti Pueblo illustrates. Antonio Montoya complained that it was unfair to allow those who engaged in pueblo dances to be excused from work on the acequia. Montoya was a progressive who did not believe in the ceremonial life of the pueblo and felt his freedom of religion was violated because he was not excused from ditch work. Therefore, he claimed, he and the others had to work harder. The outcome of his case is not known.[40]

It is interesting to compare two similar cases—one decided by Governor Juan Rey Juancho, the other by Judge Abeita. In case no. 16, dated September 18, 1922, Governor Juancho assessed fines on ten parents who failed to send their sons to work on the acequia. All but two—former governor Juan P. Lente and Santos Chiwiwi—settled with Governor Juancho who kept the fines himself. On October 30, 1922, Judge Pablo Abeita tried a similar case against thirteen people who refused to report to work on the acequia. The governor and his two lieutenant governors were present in court, and they reported the number of days each defendant failed to show up. Judge Abeita assessed fines totaling fifteen dollars and asked Superintendent Marble whether he should send the money to the governor, and, if so, whether he should have to make a report of all the fines received and how they were spent. Judge Abeita sought Marble's advice about "how far I can go with court matters and what I should do and what I should not."[41] He was being cautious as Marble continued to restrict his jurisdiction.

PROPERTY RIGHTS AND INHERITANCE

Prior to the establishment of the Court of Indian Offenses, Pueblo governors usually decided questions of inheritance according to tribal tradition. Sometimes, when the parties did not agree with the governor's ruling, they appealed to the Indian agent to resolve the matter. For example, in the late 1800s, Indian Agent Benjamin Thomas decided a dispute at Isleta within Juan Rey Jojola's family, which neither the governor nor the tribal council had been able to settle. With the establishment of the Court of Indian Offenses, however, judges like Pablo Abeita began to follow New Mexico property law instead of tribal custom, as called for by the rules that governed the operation of the court.[42]

Inheritance was the most controversial category of cases within the pueblo because conservative governors such as Juan Domingo Lucero (1911 and 1912) and Jose Padilla (1921, 1923, 1927, 1928, and 1932) believed it was their prerogative to decide these matters. When they did, the rules they used were often obscure and arbitrary, based more on favoritism than property law. Late in Abeita's term as judge, Governor Padilla was successful in having inheritance cases assigned to him, particularly because Superintendents Crane and Marble believed that the governor should decide such cases. Superintendent Lonergan, however, took the position that Judge Abeita had ample jurisdiction to decide all cases that came before him. Leo Crane (1920–1922), who succeeded Lonergan as superintendent, thought differently. In 1920 he wrote to Abeita questioning whether in the future matters of inheritance should be decided according to New Mexico State law or pueblo custom. Crane asked for a ruling from the Indian Office on the question. Whether that ruling ever came is not clear, but the mere suggestion that pueblo custom rather than New Mexico law should be the basis of decisions began to undermine the authority of the Court of Indian Offenses and of Judge Abeita. It called into question the very principles upon which the court was founded.[43] When Superintendent Marble took office from 1922 to 1924, he failed to support Judge Abeita as had Lonergan. Thus, in many inheritance cases dating from late 1922 to early 1924, litigants, when not satisfied with Judge Abeita's decision, appealed to Superintendent Marble or circumvented the court entirely by taking the case to the governor. This led to a period of uncertainty and a loss of respect for the decisions of both the governor and the Court of Indian Offenses.

In 1919 Judge Abeita tried to protect himself from criticism by forwarding three disputes over property succession to Richard Hanna, special attorney for the Pueblo Indians. Hanna, a lawyer and later a judge, emerged as one of the strongest advocates for the Pueblos, especially during the time of the Pueblo Lands Board and its aftermath.[44] Hanna's recommendations regarding inheritance, forwarded to Judge Abeita through Lonergan, were based entirely on New Mexico statutes and not on community custom.[45]

Pueblo customs regarding marriage, divorce, adoption, and inheritance rights differed among Pueblos as well as between Pueblos and other Indian tribes, causing much confusion. In 1912, in an attempt to clarify matters, the commissioner of Indian affairs asked all the local superintendents "to call together a few . . . older members of the tribes . . . under your charge" and learn from them the custom regarding inheritance rights and other domestic matters. Misunderstandings had arisen due to a common custom that "in some tribes it was usual for a man to speak of his brother's children as his own 'sons' or 'daughters'. . . . The failure of witnesses to distinguish whether the relationship was the lineal one of parent and child or the collateral one [of] 'uncle' and 'nephew' or 'niece', had frequently been a source of confusion."[46] Whether Superintendent Lonergan replied to this request is unknown, but we do know that Lonergan advocated for a Court of Indian Offenses governed by state laws that would have precedence.[47]

The following cases illustrate the comparison between Judge Abeita's earlier adjudications of inheritance cases and the later period when the governor and Superintendent Marble attempted to decide inheritance without the judge's participation. The first case concerned a female Navajo (Diné) student, Bahe Guerro, who sought Judge Abeita's help with an inheritance question. Guerro, from Puertecito on the Navajo reservation, was attending AIS. She had inherited some horses, cattle, sheep, and goats from her father, which were all in her stepfather's possession; she, however, wanted her uncle Juan Guerro to hold the livestock for her.[48] When the Navajo girl, along with her uncle and a Navajo policeman, came to Isleta policeman Louis Abeita's home, with Pablo Abeita present and acting as a judge of arbitration, they heard another side of the story. Apparently Bahe Guerro was one of eight children, all of whom had an interest in the livestock. The Navajo policeman reported that the family's livestock herd (particularly the sheep) had been substantially diminished, and if Guerro were to receive the 112 sheep she claimed "there would not be any left for the other children." So, Judge Abeita, after hearing everyone's testimony, induced the parties to settle as follows: Bahe Guerro would receive thirty sheep, two cows, and three calves to be held by her uncle as her guardian. The Navajo policeman was "to witness the transfer and to see that the stepfather got a receipt." Guerro's siblings would receive their proportionate shares. Superintendent Crane approved this settlement although he was somewhat miffed that the parties came to Louis Abeita and Judge Abeita, following "the usual Indian custom of running somewhere else for another decision."[49] This case was unorthodox because, in effect, Judge Abeita was holding court in policeman Louis Abeita's house rather than his court room. Apparently, the parties felt more comfortable there, especially the Navajo policeman. Also unusual was the extension of Judge Abeita's jurisdiction into the Navajo reservation, using the Navajo policeman as an adjunct of his court just as he did with Louis Abeita.

Another case, *Jiron vs. Jojola*, involved a convoluted inheritance question that came down to the issue of ownership of a barn/corral and a peach tree. After Governor Padilla and Judge Abeita rendered their decisions, the governor pleaded with Superintendent Marble to decide the case because he feared that "worse things may take place when some parties start fighting for property."[50] This was more than a simple inheritance question because Juan P. Lente, former governor and leader of the conservative, anti-Abeita faction, represented one of the parties in the case. Judge Abeita had just had a direct confrontation with Lente a few months earlier when the judge arrested Lente for making threats against witnesses in another case.[51]

Yielding to the pleas from the pueblo governor, Superintendent Marble called for a hearing at Isleta on October 23 at which all parties were to be present along with Special Attorney for the Pueblos F. C. H. Livingston. From the ensuing testimony, it developed that Marcelina Jiron owned part of a house and a nearby corral/barn after the death of her husband. The widow sold her share of the house to Dolores Jojola and conveyed part of the corral/barn to her children, Transita and Seferino. The children sold their share of the corral/barn to Jose Felipe Jiron who made improvements to it. When Juan P. Lente, acting as Jiron's attorney, argued the case before Governor Padilla, he complained against Lieutenant Governor Antonio Abeita: "when I was making my argument, Antonio was acting as a lawyer. I told [him] . . . he better not act as a lawyer, he should not help the other side until a decision was issued." As Judge Abeita prophesized, Lente was obfuscating the central issue of the case: who owned the property initially and to whom had they sold it? Although the testimony was somewhat confusing, it was clear that Marcelina Jiron owned the property and had sold the house to Dolores Jojola and conveyed the barn/corral to her children who in turn, sold it to Jiron. The lack of written documents such as deeds or sale agreements made the situation worse, but the interjections of Juan P. Lente and Antonio Abeita into the case made a simple question of property ownership into a bitter partisan dispute. And perhaps the most interesting question remained:

Who owned the peach tree? Although barely mentioned at the hearing, Jose Felipe Jiron claimed it because it was on his property, and Dolores Jojola claimed it because she had been eating the peaches and had taken care of the tree.[52]

It was up to Superintendent Marble to decide the case, and he would now engage in some bureaucratic legerdemain making the final decision himself while appearing not to. After a nine-page transcript of the hearing was prepared (probably by Pablo Abeita), Marble sent it to attorney Livingston with the cryptic request, "I will thank you for an early opinion regarding this case." Did he mean an opinion regarding the legal issues, or did he mean a final resolution? That was up to Livingston.[53] Livingston sensed the ambiguity in Marble's request and the superintendent's reluctance to be the one to make a final ruling in a factional dispute. After outlining the law and facts regarding ownership of the house and barn/corral, Livingston got to the peach tree. He suggested that Marble send the government farmer to the land to determine whether the peach tree was on Jiron's land. If it was on Jiron's land, Livingston told Marble, "then it is up to you to find in his favor." As to the rest of the case, Livingston opined that Jose Felipe Jiron owned the corral/barn. He was clear, however, that it was up to Marble to render a final ruling: "I am sure that you will not let my opinion as to the evidence and facts sway you in any way, and that your decision . . . will be according to your own good judgement and conscience." So, the ball was back in Marble's court.[54] But instead of deciding the case, Marble referred it to Padilla, sending him Livingston's opinion and asking him to "Kindly use your influence to end this controversy along the lines indicated." Padilla had asked Marble to decide the case to avoid bloodshed, and now Marble was telling him to "end the controversy" himself. Whether Governor Padilla was able to do so is not clear,

Figure 35. *Jose and Dolores Padilla,*
n.d., Charles Lummis, photographer. Courtesy of the Pueblo of Isleta Tribal Archive, Yonan Cultural Center, Negative no. YACC00900.2008. Original print housed at the Autry Museum of the American West, Negative no. P7387

but there would be no shortage of factional bickering during Superintendent Marble's remaining term of office before Superintendent Chester E. Faris succeeded him.[55]

Some defendants on the losing end of Judge Abeita's decisions accused him of bias. In all civil cases there is generally a winner and a loser, and the latter often charged the judge with unfairness, occasionally holding a grudge against him personally. That was as true of tribal judges as it was of tribal policemen. As early as 1886, when the Standing Rock band of the Lakota was the only tribe to have a functioning Court of Indian Offenses, a Lakota tribal policeman pointed out the perils of serving as tribal policeman and as judge: "to act as judges over our own people and condemn them to punishment when necessary will further endanger our lives and increase their [the people's] enmity."[56] Pablo Abeita felt the same way. In 1923 he told Commissioner of Indian Affairs Burke, "when I first took the position as judge, I was opposed and was always in danger of assault . . . I have endured all kind of criticism and have been assaulted, cursed, [and] swored [sic] at just because I have been a help to the Indian Office towards a betterment of conditions among my own people."[57]

Part of the opposition to the Court of Indian Offenses came from the Isleta governor, whose power began to diminish as that of the court increased. In 1921 Governor Jose Padilla declared open war on the Indian superintendent, the Court of Indian Offenses in general, and Pablo Abeita in particular. Padilla's concern over Judge Abeita's growing influence was exacerbated in September 1921 when Abeita brought Governor Padilla's daughter-in-law, Lugarda C. Padilla, to trial on charges of slander filed by the litigious Emily L. Carpio. Carpio, who seemed to have a proclivity for getting into fights with other women, claimed Padilla had called her "bad words." Abeita believed Carpio's testimony despite the case made by Lugarda Padilla, whose lawyers, according to the judge, "made more noise than a dozen brass bands." The defense attacked the jurisdiction of the court and Abeita, arguing that the judge "was a crook and had no right to try . . . this case." Abeita sentenced Padilla to ten days in jail and fined her ten dollars. This incensed Governor Padilla who still believed that he, as the governor, "should have authority as judge, to hold hearings and assess fines in civil and probate cases, without permitting any appeal."[58]

THE DORRINGTON INVESTIGATION

In December 1921 Governor Padilla led a delegation to Washington, DC, where he voiced his complaints against Judge Abeita. Commissioner of Indian Affairs Charles H. Burke did not support the delegation's petition criticizing Abeita. Nevertheless, the secretary of the Interior's office agreed to send a special investigator to New Mexico to investigate the complaints raised in the petition. Burke, however, wrote a scathing letter strongly criticizing the delegation for its baseless vendetta against Pablo Abeita. When the delegation returned to Isleta, satisfied with Interior's promise of an investigation, Governor Padilla did not mention Commissioner Burke's letter "castigating their proposals as well as their approach." Pueblo members did not hear of this letter until Superintendent Crane read it to them at the ensuing meetings held at Isleta and led by Inspector Lafayette A. Dorrington.[59]

The first day of the meeting convened at the pueblo with Dorrington, Inspector John W. Atwater, and Crane all in attendance. Governor Padilla called the meeting to order at 2:00 p.m. on December 15, 1921, and introduced the inspector (who he called Colonel Dorrington), and referred to him as "an honorable man." Dorrington, in turn, alluded to the friction at the pueblo and asked everyone to "refrain from any unpleasant statements and . . . [to] conduct [themselves] in a thoroughly businesslike manner . . . for the benefit of [the] pueblo and the people." This high-minded admonition was generally followed throughout the first day of the meeting, which did not adjourn until 10:30 p.m. During the second day, however, the meeting degenerated into such a bitter confrontation that Dorrington announced, "unless you conduct this meeting in a thoroughly businesslike manner, it will be necessary for me to withdraw."[60] Although Dorrington stayed throughout the meeting, it remained a partisan affair between the faction supporting Governor Padilla and the one supporting Pablo Abeita. Only at the end of the second day, at Abeita's urging, was there a discussion of matters of concern to the whole pueblo, such as land rights.

Governor Padilla made most of the complaints against Judge Abeita and the Court of Indian Offenses. Due to his focus on Abeita and the court, he only briefly mentioned non-partisan business such as the pueblo's claim for land to the crest of the Manzano Mountains, the fencing of the grant, and the continuing problem of transportation of the schoolchildren at Chical, an Isletan village across the Rio Grande, five miles away from the Isleta plaza.[61]

Governor Padilla began by noting that Superintendent Lonergan started the Court of Indian Offenses in 1914 and appointed Pablo Abeita as judge. "Since then," said the governor, "there has been no harmony in our affairs." Previously "the position of governor was considered an honorable position," Padilla continued. To illustrate his concern, he told the following stories about the impounding of horses.[62] The first incident involved a stray horse Padilla ordered his sheriff to take to the governor's house until the owner arrived. The next day when the owner did not appear, Judge Abeita's policeman arrived with orders to take the horse. When Governor Padilla refused, the unnamed policeman told him that "[if] he could not take the mare he would take [the governor]." Padilla relented to avoid trouble, but lamented to Inspector Dorrington, "I think . . . that the judge has more authority than I have as governor."[63] Now it was clear that this conflict was about political and judicial power.

In the second confrontation, Pablo Abeita's horses got out one night and ran loose through the village. Governor Padilla impounded them and sent word to Abeita through his sheriff that he would have to pay a six-dollar fine (one dollar for each horse) to have them released. When the sheriff told the governor that Abeita would not pay the fine, Padilla ordered the sheriff to put a lock on the gate where the horses were held. Undaunted, Judge Abeita (or one of his sons) later approached Padilla's house, cut the wire, and released the horses. Stung by this affront, Padilla sent his sheriff to order Judge Abeita "to report to the courthouse and explain . . . what he did," an order Abeita ignored. This led Governor Padilla to again lament to Inspector Dorrington, as he had to Superintendent Crane, "because he is a judge he is under no one because he refused to answer my call to come and explain."[64] Padilla wanted the governor to have supreme power, even over Judge Abeita and the Court of Indian Offenses; instead, he complained that he had only a sheriff and no jail, whereas Abeita had several policemen and a jail.[65]

In none of his complaints, however, did Governor Padilla charge that Judge Abeita's decisions were unfair, although he did believe the Court of Indian Offenses gave Abeita too much authority.[66] Padilla objected to Abeita's issuing permits for those operating concessions at the annual feast day. He complained that issuing permits and collecting the fees had always been the governor's prerogative, but now Abeita, with Crane's support, was usurping that as well. This was an old complaint that went to the heart of the governor's concerns. According to Padilla and his supporters, such as Juan Lente, "the collections from the concessions . . . are the only funds from which the pueblo officials are paid a salary."[67] Most of those present at the investigation agreed that this had always been the custom. Pablo Abeita, however, did not claim a right to the funds collected; rather, he believed the funds should be deposited in the pueblo bank account for the benefit of the entire village.

When Padilla finished his statement, Abeita made his only defense to the multiple charges by telling the governor, "I will make answer to all that has been said against me or my position at the proper time in writing. [As to the concessions] I had the authority to issue permits but not to collect money."[68] Superintendent Crane supported Abeita against Padilla's charges and complaints. With regard to Padilla's recent delegation to Washington, when Crane authorized payment of Abeita's expenses to accompany the delegation, he said, "Pablo Abeita has worked in [Isleta's] interest, both here and at Washington and has largely kept this pueblo alive."[69]

Several of those complaining at the meeting directed their concerns at Superintendent Crane, as they had less to do with Pablo Abeita. Often the complaints related to children kept in school too long or returned to school after they had run away. For example, Jose Lucero complained that his son was forced to stay in school past age eighteen, and when he went to see the superintendent, "he shook his finger in my face and told me to get out of his office." When Lucero contacted Abeita and asked him to take the case, the judge told him that the boy had signed a contract agreeing to stay in school and, in any case, he did not have jurisdiction.[70]

Matters relating to the general concerns of Isleta Pueblo were rarely discussed at the Dorrington meeting. But finally on the second day, after Dorrington had threatened to leave the meeting, Pablo Abeita spoke for only the fourth time: "All this wrangle is getting us nowhere. . . . We should get together here and give Colonel Dorrington information on matters of importance to us as a people and a Pueblo. We should here be taking up matters pertaining to our land rights and other community matters."[71] Abeita was undoubtedly thinking of the two-decades-long quest for a survey, patenting, and transfer of the Isleta tract, east of the pueblo, running to the crest or spine of the Manzano Mountains. Governor Padilla had mentioned the claim at the beginning of the meeting but only ancillary to his primary goal of attacking Judge Abeita and the Court of Indian Offenses.[72] Bautista Zuni then recommended that one way to avoid the bickering was to let the young people speak because the older ones brought up long-standing rivalries. Earlier he had summed it up: "I do not approve of much that has been said here by others. I have no charges to make against any of the officials of the government, neither Mr. Crane nor Judge Pablo Abeita."[73]

Finally, the Dorrington meeting, or investigation, adjourned inconclusively. Even after the members became more reasonable and businesslike near the end, they could not resist the urge to argue even while praising the superintendent. At one point Antonio Abeita said, "I want to protest against the statement of Superintendent Crane . . . [that] Pablo Abeita was entitled to more credit than any other person for getting things for this Pueblo. I think Superintendent Lonergan is deserving of more credit than anyone." In response, Crane, who perceived the barb wrapped within this apparent praise, said, "I

Figure 36. *Bautista Zuni, 1918,* Albert E. Sweeney, photographer. Courtesy of the National Anthropological Archives, Negative no. BAE GN 01987 06337000

wish to ask which side you are on." Soon after this exchange, the meeting was adjourned with no final statement or report. Apparently, Colonel Dorrington achieved his mission of calming the tension in the pueblo, at least temporarily, by letting everyone have their say. In the end, no charges were brought against Judge Abeita, and the Court of Indian Offenses continued for three more years.[74]

THE AFTERMATH OF DORRINGTON IN THE COURT OF INDIAN OFFENSES

For a few months after the Dorrington investigation, Judge Abeita did not hold court, but by the spring of 1922, he decided one controversial case and requested advice from Superintendent Crane on two others. This was the beginning of a trend whereby the superintendent exercised closer scrutiny over the court and began to limit its jurisdiction. In the first dispute Abeita asked Crane for his opinion on the case of Jose Santos Olguin, age twenty-four, who complained of abuse at the hands of his mother and of Juan P. Lente, his stepfather and Pablo Abeita's nemesis. The young man planned to leave home and wanted to take with him "things he had bought for future use, such as horses and harness, and blankets," but Lente refused to let him. Judge Abeita was careful to refer this politically charged case to Crane whose response was equally cautious. "I would be careful to ascertain whether or not any of the property was acquired during the minority of the complainant," he said, for if it was, the mother would have an interest in the property and could prevent Jose Santos from taking it. Crane told Abeita to determine whether Olguin's statement that he had acquired the property was true and if there was any doubt, to obtain an opinion from F. C. H. Livingston, the pueblo counsel at Belen. The outcome of this case is unknown, but it clearly shows how cautious Superintendent Crane was becoming over what might seem to be a simple case of a young man seeking to free himself from parental abuse.[75]

In another case Crane imposed even stricter limitations on Judge Abeita's jurisdiction. The case involved the fencing of a road considered public for more than fifteen years. There were fifteen plaintiffs led by Pedro Lujan who first encountered the fence when bringing the children from Chical to the day school. Judge Abeita heard the case and decided in favor of the plaintiffs, ordering the defendants to remove the fence in one week. Abeita based his decision on testimony from members of a committee, established by previous governors, which had determined which roads were public and which were private.[76] When Superintendent Crane read about this convoluted set of facts and the possibility that he would have to untangle the mess, he advised Abeita to back off. Crane recognized that the parties on each side represented the two factions of the village who, he said, "with little else to do . . . [just wanted] to see who will win." Crane advised Abeita to "let the governor sweat-out these wrangles" because of the confusion over when a private road legally became public and because of doubt over the extent of the court's jurisdiction.[77] Crane reminded Judge Abeita that although the jurisdiction of the Court of Indian Offenses "had been strictly upheld as to minor criminal cases and perhaps domestic disputes, its authority was not clear as to civil cases involving inheritance and land matters."[78] It seems that Crane was still smarting from the Dorrington investigation—he sent Colonel Dorrington a copy of his letter—and did not want to get involved in another squabble at the pueblo. In addition, Crane could see that despite the fiasco of the Dorrington investigation the conservative faction led by Lente and Padilla still had the support of many Isletans determined to curb Judge Abeita's power by eliminating the Court of Indian Offenses. By November 1922 Harmon P. Marble replaced Leo Crane as superintendent, and the criticism of Pablo Abeita intensified.

JUDGE ABEITA UNDER SIEGE

Pablo Abeita bore the brunt of numerous attacks, both personal and political, because of the growing power he wielded as judge of the Court of Indian Offenses. As we have seen, he was sometimes challenged regarding the fairness of his decisions and the propriety of his handling court fines. An example of an attack on his fairness occurred in 1922 when the litigious Emily Carpio complained to Superintendent Marble about Abeita's handling of a criminal complaint against her for fighting on the streets of Isleta and disturbing the peace. The case was a minor misdemeanor but highly sensitive because of the bad blood between Carpio and the other defendant, a Mrs. Lucero, who was married to Judge Abeita's first cousin. To avoid an appearance of favoritism, Abeita requested that another judge hear the case alongside him. Judge William Paisano from Laguna received the appointment, and although he was not related to either party, Carpio was still dissatisfied. The facts of the case were mainly undisputed: one evening as the two women were walking the streets, they crossed paths, exchanged some heated words, and then came to blows. Neither was seriously hurt; it was more a matter of pride or even honor. Also important were the questions of who started the fight and whether Carpio was armed with a stick. Since the judges could not determine who was telling the truth, they fined both women. Carpio complained that the judges fined her five dollars while fining Lucero only two dollars. Besides the discrepancy in fines, Carpio complained that Judge Abeita favored Lucero by not allowing Carpio's witnesses to testify, by not admonishing Lucero when she interrupted Carpio's testimony by calling her a liar, and by not accurately translating the testimony of both parties. Apparently, Judge Abeita was translating from Tiwa for the Keres-speaking Paisano. Carpio claimed that although Abeita faithfully translated Mrs. Lucero's words, he left out crucial parts of Carpio's testimony. Perhaps most damning was the charge that Judge Abeita and Judge Paisano had planned the outcome of the case when Paisano was staying at the Abeita compound.[79] In fact, it seems that Judge Abeita was not responsible for the disparity between the fines levied against Carpio and Lucero. Paisano told Abeita that, "You know that I didn't [reverse] your decision. I only added one more on Carpio."[80] It is doubtful that Superintendent Marble changed the sentences of Carpio and Lucero meted out by the two judges or took very seriously the charges of bias against Judge Abeita.

Initially, Marble relied heavily on Abeita and had faith in his impartiality, as can be seen in other cases. In addition, he was used to disgruntled losers coming to him for a different decision. It was not until Marble had to decide factional disputes himself between the progressives and the conservatives that he and Abeita crossed swords. Pablo Abeita regretted losing the working relationship he had built up with Superintendents Lonergan and Crane. They had upheld his authority and jurisdiction for the most part, a fact that litigants recognized. Not only were there fewer appeals, but claimants generally respected and abided by his decisions. Lonergan and Crane not only upheld Abeita's authority; they were quite firm in their resolve to avoid becoming involved in purely factional disputes. Marble, on the other hand, gave lip service to non-involvement but lacked his predecessors' resolve. The saga of the *Pueblo of Isleta vs. Carpio and Lucero* is illustrative of the difficulties Abeita faced during the ten years he sat as judge of the Court of Indian Offenses.

The third case discussed between Judge Abeita and Superintendent Crane dealt with the lax conditions at the jail and seemed to signal a deterioration in the effectiveness of the Court of Indian Offenses as well as the interference of a new government official at Isleta, John Shafer, the resident farmer. Conditions at the jail were so lenient that prisoners came and went at will; they were seen chatting with passersby and talking with "women of bad character . . . seen coming in and around the jail." The policeman Seferino Jojola pointed out that he "worked enough to get [these prisoners] . . . arrested and then to have them tried and convicted [so that] any punishment imposed should be a punishment and not a picnic." Judge Abeita said that the problem was caused in part by Shafer, who often had the prisoners work for him even when Abeita had ordered them locked up. Shafer seemed to be taking sides with the conservative faction, making things difficult for Judge Abeita.[81] The lax situation at the jail did not improve, which impacted negatively on the operation of the court.

Personal attacks on his character, which even extended to his wife, also hampered Judge Abeita. In May 1923 he happened to encounter Maria Olguin at the windmill and water tank as he was walking to his store/house after leaving the courthouse. Olguin asked the judge about a plastering trowel her sister had left at Abeita's house. When he got home, Pablo told his wife, Maria Dolores, and she returned the trowel to Maria Olguin's sister. Normally this would have been the end of the matter, but somehow, even though Olguin got her plastering trowel back, she was not satisfied; she was enraged. Apparently, Olguin's sister told her that she should not have asked Abeita for the trowel, because "men don't know nothing about those things." Although it is true that the job of plastering and replastering houses with a mixture of mud and straw was traditionally a woman's responsibility, this alone did not warrant the attack that followed.[82]

Maria Olguin went to Judge Abeita's store, which was attached to his house, and when his wife came out to wait on her, Olguin began cursing her and her husband, which led to blows reminiscent of the melee of Emily Carpio and Mrs. Lucero. When Abeita came to see what the yelling was about, he found Olguin pulling his wife's hair and screaming obscenities. He forced Olguin to release her grip on Mrs. Abeita's hair, at which point Olguin lunged at her, breaking two of her necklaces. Olguin finally left the store cursing. Judge Abeita told Superintendent Marble he wanted to file charges against Olguin, at his son's urging. Abeita told Marble that this was "the first time anyone has had the audacity to assault my wife." Later, Judge Abeita hinted that community factionalism was behind the attack, as his enemies "have been trying to find some fault with me, both as an Officer and as personal [*sic*]."[83]

Olguin pinpointed what was behind the altercation in a letter to Marble, noting that her sister "had gone as a witness to Santa Fe in Pablo's case." This was the sexual assault case heard just ten days earlier in Santa Fe when Teresa Lente charged Judge Abeita with assault when they were staying in town as part of another case. Judge Raymond R. Ryan of Silver City dismissed the case after the presentation of the prosecution's evidence,

Figure 37. *Pablo and Maria Dolores Abeita, 1936*, Isabella Edenshaw, photographer. Courtesy of the National Museum of the American Indian, Negative no. N47788

allowing Abeita to go free. Judge Ryan ruled that the state's attorney (Alois B. Renehan) had not presented sufficient credible evidence, especially after Abeita's defense attorney brought out the existence of bitter factionalism at the pueblo between conservatives and progressives, and suggested that Teresa Lente, the complaining witness, was part of the conservative faction. Although the press agreed that Judge Abeita was "set up" as part of the conservative's long-term effort to discredit him, Isletans continued to attack Abeita and his family. It is not clear whether charges were ever brought against Maria Olguin for her assault.[84]

Throughout the summer and fall of 1923, Judge Abeita—clearly under siege—tried to remain impartial as the factional fighting reached a point where claimants, disgruntled by the governor's decisions, began resorting to violence. As Antonio Abeita noted, speaking on behalf of Governor Padilla, "some Indians are getting impatient and are using physical force to get what they think is rightfully theirs." Even though Superintendent Marble undermined Abeita's jurisdiction and prestige, litigants still took their cases to Governor Padilla and Judge Abeita, although they were usually not satisfied with their decisions.[85] In the midst of the turmoil at Isleta, Judge Abeita continued to hear cases, trying to maintain some order at the pueblo. He also wrote Marble on an almost daily basis, reporting the details of cases and "attempting to carry out [his] orders to the letter."[86]

Judge Abeita was careful to refer almost every case to Marble to determine if he had jurisdiction. In August, when Abeita asked Marble whether he thought the Isleta council could pay out money without the approval of the governor, Marble demurred saying, "I do not wish to enter into a controversy over this point."[87] In September, when Agency Farmer Howard V. Smith inquired about a complaint by Jose Jojola and Juan Rey Zuni that Governor Padilla treated them unfairly, Marble responded, "unless there is a very clear case of fraud or injustice . . . I do not care to interfere in cases of this sort."[88] In other disputes, however, Marble *was* willing to venture an opinion and even decide cases dealing with property ownership.

During the final months of Marble's term as superintendent, his relations with Abeita became more and more strained. Whereas Lonergan and Crane had often visited Isleta and taken pleasure in developing relationships with Abeita and other village leaders, Marble stayed in his office. He mainly came to Isleta for formal hearings such as the Dorrington investigation and the hearing on the *Jiron vs. Jojola* case. Part of the testiness that developed between the two stemmed from a letter Abeita wrote in mid-December 1923 to recently appointed Commissioner of Indian Affairs Charles Burke, complaining about several of Superintendent Marble's policies. Judge Abeita bemoaned changes to "the system adopted by Supt. Lonergan and improved and continued by Supt. L. Crane." Though never written down officially, numerous letters reveal that it entailed a democratic system of checks and balances that spread the political and judicial powers evenly among the governor, the council, and the Court of Indian Offenses. Among these changes was "giving the governor authority over the irrigation ditches, instead of leaving that jurisdiction with the majordomos [*sic*] as tradition dictated." This is an example of changes that, according to Abeita, resulted in the pueblo "drifting back to the old time system of one man domination."[89] He expanded on his concerns in a letter to Marble in February 1924: "it would be good to have [a] legal opinion from Livingston as to the water rights and ditch work. They should be the same as old times. . . . These matters are important and should reach some sort of settlement before it goes beyond repair."[90]

Marble responded defensively to such criticism. He told Burke that the dissension at Isleta was partly Pablo Abeita's fault for involving himself in factional disputes. This was unfair, for as we have seen, Abeita made every effort to ask Marble whether he had jurisdiction in most cases. Moreover, he removed himself from the *Jiron vs. Jojola* dispute, letting Marble handle it, and he usually identified cases where Lente, Padilla, Antonio Abeita, and other conservatives were using the Court of Indian Offenses for their own purposes. Judge Abeita suggested that the governor try those cases. Abeita told Marble that the recent factional fights at Isleta "are not the usual type but rather a fight for decency and equality for all, to promote a better way of living. It is not a fight to abandon the old-time usages and customs, but to improve them wherever and whenever necessary."[91] In this eloquent statement, Pablo Abeita defied the labels of conservative and progressive as he noted what he and his followers stood for. He wanted to preserve the pueblo traditions and religious ceremonies, but reform and improve the governance of the pueblo where necessary to promote "equality for all . . . and a better way of living."[92]

As Marble defended himself against Abeita's charges, their relationship became increasingly strained. In the latter part of 1923 and the early months of 1924, Marble ignored Judge Abeita's complaints against Governor Padilla and his successor, Lalo Lucero, while often undermining Abeita's authority. In most cases where there was a question of jurisdiction, as between the governor and the Indian court, Marble deferred to the governor. When Francisco Lujan complained that Governor Padilla took his land from him unjustly, Marble wrote Abeita that "disputes involving lands belonging to the community must be settled by the governor and council."[93] When Jose Lucero complained to Marble about the governor, the superintendent wrote to Agency Farmer Smith, asking him to investigate but noted that since community property was involved, "it should be passed upon by the governor and council."[94] Superintendent Marble further undermined Judge Abeita's authority by referring more cases to Smith, just as he had done with Smith's predecessor, John Shafer.

Aftermath of the Court of Indian Offenses

By February 1924 Pablo Abeita would no longer be Judge Abeita because in that month, the Interior Department abolished the position of judge of the Court of Indian Offenses. This was due in part to Governor Padilla's longstanding opposition and to a 1922 petition to the BIA by a council of southern Pueblos seeking "to have all Indian judges withdrawn from Pueblo country."[95] Abeita had been fighting to retain the Indian court in the face of protests by Governor Jose Padilla and others, but he had lost Superintendent Marble's support. Although Superintendents Lonergan and Crane had seen the benefits of the Court of Indian Offenses in quelling factional bickering, Marble had seen Abeita and the court as the cause of such strife. Abeita tried to explain this to Marble, but by January 1924, he gave up, telling the superintendent that he would never understand the factional trouble.

Pablo Abeita was beginning to withdraw from Isleta politics "for the simple reason that a lot of the blame has been laid at my door for this faction trouble," as he noted in

January 1924. He was concerned, however, about what would fill the gap left by the absence of the Indian court. Marble had presumed that "the Indian office will provide substitute means for enforcing the regulations governing minor offenses," and suggested to Abeita that there was "nothing for us to do but wait in patience."[96] Marble would see the benefits of the Indian court belatedly as Isletans began to take their claims directly to him.[97] Abeita had many other concerns in early 1924, not least of which was the fight against the infamous Bursum Bill for adjudicating non-Indian claims to pueblo land. But he would continue to seek an alternate means of achieving the relative harmony and respect for law that the Court of Indian Offenses had brought to Isleta Pueblo.

Abeita did not accept the abolition of the Court of Indian Offenses easily and continued to lobby for the court's reinstatement. He wrote Commissioner of Indian Affairs Burke in March 1925, noting that after the abolition of the Indian judges, "it was like teachers going away from the classroom." Elected officials were unable to control the people; he continued, "we are like a scare-crow in the middle of a field, we can crow and wave, but cannot hurt the intruders in the field." Abeita asked Burke to reinstate the Indian judges, but to no avail.[98] When Chester Faris replaced Superintendent Marble in 1924, Abeita found an official more supportive of his vision for Isleta Pueblo. Abeita wrote Special Attorney Livingston asking his advice about applying for the prestigious position of US commissioner for the Pueblo Indians, noting that Superintendent Faris approved of the move, boasting that "I can get high recommendation from men of the highest class in Law."[99] Nothing came of that effort either, but the letter shows that Abeita had found a superintendent who supported him, even though Faris was only in office for a year, but he returned in 1929 for another year and was instrumental in bringing a semblance of harmony to Isleta.

In the meantime, Pablo Abeita was elected to serve in Isleta in governmental capacities (lieutenant governor in 1925 and 1929), but without a Court of Indian Offenses, the superintendent was flooded with cases the governor could not resolve. On the local level, many of the cases Abeita pursued were appeals on behalf of those who he believed were being punished unfairly. In 1925 he complained to Superintendent Faris and AIS superintendent Reuben Perry about treatment of boys by the school disciplinarian, stating that, "they are punished severely for very small offenses."[100] In 1927 Abeita wrote to Superintendent Lemuel Towers advocating for two men held in the county jail without a fair trial. Towers said the trial was fair, but he would not object to releasing the men from jail.[101] In 1928 Abeita again wrote to Towers advocating for the grandchildren of Bautista Zuni, whose wife Dominga had died, noting that, "Jose Padilla is taking the children's property."[102] And finally in 1932, Pablo Abeita advocated for Jose Chiwiwi, who had been in jail for seventeen days for using strong language against pueblo officials.[103] No longer judge of the Court of Indian Offenses, Abeita could not determine the outcome of a case, but he continued to plead on behalf of those he believed were being treated unfairly.

The court had served as a moderating, although controversial, influence for a decade. By rendering fair, pragmatic, and impartial decisions followed up with fines and/or jail time, Judge Abeita brought to Isleta Pueblo a period when most of its people respected traditional rules of law and order.[104]

CHAPTER NINE

Pablo Abeita as Advocate for the Pueblos

I see that the famous Bursum Bill looks like . . . a cyclone struck it after a
thunderstorm had gone over it.
Pablo Abeita to Charles S. Lusk, March 10, [1923?]

No one doubts Mr. Collier's sincerity. One may reasonably question his
judgment. His idea of restoring to the Indian his dignity and self-respect
seems to take away land from the white man and give it the Indian. . . .
Out of a wide acquaintance with Indians in this state, we do not know of
any who are lacking in either dignity or self-respect.
New Mexico Stockman 4, no. 4 (April 1939): 1, 3

A s Pablo Abeita was growing up and learning about Isleta Pueblo culture from the elders, he saw the injustices Native peoples suffered; as a result, he began to advocate for the pueblos as well as for himself and his family. At a relatively young age (mid-twenties) he became a go-between or cultural broker on behalf of Pueblo causes, reaching out to government officials, lawyers, judges, and even the President of the United States.[1] Abeita knew many of these officials personally and considered some of them friends. He knew and corresponded with many lawyers, including George Hill Howard, Elmer Veeder, Francis Wilson, and Richard Hanna, to name a few.[2] Pablo's training in Isleta and his superb education made him well equipped to carry on the advocacy of his grandfather, Ambrosio Abeita. He became a master negotiator and champion of Isleta.

Abeita recognized that Isleta's core strength was the land and the water that irrigates it. Isleta was blessed with a relatively large land grant (which Congress confirmed in 1856 at 110,000 acres) and had increased its holdings in 1751 and 1808 with the purchase of the Lo de Padilla grant and the Gutiérrez-Sedillo grant, respectively. But Isleta's land holdings were compromised by the improper, even biased, survey of its eastern boundary and the massive encroachment of non-Indian squatters, especially on lands it had purchased. The Joseph case, which is discussed below, had given these Anglo and Hispano settlers a green light to move onto Indian land and to dare the Pueblos to challenge them in court. Abeita soon realized that Isleta needed a lawyer to represent it and fight the encroachers.[3]

Pablo Abeita was born into a society deeply prejudiced against Native Americans, a society whose courts reflected that bias. In the decade before his birth in 1871, New Mexico courts handed down a series of cases addressing the question of whether the

Pueblos were wards of the federal government and hence entitled to US protection in their fight against encroachers on their land. Abeita inherited a tradition of advocacy from his grandfather, Ambrosio Abeita, a former governor of Isleta Pueblo. Ambrosio, an anomaly among Pueblo Indians, was a wealthy sheep owner and businessman. When Ambrosio learned about the court decisions rejecting federal wardship and protection of the Pueblos, he and other Pueblo leaders understood clearly that they were engaged in a life-or-death struggle for their survival. In 1868 Ambrosio traveled to Washington, DC, as part of a delegation led by Indian Agent John Ward to lodge a complaint about the recent court cases that they said would "unmake them as a distinct and separate peoples, dispossess them of their ancient customs and rights, and will also deprive them of their land." Later, Commissioner of Indian Affairs Ely S. Parker, a Seneca Indian and the first Native commissioner, wrote to Isletans Juan Andres Abeita and Juan Rey Lucero to assure them that the government still cared about them. But their promises rang hollow in light of the extreme nature of the pueblo's plight.[4]

In 1876, eight years after Ambrosio's delegation to Washington, the United States Supreme Court handed down its decision in *US v. Joseph*, which ruled that Pueblo Indians were not entitled to protection by the federal government under the 1834 Non-Intercourse Act because they were not "wild Indians," but civilized, and because they had been absorbed into the general mass of the population. The Joseph decision determined that the Pueblo Indians had title to their land and could transfer it without the approval of the federal government and must turn to New Mexico state courts for protection, courts that almost uniformly decided against the Indians and for the squatters.[5] The Pueblos, having received protection from the Spanish and Mexican governments, now felt betrayed and abandoned.[6]

In 1899 Pablo Abeita, as a twenty-eight-year-old, drafted and wrote a letter to the recently appointed special attorney for the Pueblo Indians, George Hill Howard, on behalf of Isleta's lieutenant governor, Antonio Jojola, to congratulate him on his recent appointment and to outline the two main claims with which Isleta needed help. Those claims concerned the failure to survey Isleta's eastern boundary to the top or crest of the Manzano Mountains and the encroachment on the recently confirmed Lo de Padilla grant by the town of Peralta. In his letter to Howard, Abeita asked for a boundary survey to run to the peak of the mountain and requested that the Peralta settlers be required to produce their deeds so that their land could also be surveyed and segregated from Isleta's Lo de Padilla grant. It would take over two decades before the Pueblo Lands Board settled these claims in Isleta's favor, mostly due to Pablo Abeita's perseverance.[7] Characterized as the quest for the crest, we discuss in chapter 10 his crusade to acquire for Isleta the roughly 21,000 acres of land on its eastern boundary running to the peak of the Manzano Mountains.

George Hill Howard advocated for Isleta for a few more years until Francis C. Wilson replaced him as special attorney for the Pueblo Indians around 1909. Abeita developed a close relationship with Wilson who not only advocated for Isleta in specific cases, but also joined Abeita in testifying before Congress prior to the 1913 Sandoval decision. Besides Wilson, who will be discussed later in more detail, Abeita corresponded most often in the early days with Las Vegas, New Mexico, attorney Elmer Veeder, hired by the pueblo

Pablo Abeita as Advocate for the Pueblos 109

Figure 38. *Pueblo delegation to Washington protesting the Sandoval decision. Abeita is standing to the left a little apart from the others holding a pencil in his hand. His brother Marcelino is second from the left in the first row. Washington, DC, Delegation, 1913*, photographer unknown. Courtesy of the National Anthropological Archives, Negative no. BAE GN 2860 N

to prosecute claims by individual Isletans against the US government, mostly for livestock losses due to Navajo raids. Veeder agreed to take these cases on a contingency basis, charging the Indians a percentage of what he recovered. If the claim was unsuccessful, the Indians paid nothing.[8] It was more of a gamble for the lawyer than for the pueblo.

Abeita was still in school during the surveyor general period (1854–1879) and the early part of the Court of Private Land Claims adjudications (1891–1904), but he became aware of Isleta's disadvantages before the court and its lack of legal representation. The pueblo was fortunate, however, to have the lawyer Gustave L. Solignac representing it in the land claims court cases. But Solignac was not always notified of trials in cases involving Isleta, causing him to be late entering into the proceedings. Solignac successfully defeated the claim to the overlapping Ojo de la Cabra grant and defended the Isleta purchase of the Lo de Padilla and the Gutiérrez-Sedillo grants. Issues arose with the Peralta tract and the Bosque de los Pinos tract overlaps, which might have been avoided if Isleta had had more consistent, full-time legal representation. Abeita perceived that Isleta needed several lawyers since the numerous non-Indian squatters and their lawyers, like Frank Clancy, put Isleta at a disadvantage.[9] Yet pueblos could not always afford to pay attorney fees. Moreover, the pool of lawyers from which pueblos could select was small since many members of the bar, like Thomas B. Catron, were themselves land speculators. Catron routinely sued other pueblos such as Jemez, Santa Ana, and Zia, and defended Hispano encroachers on Pueblo land.[10]

CLAIMS FOR LIVESTOCK LOSSES DUE TO NAVAJO RAIDS

Elmer Veeder, one of the lawyers working for Isleta, had a record as one of the few lawyers willing to represent clients with land grants without taking land in payment. Starting in July 1907, Abeita and Veeder corresponded frequently about the claims Veeder was pursuing for Isleta. Most of the claims were over fifty years old, and many of them were made by members of Pablo Abeita's extended family. Although it is doubtful that Veeder succeeded in getting payment, the claims reveal many details about the pueblo and its customs of inheritance and sheep raising. Veeder's first filings were on behalf of three deceased Isletans whose claims spanned a ten-year period in the 1850s and 1860s, all involving Navajo raids. For each claim, Veeder recorded the exact month and year and the precise number of livestock lost.[11]

The story of Ambrosio Abeita's claim must have been passed down through several generations of Abeitas, probably written down by Ambrosio himself along with details of other claims. In an earlier raid on November 5, 1856, Navajo raiders stole Ambrosio's sheep at the Rio Puerco, the western boundary of the Isleta grant. Although Abeita was unclear about the exact location of the raid, he was precise about the number of sheep stolen—3,200 ewes—which must have comprised most of Ambrosio's flock. A group of men followed the Navajos and came in sight of them at which time the Navajos were able to take Jose Manuel Lujan captive. Fifty-one years later Veeder asked Pablo Abeita to round up witnesses to these events, including Lorenzo Jojola and Juan Felipe Jojola.[12] It is likely that many of the witnesses whom Veeder sought to substantiate the claim were deceased, but one important witness, Juan Felipe, who had testified in a 1903 hearing on the claim, was still alive. He is listed in household 132 in the 1910 census that Abeita recorded. He was eighty years old (which would make him twenty-six years old at the time of the raid) and living with his seventy-eight-year-old wife, Dominga.[13]

Veeder was optimistic that, with the proper witnesses, he could "push the claims to judgement and get them paid shortly thereafter," as he told Abeita in July 1909.[14] Sometimes Veeder returned to Abeita after the claims had been submitted to the court with questions like, "we have been advised from Washington that we will need more testimony about citizenship. Need to prove that the claimants were living in New Mexico at the time of the 1848 Treaty of Guadalupe Hidalgo."[15] Abeita gave answers, just as he had outlined the facts of the claim. Abeita, who had provided the witnesses to substantiate these facts in the first place, made sure they kept the many appointments for interviews in Albuquerque. Because of Abeita's organizing and advocacy skills, Veeder was able to pursue these claims. He realized that Abeita was indispensable. He was not as fortunate at Cochiti Pueblo, where the contact Abeita gave him refused to answer his letters about claims. In January 1908 Veeder asked Abeita to recommend someone else, "who could take hold of these cases there and help the people secure witnesses."[16] This is exactly what Abeita did for the Isleta claims.

Pablo Abeita as Advocate for the Pueblos   111

It does not appear that Veeder collected on any of these claims. The court seemed skeptical about several issues, such as the authority of the administrators like Marcelino Abeita, representing the deceased Ambrosio Abeita, and the age of the claims. The government had already paid the most promising claim. In 1862, when Ambrosio famously loaned the US Army $18,000 in gold to pay troops stationed near Isleta who had been called to fight the Confederate Texans who had marched into New Mexico, he accepted a government IOU. The government finally repaid the loan when the elder Abeita traveled to Washington, DC, and met with President Ulysses S. Grant.[17] Since Veeder had little success in pursuing the claims for lost property due to Navajo raids, it is doubtful that Isleta had to pay him any attorney's fees, which were based on the amount collected. Nevertheless, Pablo Abeita gained valuable experience, learning how lawyers operated and how the legal process worked.

THE ASSAULT ON PUEBLO LAND THROUGH STATE TAXATION

In the decade prior to statehood in 1912, the Territory of New Mexico launched an attack on Native sovereignty by attempting to tax Pueblo lands. This had been going on for some time since statutes and court rulings had classified Pueblo Indians as citizens with title to their lands. In 1885 New Mexico governor Edmund G. Ross received a letter from Interior secretary Lucius Quintus Cincinnatus Lamar, noting that the Pueblos were not prepared for the duties of citizenship such as the election franchise and taxation. As a result, Ross told his tax collector to suspend collection of property taxes on the Pueblos. Nevertheless, in 1904 the territory sued the Pueblos to collect delinquent taxes in the case of *New Mexico v. Delinquent Taxpayers*. New Mexico Supreme Court judge Jonathan W. Crumpacker held that the Pueblos were subject to taxation because they had title to their land and could alienate it.[18] In response, the northern pueblos drafted a letter in March 1904 to the southern pueblos seeking support in their resistance to citizenship and taxation. It can be assumed that the southern pueblos agreed. Soon, however, Congress passed a law overriding *New Mexico v. Delinquent Taxpayers*, stating that all Pueblo real and personal property was exempt from taxation.[19]

But this development did not reassure Pablo Abeita. He went to Washington on another delegation and wrote letters protesting New Mexico's attempt to increase its revenue by taxing Indian lands. In a letter to Father Ketcham in June 1913 he noted that the state was again attempting to tax Indian lands: "something is wrong somewhere, else I cannot see why a state can have more power than the U.S. itself," referring to the state's belief that it had the power to tax Indian land even when the federal government said that land was exempt. In the same letter Abeita warned, "this is a matter where the Indians are getting indignant . . . [so] if the Indian Office don't [*sic*] hustle a little [to protect the Natives] there will be trouble."[20] Ketcham passed the letter on to Commissioner of Indian Affairs Abbott because of its serious tone. The commissioner responded with a five-page letter to Father Ketcham at the Bureau of Catholic Indian Missions, outlining the cases and statutes governing the taxation of Pueblo land in New Mexico. Pueblo land was historically exempt from taxation and the Enabling Act of 1910 had reiterated that exemption, but Judge William Hayes Pope's decision had declared the Enabling Act void.[21] The secretary of Indian affairs concluded that the question of taxes on Pueblo land was for the courts to decide.[22] These explanations rang hollow to Abeita as state taxing authorities repeatedly threatened to tax the Pueblos. In response to his concern that the Pueblos might resort to extreme measures if New Mexico persisted in its attempts to tax their land, Ketcham wrote, "I trust that the pueblos will not resort to violence because this will result not only in the loss to them of property, but likewise in the loss of life."[23] Abeita had tried everything in his advocate's toolbox, but now the veiled threat of violence got the attention of the Indian Office.

PABLO ABEITA AND FRANCIS C. WILSON

Pablo Abeita had a long relationship with the lawyer Francis C. Wilson who served as special attorney for the Pueblo Indians beginning around 1909. Although Wilson devoted himself to numerous claims on behalf of Isleta, he was also responsible for the other eighteen pueblos and was often absent from Santa Fe as he visited them.[24] Abeita assisted him in filing ejectment lawsuits against trespassers on Isleta land, among other claims. For example, Wilson promised in 1911 to file an ejectment action against Jose Lucero if Abeita determined that Lucero lacked a deed to the land, had not filed a small holding claim, and no one had lived on the land prior to Lucero.[25] Wilson also sent a letter to Sylvester and Jesus Padilla in 1910, threatening an ejectment lawsuit against them. In both cases Wilson relied on Abeita to gather and verify the facts behind these claims.[26] The two worked closely on a variety of cases ranging from a boundary dispute with Santa Ana Pueblo to the two claims closest to Pablo Abeita's heart: the Peralta overlap on the Lo de Padilla grant and the survey of Isleta's eastern boundary to the crest of the Manzano Mountains. As to the Santa Ana claim, Wilson believed that it was just and that a survey should be performed to settle the matter.[27] As to the eastern boundary claim, Abeita kept pressuring Wilson who at one point told Abeita that Assistant Commissioner of Indian Affairs Abbott "assured me that the matter of your eastern boundary will be pushed."[28] It would take over two decades more of persuasion before Isleta received a patent to the land. As to the Peralta overlap to the Lo de Padilla grant, even though Wilson intervened in the quiet title suit to settle the issue, the decision in that case was ambiguous.[29] Wilson worked diligently to resolve these claims. But it took the Pueblo Lands Board to settle the Lo de Padilla claim, nudge the federal government into issuing a patent for the Isleta mountain tract (adding about 21,000 acres to Isleta's landholdings), and move toward a monetary settlement of the Peralta claim.

Francis Wilson encapsulated their close relationship in a 1914 letter to Pablo Abeita informing him that he was resigning his position as special attorney for the Pueblo Indians so he could run for Congress. Wilson wrote, "I have their [the Indians'] interest at heart and will never forget the co-operation of men like yourself in the work we have undertaken to do for them."[30]

THE SANDOVAL CASE

In 1912 Pablo Abeita became aware of a major problem on the horizon, as the case of US v. Sandoval, challenging the wardship status of the Pueblo Indians, began working its way up to the Supreme Court of the United States. The narrow issue faced in the New Mexico Federal District Court by Judge William H. Pope was whether the 1834 Trade and Intercourse Act, prohibiting liquor sales to Indians, applied to the Pueblos. If it did, that would make the actions of defendant José Sandoval's selling liquor at San Juan

(Ohkay Owingeh) Pueblo illegal. As mentioned earlier, the 1876 landmark case of US v. Joseph held that the 1834 Act making Indians wards of the federal government, protecting them from non-Indian encroachment, and prohibiting liquor sales to them, did not apply to New Mexico Pueblos. However, the 1910 Enabling Act that granted New Mexico permission to organize as a state required the state to recognize land owned or occupied by the Pueblos as "Indian Country." Since this was contrary to the Joseph holding, Judge Pope had to decide which would prevail: the Enabling Act or the Joseph decision.[31]

Sandoval's attorney, A. B. Renehan, argued that Congress lacked the power to impose the "Indian Country" designation as a condition for New Mexico entering the Union.[32] The Pueblo Indians in general and Pablo Abeita in particular opposed Renehan's argument. They disagreed with most of his statements, because Renehan usually represented non-Indian encroachers. Abeita believed that the lack of federal wardship protection over the Pueblos left them vulnerable to encroachers. Judge Pope's ruling that the Enabling Act was void with respect to the provisions concerning "Indian Country" greatly disappointed Pablo Abeita. In the late summer of 1912, he wrote Judge Pope a personal letter telling him so.[33] It was highly unusual for Abeita, who was familiar with the Joseph decision and its implications, to write directly to the judge. It was even more extraordinary that Pope, who had said that "it is not my rule to answer letters bearing upon my decisions," had indeed answered Abeita's letter. Pope, who had served as a US attorney under Matthew Reynolds in cases involving Isleta in the Court of Private Land Claims, told Abeita, "I am sorry that my decision in the Indian case does not meet your ideas of justice." He explained, however, that Abeita may have misunderstood the scope of the decision as it did not deal with taxation of Indian lands. He told Abeita, "I know you to be an earnest man, and I am unwilling for you to remain under a misapprehension as to the scope of my decision." Whether this satisfied him is unlikely, but this letter from a federal judge shows Pablo Abeita's interactions with those in authority and his willingness to stand up for his beliefs.[34] His main concerns with Pope's decision in the lower court was that it could lead to the taxation of Indian land and raised the broader questions of Pueblo wardship and protection of their lands.[35] Because of his communications with lawyers like Francis Wilson and his familiarity with the legal decisions they sent him, Abeita felt at ease discussing this case with the judge.

Judge Pope enclosed in his letter to Abeita a syllabus or outline of his decision in the federal district court's Sandoval case. The point about which Abeita most disagreed with Pope was the holding that "the Pueblo Indians of New Mexico were considered citizens of the Republic of Mexico, and under the treaty of Guadalupe Hidalgo of 1848 they became citizens of the United States." To Abeita, this meant taxation of Pueblo lands. After non-Indian encroachment had caused significant land loss at Isleta and other pueblos, taxation could result in the complete loss of their lands. Most Pueblo Indians, as Pablo Abeita recorded in the 1910 census, were engaged in subsistence farming to support themselves and their families and had little cash with which to pay taxes. Francis Wilson, in his capacity as special attorney for the Pueblo Indians, had presented the case for the government in Judge Pope's court, and when the case was decided against him, Wilson prepared the papers for an appeal to the United States Supreme Court and then turned the case over to the Department of Justice.[36]

Aware of federal policies under the Dawes Act that had resulted in privatization and loss of land to tribes in Oklahoma, Abeita decided that the time had come, while the Supreme Court was considering the Sandoval appeal, for an Indian delegation to Washington, DC. He hoped to gain a hearing before Congress to bring the Pueblos' plight to light. The delegation would need an eloquent Pueblo spokesperson, one who could present the case for the Pueblos and stand up to, often hostile, questioning by unsympathetic congressmen. Pablo Abeita would rise to the occasion.[37]

Although he had been to Washington many times, Abeita's appearance at the February 1913 hearings gave him the opportunity to present the case for the Pueblo Indians in his own words and with historical background that only he could deliver. The hearings dealt with Wilson's proposal for the Pueblos to deed all their land to the United States to be held in trust to provide federal protection in case the court determined these lands to be subject to taxation by the states. If the Supreme Court failed to overturn Justice Pope's decision in the Sandoval case, the Pueblos' trust status with the federal government would be in jeopardy. Senate Bill 6085 was designed to provide federal protection from state taxation for those lands transferred from the Pueblos into federal trust status.[38]

Wilson testified at the hearing that according to the 1910 census there were about 7,400 Pueblo Indians in New Mexico and that they owned about 765,000 acres of patented land and almost 400,000 acres of Executive Order Reservations. Of this land about 50,000 acres were being deeded to the United States by individual Pueblos. Not all the Pueblos had agreed to this plan, however. In fact, only Santa Clara, Cochiti, and Taos were prepared to deed their lands to the government. Wilson was subjected to intense questioning, mostly by Senator Thomas B. Catron, who opposed the trust idea and believed the Pueblo Indians should pay taxes on their lands.[39]

Now the time had arrived for Pablo Abeita to present a statement that provided a Native American perspective. This was his first extensive appearance on a national stage, and he must have caused quite a sensation. He opened his remarks with a brief history lesson:

The white people came into this country without our invitation . . . they appropriated our land without asking for it. . . . We protested against them but they were stronger and much more in number. They rounded us up; they settled around us, took our land, our hunting grounds, our water, and all they could lay their hands on . . . Our land will not be safe if we are left alone under the state laws. There . . . never was a law made in New Mexico in favor of us, but New Mexico has always . . . made laws by which we would lose our lands. . . . I could put an argument 2 miles long and in the end I would conclude by saying that we ought to tax the white people for the land they took away from us instead of the white people taxing us for what land they never gave. . . . So no matter what you do or say, you will never pay back enough for what you took away from us.[40]

As soon as Abeita finished his eloquent statement, Senator Catron, who should have been representing all New Mexicans, including the Pueblos, immediately began a withering cross-examination seeking to show that Pablo Abeita and Pueblo Indians in general were relatively well off, that they had not lost that much land, and that Isleta Pueblo in particular was not subject to excessive encroachment. As to his supposed wealth, Abeita held his own.

Q: "You have considerable property there outside of your land, have you not?"
A: "No, sir."
Q: "You are a merchant down there, are you not?"
A. "I have a little store."
Q: "A very good-sized store, is it not?"
A: "A little store."

As to land loss, Catron asked Abeita what lands had been taken from him and the pueblo. Abeita answered that there were over ten thousand acres that Hispanos were trying to take away and five hundred acres they were living on. The ten thousand acres referred to the Peralta tract, which covered the western part of the Lo de Padilla grant.[41] Abeita also held up well as Senator Catron continued to press him about Isleta's claim to the twenty-one-thousand-acre Isleta mountain tract. At one point, Wilson interrupted Catron to explain Isleta's claim that their grant document called for the spine of the mountain as their eastern boundary.[42]

Finally, Abeita did so well in his presentation that some senators did not believe he had written it himself. At the end of his testimony Catron and Abeita had this exchange:

Q: "Mr. Abeita, who wrote that paper, which you read, for you?"
A: "I wrote it myself."
Q: "Who wrote the original from which you copied? You copied it—who wrote that original?"
A: "I did not copy it."
Q: "Who wrote it for you so that you could copy it?"
A: "I did not copy it from anyone. I wrote it myself."

In the face of Catron's arrogant insistence that Abeita could not and did not write his own statement, the Isletan remained cool and did not respond to the argumentative tone of the senator's questions. Finally, after Catron's attack, Father Ketcham came to Abeita's defense. Ketcham said he had been corresponding with Abeita for more than four years and that his letters indicate that "he could write not only that statement, but a far better statement than that if he undertook to do so." In fact, Abeita would write many more eloquent statements, as the fight to protect Pueblo lands continued into the next decade. In a final statement to the committee, Abeita told the senators, "we hope the white people will remember that they are living in a country once owned entirely by us Indians."[43]

During the summer and fall of 1913 the Pueblos, along with their friends and enemies, many of whom had testified at the senate hearings in February, waited anxiously for the United States Supreme Court's ruling on the appeal of Justice Pope's lower court

Sandoval decision. This was a period of great uncertainty as the courts grappled with a question important to Pablo Abeita and crucial to the relationship between the federal government and the New Mexico Pueblos. Simply stated, the question faced in both the Joseph and the Sandoval cases was whether the Pueblo Indians fit the definition of an Indian in the 1834 Trade and Intercourse Act and were therefore entitled to its protection. Joseph said they did not fit and were not wards. Shortly after Justice Pope's New Mexico Supreme Court decision, holding that the 1912 Enabling Act was void, Superintendent Lonergan revealed his consternation when he wrote to Abeita, "that decision has knocked me flat, Pablo and I don't know just what to do."[44]

Many who had believed that Pope's decision would not be overruled were surprised when the United States Supreme Court handed down its Sandoval decision, written by Justice Willis Van Devanter. The Joseph case, holding that the Pueblo Indians were too civilized to be considered Indians covered by the 1834 Trade and Intercourse Act, was overruled. Now the Pueblos were considered less civilized and thus entitled to the Trade and Intercourse Act's protection. As one historian noted somewhat ironically, "in the Joseph decision the court had rewarded their civilization by removing [their] protection. In the Sandoval appeal the Pueblos won back that protection only by proving their inferiority." Judge Van Devanter had obviously never met Abeita or other Pueblo people when he so broadly characterized the Pueblos as "a simple, uninformed, and inferior people."[45] Most people did not understand the decisions at all; Pablo Abeita was one of the few who did.

The Sandoval decision resolved many of the concerns Abeita and the Pueblo delegation raised when the court laid the tax question to rest and restored federal trust status to the Pueblo Indians. Superintendent Lonergan wrote the commissioner of Indian affairs in Washington that the Pueblos need worry no longer about state taxation because, "local authorities have desisted in all their efforts to collect local taxes." The superintendent did not "contemplate any further difficulty along this line."[46] But many more issues remained unaddressed.

As Pablo Abeita had told the senators in Washington in 1913, it was not only taxation that concerned the Pueblos; it was also encroachment on their lands, and erosion of their tribal sovereignty. When Abeita reminded the lawmakers that they were living in a country his ancestors once owned, he was talking about Pueblo sovereignty, the right of Pueblos to govern themselves and control their lands. Mindful of the travesties of the 1887 Dawes Act that required the privatization and allotment of former communally held land, Abeita was determined to do everything in his power to avoid a similar fate for Isleta.

After the 1913 Sandoval decision, non-Indians in possession of Pueblo lands used every available means to evade its consequences. Tensions were growing after Richard Hanna, the new special attorney for the Pueblo Indians, began filing ejectment suits in 1919 against non-Indians residing on Pueblo land. Tensions also mounted as Francis Joy completed his surveys of non-Indian claims to Pueblo land. Although the surveys were meant only to show the extent of the claims, the settlers viewed Joy's surveys as confirming their titles. They began erecting fences on the boundaries shown on Joy's plats. The Indians tore them down in many pueblos.[47] The most notorious example occurred on February 8, 1922, at Tesuque Pueblo when Martín Vigil led a group of peaceful Indians in dismantling an illegal fence erected by settler Ed Newman. Newman complained to federal officials and even threatened violence. After a number of investigations and vociferous protests, which gained national attention, the Tesuque protesters were vindicated.[48]

Pablo Abeita was aware of the Joy surveys at Isleta and could see where they were leading. He apparently did not like the surveys and did not like Francis Joy. Abeita told Joy that a kiva ladder, quite important for Isleta's religious observances, had been missing ever since his surveyors were working in the area. Joy responded in a curt letter to Mr. Abeita, disclaiming all responsibility for the missing ladder. The subtext of the exchange was that Abeita did not welcome Joy and his crew whose surveys would form the basis for adjudication of those claims (mostly against Isleta) a little over a decade later.[49] The challenge of the Bursum Bill to resolve the Pueblo land title controversy became a high priority after the Tesuque Fence War brought the concerns of the Pueblos to national attention. When the Bursum Bill was proposed as the answer, it galvanized the Pueblos into action and engaged Pablo Abeita in the fight of his life.

When New Mexico senator Albert B. Fall was appointed secretary of the Interior, Holm Bursum was appointed to fill the vacated Senate seat. Subsequently, Bursum became the champion of the non-Indian settlers in his winning campaign to retain his Senate seat against challenger Richard Hanna. The first bill he offered to settle Pueblo land titles would confirm all non-Indian claims for no less than 160 acres if the claimants could show continuous possession for ten years prior to the date of the enactment of the law. The Indians would receive no compensation for lost land. This bill was blatantly one-sided and went nowhere. Then, Representative Homer Snyder reintroduced a pro-Indian bill that former Interior secretary John B. Payne had drafted. Believing that neither of these bills was workable, Bursum commissioned a report by historian Ralph Emerson Twitchell regarding Pueblo land titles. Twitchell noted that non-Indian encroachment had increased since US sovereignty, but his specific proposals showed that he sympathized with the non-Indian settlers. Finally, Secretary Fall brought Twitchell and Renehan to his office, and they hammered out what would be called "the infamous Bursum Bill." There was no consultation with Indian leaders or with lawyers like Hanna and Wilson who represented them. Yet when introduced in the Senate, Bursum falsely told Senator Irvine Lenroot, chairman of the Public Lands Committee, that the bill was a compromise, and all parties supported it. On September 11, 1922, the Senate unanimously approved the Bursum Bill. Then came the firestorm.[50]

Last to be consulted, if at all, the Pueblos needed a national advocate. That is when John Collier entered the scene. When Mabel Dodge, soon to marry Taos Indian Tony Lujan, invited Collier to New Mexico, she introduced him to Pueblo society and culture; this changed his life. He would learn about the Pueblo land dispute and soon adopted it as his all-consuming cause. Collier and Stella Atwood, chairwoman of the two-million-strong General Federation of Women's Clubs, began organizing a campaign to defeat the Bursum Bill. Together with allies in the Taos and Santa Fe arts community, they began a letter-writing campaign that stirred up a storm of controversy.[51]

Collier began meeting with Pueblo leaders and explaining how the Bursum Bill would affect them. These efforts culminated in a two-day meeting at Santo Domingo, starting November 5, 1922, attended by 121 delegates representing every New Mexico pueblo. Collier, Wilson, and other Pueblo advocates from Santa Fe also attended. The attendees heard detailed explanations of the bill, and, after temporarily dismissing the whites from the meeting, the Pueblo leaders came up with a memorial that Pablo Abeita drafted titled "An Appeal by the Pueblo Indians of New Mexico to the People of the United States." News of the meeting traveled swiftly across the country, making headlines in the major newspapers. The text of the memorial was printed in a booklet and appeared in the *New York Times.*[52]

The appeal to the people of the United States outlines Abeita's attempts to get information about the Bursum Bill by contacting everyone from the commissioner of Indian affairs to Ralph Emerson Twitchell. Abeita summarizes these activities in a letter to Father Hughes that includes a graphic description of his altercation with Twitchell:

> I am sure you have heard of the infamous Bursum Bill. From the first time I saw and read a copy of the Bill, I did not like it, and I at once started to write to those who I thought were my friends, the Coms. of Indian Affairs, who answered my letter and told me the Bill was a good one, as it would do away with all the land troubles we the Pueblos were having with our neighbors etc. Next I wrote another letter to our Atty. for Pueblos, but did not get any encouragement, next I wrote to Col. Twitchell who was pointed out to me as looking after our interest. Col. Twitchell answered me a fine letter and so with these hopes I went to see him in Santa Fe to have a talk with him, and all I got out of him was to call me names, and tell me that I was an ungrateful Indian, that I did not appreciate what he was doing for us Pueblos; of course for answer I told him that if that was all he could do for us Pueblos, he could . . . go straight to <u>HELL</u>. After that I went from Pueblo to Pueblo and told all those would listen to me what was coming to us through the Bursum Bill.[53]

After all the petitions, op-ed pieces, and letters to Congressmen, one of the most effective weapons against the Bursum Bill was the Pueblo Indians themselves. In 1923 and 1924, leaders from ten pueblos, including Pablo Abeita and John Collier, took to the road, giving speeches before clubs and town meetings, before arriving in Washington, DC, to testify before Congress against the Bursum Bill. Abeita's eloquent testimony was one of the highlights.[54] His advocacy was quite effective on the national level with the general public but less so in the halls of Congress. He had little faith in any of the bills submitted to Congress because they all included a statute of limitations provision that confirmed title to non-Indian settlers if they had possessed the land they claimed for a period of time, such as ten years. Abeita saw how this provision could work against the Indians with a pro-settler Pueblo Lands Board, and his worries were confirmed. He told Charles Lusk of the Bureau of Catholic Indian Missions that the best solution, in his view, was to appropriate $10,000 and buy out the settlers' claims; those who would not sell could take their cases to federal court. But that was not to be.[55]

Pablo Abeita's efforts, along with his allies', were enough to defeat the Bursum Bill but not sufficient to stop the Pueblo Lands Board's unfair adjudication of non-Indian claims to Pueblo land. Abeita's efforts in defeating the Bursum Bill attracted influential reformers to his cause during the 1920s.[56] One of those reformers was D. H. Lawrence, the English writer who also became enamored of the Pueblo Indians. He wrote a full-page plea in the *New York Times* analyzing the Bursum Bill in a witty, self-deprecating manner. After including the full text of the bill with comments on each section, he summarizes, "The Bursum Bill is amusing in its bare faced-ness—a cool joke. . . . Surely the great Federal Government is capable of instituting an efficient Indian Commission to inquire fairly and settle fairly." In fact, the Pueblo Lands Board established in 1924 was neither fair nor efficient.[57]

As it turned out, the Pueblo Lands Board's decisions were uniformly anti-Indian. Pablo Abeita would spend part of the last decade of his life advocating for compensation to the Pueblos and in making the most of the reform policies of John Collier, especially the 1934 IRA.

PABLO ABEITA AND THE ALL PUEBLO COUNCIL

The All Pueblo Council, organized in 1922, was a response to the looming threat of the Bursum Bill. As discussed earlier, Collier met with Pueblo leaders, told them of the proposed legislation, and helped organize the November 5, 1922, meeting at Santo Domingo Pueblo. After drafting the "Appeal to the People of the United States" and lobbying successfully for the defeat of the bill, Abeita set about making the All Pueblo Council a permanent institution. In 1925, while serving as lieutenant governor at Isleta, Abeita wrote to Special Attorney for the Pueblo Indians Livingston seeking help with running the council. Livingston offered procedural details for running the meetings. Abeita applied those rules as the long-time secretary of the All Pueblo Council, which is still operating today. The council was so effective that the US government began a long campaign to blunt its power by forming the alternate United States Pueblo Council and assuming control of the appointment of delegates.[58]

At a meeting of Pueblo governors called by representatives of the federal government and by former New Mexico governor Herbert J. Hagerman, Pablo Abeita used all his negotiating skills to oppose the idea of substituting one council for the other: "Where your president takes the place of our governor, and your councilmen take the place of ours . . . we do not want our governors to be merely scarecrows, we want them to have some authority among their people."[59] When it became apparent that the new council would be forced upon the Pueblo leaders despite their wishes, Abeita shifted his tactics: let them have their council, but let us keep the All Indian Pueblo Council, as he called it. Abeita spoke of the meeting of the council at Santo Domingo in 1922 saying, "we made a solemn pledge . . . that in the future if any disagreements should come up between any . . . of the Pueblos, these things should be settled in the council. . . . If the present council [the United States Pueblo Indian Council] has been called here to do away with that solemn pledge, I might as well go home." In the end, the new organization was a rival of the All Indian Pueblo Council, but none of the Pueblo leaders ever attended a meeting, and the organization atrophied but did not die. The All Indian Pueblo Council continued, and Pablo Abeita remained as its secretary.[60]

Finally, on January 30, 1931, the Senate Subcommittee on Indian Affairs held hearings to determine the fate of the new council. Present were Commissioner of Indian Affairs Charles Rhoads, John Collier, Assistant Commissioner Lawrence Elkus, Judge Richard Hanna, Charles F. Lummis, and the members of the subcommittee. Controversy had arisen over Herbert Hagerman's role in establishing the United States Indian Pueblo Council. Lummis, along with Collier, charged that the Pueblos were "led into a trap at the meeting in Santa Fe [in November 1926] . . . to induce the Pueblos to form a 'United States Pueblo Indian Council' under supervision of the Indian Bureau."[61] Elkus put the question more succinctly: "Is it right for Hagerman, a judge of the land court [Pueblo Lands Board] to step down from the bench and organize a council of Indians . . . when that council shall decide to overturn the verdict of Hagerman as judge?" He explained further, "the United States All Pueblo Council is not looked on kindly [by the Pueblos], nor have they confidence in it, in the manner of its origin, or in the manner in which it was carried on."[62] In fact, Pablo Abeita's All Pueblo Council resolved not to attend meetings of the other council, which it saw as an attempt to do away with their tribal customs and their right to self-government. Some saw those January 1931 hearings as an attempt to force the Pueblos to deal with the US government only through the United States Indian Pueblo Council. Although cordial on the surface, this was a fight for self-determination and Pueblo sovereignty.

Although Pablo Abeita was taking a conciliatory approach at these hearings, in a way he was leading that fight. He had opposed the new council from the beginning in several eloquent speeches. Now, he expressed the view that there could be two councils: "We feel we are between the devil and the sea. . . . It is the same thing as if we were in the ocean between two ships; which should we take help from?"[63] Abeita faced the implicit conflict these hearings posed: accept the US Indian Pueblo Council, which the Indian Service controlled, or there would be no more cooperation between the Pueblos and the BIA. He did not want to be forced to choose. Finally, a vote was taken on which council the Pueblos wanted to represent them and the unanimous conclusion, with two pueblos abstaining, was the traditional All Pueblo Council. Now Abeita did not have to choose, the All Pueblo Council would continue with him as its secretary, and later its president, and the Pueblos were free to both cooperate with the Indian Service and challenge it over the unfairness of the Pueblo Lands Board.[64]

THE PUEBLO LANDS BOARD

Once the specter of the United States Indian Pueblo Council had been eliminated, the Pueblos were free to challenge the unjust decisions of the Pueblo Lands Board, which had taken thousands of acres of Pueblo land and applied reduced valuations in determining compensation. Both Indians and non-Indians were entitled to compensation for lost land, but the board, led by Herbert Hagerman, used a per-acre valuation for the Indians' awards that was one-third of the valuation for non-Indians' awards. Pablo Abeita worked, along with Judge Richard Hanna, in laying the groundwork for the claim for compensation. Both men testified before the Senate Subcommittee on Indian Affairs in 1931. Abeita talked about issues particular to Isleta, such as the Peralta encroachment on Isleta land, and Hanna addressed the valuation problem.

Pablo Abeita as Advocate for the Pueblos   121

Hanna worked hard to prepare the pueblo's challenge, in part by hiring a bright young Isletan, Diego Abeita, to review all the monetary awards to the Pueblos and compare them with the awards made to non-Indians. Hanna testified before the Subcommittee on Indian Affairs that initially the Pueblo Lands Board awarded compensation to the Pueblos of $100 per acre, the same as non-Indian awards, but later they reduced Pueblo awards from $25 to $35 per acre. Hanna highlighted the unfairness of this situation when he pointed out that Indians who were awarded $25 per acre for lost land would have to pay $500 per acre to purchase that land from the non-Indian encroacher. As Hanna said at the May 2 hearing, "[The Pueblo Lands Board] has taken over 20,000 acres of land away from the Pueblo Indians that they have not compensated them for [except] to the extent of a cancelled postage stamp; and if that constitutes due process of law, why, I ought to go back and resume my work as a freshman in law school."[65] At the end of the first day of hearings regarding the Pueblo Lands Board, Senator Burton K. Wheeler summed up the situation, noting that the board construed every provision of the act against the Indians and in favor of the government. Senator Wheeler was one of the sponsors of Collier's 1934 IRA, also known as the Wheeler-Howard Act.[66] Pablo Abeita said something similar: "We want to live and let the other fellow live, observe the golden rule which is now out of fashion. . . . The golden rule is now the silver rule; the religion of the white people is the silver dollar."[67]

The testimony was overwhelming regarding the injustice of the awards the Pueblo Lands Board made to the Pueblos, so the Senate Subcommittee on Indian Affairs drafted a bill increasing the amount of compensation. But when it was submitted to Congress in the fall of 1931, it died due to President Herbert Hoover's lack of support. Finally, when Franklin Delano Roosevelt was elected in 1932, and John Collier became commissioner of Indian affairs, Congress passed the compensation bill, and Roosevelt signed it into law on May 31, 1933. Now another battle was won. The bill added nearly $800,000 to the $621,000 previously awarded, but still not sufficient to bring the awards up to the land's appraised value.[68]

THE INDIAN NEW DEAL AND THE INDIAN REORGANIZATION ACT OF 1934

Soon after John Collier became commissioner of Indian affairs on April 21, 1933, he went to work to ameliorate the disastrous situation on reservations resulting from the drought and blizzards of the winter of 1932–1933. He acquired $5.8 million in emergency funds through the Civilian Conservation Corps (CCC), establishing a separate Indian Emergency Conservation Works program, staffed by Natives, whose projects were located on or near reservations so that Indian employees could remain with their families. This was a popular program because it aided Indian communities directly.[69] Isletan Diego Abeita testified that this program greatly benefitted his people.[70]

Collier had a long list of legislation he wanted passed that he developed as director of the American Indian Defense Association. But he realized the importance of going slowly with the implementation of these programs so they could be explained to Indian tribes. He addressed some of the problems in Indian Country by executive action such as when he closed numerous boarding schools (Carlisle had already closed in 1918) and used Works Progress Association (WPA) funds to construct more day schools that also served as community centers.[71]

Collier secured more than $100,000,000 from the CCC, WPA, and other New Deal agencies for the benefit of Indians throughout the country. His plan to reconstruct Indian America was revealed in the Wheeler-Howard Bill (1934), which reversed the Dawes General Allotment Act and would have created autonomous Indian political communities, established special education to promote the study of Indian civilization, mandated the collective ownership of Indian land, and authorized the creation of a federal Court of Indian Affairs. However, the bill that passed Congress during the spring of 1934 differed substantially from the bill Collier submitted. For one thing, an amendment to the bill gave the tribes the right to hold a referendum on the IRA. Tribes that accepted the IRA had to draw up a constitution defining their powers of self-government and establish articles of incorporation, permitting them to borrow money from the revolving credit fund.[72] The diluted act eliminated the Indian court system and cut other provisions, leading Collier to lament that these dilutions were "a major disaster to the Indians, the Indian Service, and the program."[73] But he soon realized that many Indians had little interest in his romantic ideas about the value of their communal life. He found that many reservations were divided into factions, the mixed bloods favoring self-government to controlled tribal politics, while the full bloods, suspicious of any government, clung to their cultural conservatism, and resisted any change. The Indians who attended the meetings Collier called to gain support for the bill criticized it because it made no provision for tribal claims and failed to guarantee treaty rights.[74]

Pablo Abeita and Isleta Pueblo were also conflicted about the IRA. In January 1936 one young Isletan told Collier that Isletan leaders did not support the Indian New Deal, but by April, after a new election brought Bautista Zuni to the governorship, the solicitor for the Department of the Interior concluded that "the Pueblo of Isleta now comes under the Indian Reorganization Act." Isleta, like other New Mexico Pueblos, endorsed the part of the IRA that would purchase land for the Pueblos, but resisted the part about reorganization of tribal governments.[75] At the May 1936 hearing of the Subcommittee on Indian Affairs, Antonio Abeita, representing Isleta Pueblo, noted the provision in the IRA that authorized two million dollars a year "for purchase of lands for the Indians," and complained that "someone is blocking that part of the bill," commenting that "we were very much living in hopes of someday deriving benefits from this bill."[76] Pablo Abeita, appearing as secretary of the All Pueblo Council, representing about twelve thousand New Mexico Indians, was also focused on land, as he always was. He complained that it was not fair for the government to purchase land from non-Indian settlers so that Isleta can have it back because the settlers did not pay for it. However, he seemed to support the Indian New Deal when he testified that "during this administration [Collier as commissioner of Indian affairs and FDR as president] in the last three years more has been done for us Pueblos than in any 25 years . . . in the past to help the Pueblo to help ourselves."[77] Ultimately, 171 tribes voted for the IRA and 77 voted against it, including the Navajos, the nation's largest tribe, who associated the bill with livestock reduction. Collier was even more disappointed that of the 171 proponent tribes, only 93 adopted constitutions and only 73 drew up charters of incorporation. Former Collier aide H. Scudder Merkel insisted that the Indians' negative response was due, in part, to the IRA's imposition of rigid non-Indian economic and political concepts in a situation that called for flexibility.[78] After they learned more about the IRA and its benefits, many tribes that had rejected it changed their minds. In the end, Collier was able, through a series of administrative maneuvers, to solve the problem by extending the provisions of the act to all Indians. Although Isleta fell within the IRA, it was not until 1947 that the pueblo adopted a constitution.[79]

Overall, the Indian New Deal and the IRA, with all its limitations, made a great impact on Indian Country. It provided jobs where none had existed before. The loan fund gave credit to thousands of Indians who used it productively to improve their individual situations. In the Southwest, reduction of livestock led to improvement of range conditions, although this was hugely controversial, especially with the Navajos.[80] Although Pablo Abeita did not like the imposition of changes in tribal government inherent in the IRA, he wholeheartedly endorsed the Indian New Deal programs that returned land to the Pueblos. His crowning achievement had to do with the Isleta mountain tract, 21,404 acres of wooded uplands eliminated from the initial Isleta grant due to an erroneous survey, as described in chapter 10. Although the Pueblo Lands Board recommended that a patent be issued for this land, it took several more years of advocacy by Abeita, Richard Hanna, and others for Isleta to finally receive title. Isleta Pueblo still uses that land for grazing, timber, and ceremonial purposes.[81] Besides helping Isleta acquire more land, Abeita is credited with single-handedly advocating for the first major bridge over the Rio Grande, which provided access to the pueblo (see chapter 3), and with taking the most detailed modern census of Isleta Pueblo (see chapter 6). Pablo Abeita was the most distinguished Indian in New Mexico. He could have been an effective lawyer, he could have been governor of New Mexico, but, with all his achievements, he seemed content with his life as it was. "I ask to remain an Indian," he said, "and if I could ask to be born again, I would ask to be born an Indian."[82]

CHAPTER TEN

Pablo Abeita's Quest for the Crest

*The Great Spirit, the Supreme Being put us on this country long before the
white people came into this country. . . . The white people came into this
country without our invitation. . . . They appropriated our land without
asking for it. . . . We protested against them, but they were stronger and
much more in number. They rounded us up; they settled around us, took our
land, our hunting ground, our water, and all they could lay their hands on.*
Pablo Abeita, Statement to the Senate Committee on Indian Affairs
Hearing, February 13, 1913, Washington, DC

Perhaps Pablo Abeita's greatest accomplishment was his persistent advocacy to
obtain a resurvey of Isleta's eastern boundary to the crest or spine of the Manzano
Mountains. This would be one of his abiding concerns over the more than two decades
it took to correct the erroneous survey.

In 1856 when Pablo's grandfather, Ambrosio Abeita, appeared before New Mexico's
surveyor general to describe the boundaries of Isleta's land grant, he was careful to
delineate with precision the location of the eastern boundary: the *espinazo* (spine or
crest) of the Manzano Mountains. Although this designation of Isleta's eastern boundary was crystal clear and without ambiguity, when Deputy Surveyor John Garretson
surveyed the grant in 1859, he placed the eastern boundary in the foothills at the base of
the Manzanos, depriving Isleta Pueblo of more than 21,000 acres of mountainous land.
Pueblo members had used this land for centuries as a source of firewood, vigas, rock,
and other building materials, as well as for medicinal herbs.[1] In addition, the mountain
itself was sacred to the Isletans as the location of sacred shrines; indeed, several religious
ceremonies still performed today depend on the mountain.[2] That is why Pablo Abeita
and other Isletan leaders like Bautista Zuni fought for a return of the mountain and for a
resurvey of what became known as the Isleta mountain tract.

Abeita first challenged the government about the Isleta mountain tract indirectly
in 1899 when he was serving as secretary for the pueblo council. He wrote to the newly
appointed Special Attorney for the Pueblo Indians George Hill Howard, congratulating
him on his appointment. Writing on behalf of Isleta governor Antonio Jojola, Abeita
told Howard that one of the most important land-related challenges facing the pueblo
was the resurvey of the eastern boundary of the Isleta mountain tract to the crest or
summit of the Manzanos.[3] He laid out the reasons for Isleta's request for a resurvey in a
clear and convincing manner, but Howard ignored the request. He did, however, petition
the Court of Private Land Claims to resurvey the eastern boundary of the Lo de Padilla

Figure 39. *Bautista Zuni, Pablo Abeita, Marcelino Abeita, 1918*, photographer unknown. Courtesy of the National Anthropological Archives, Negative no. GN 02004

grant neighboring Isleta on the south. Isleta had purchased the Lo de Padilla grant, and the pueblo was asserting its claim of ownership in the Court of Private Land Claims. The land claims court approved Howard's request and ordered the Lo de Padilla grant surveyed to the crest. This resulted in the anomaly of two adjacent grants that Isleta owned being surveyed differently. The Lo de Padilla grant survey went to the crest, and the Isleta grant went to the foothills. Howard asked the land claims court to provide a uniform rule for locating boundaries where a mountain is designated as a landmark, but the court refused, leaving the issue completely confused.[4]

Frustrated at the absurdity and injustice of the situation, Pablo Abeita began his long quest to have the peak of the Manzanos designated as the eastern boundary of the Isleta land grant. He realized that until he achieved that goal, the mountainside would be considered public domain of the United States, available to non-Indians who wished to obtain parts of it as small-holding claims. In fact, several non-Indians did so, resulting in an even more confusing situation when the government finally agreed with Isleta's argument and resurveyed its eastern boundary.[5]

It is unclear why government surveyors sometimes gave preference to Hispano land grants over Pueblo grants when surveying identical boundary calls. John Garrertson surveyed the Isleta grant's east boundary only as far as the foothills. The Sandia Grant, which Garrertson initiated, and Reuben E. Clements completed, had a similar boundary call, "the Sierra called Sandia."[6] It, too, was surveyed only to the foothills of the Sandia Mountains. The Sandia and Manzano Mountains bounded each pueblo respectively on the east (though Isleta's grant specified the spine of the mountain, clearly identifying the crest) and yet both were surveyed at the foothills or base of the mountains. This was done notwithstanding a clear directive from the General Land Office to consult with the tribes regarding boundary location if there was any doubt. Overall, there seems to have been an unwritten government policy to construe boundary calls of Pueblo grants more strictly than those of Hispano land grants. Both Sandia and Isleta were bounded by Hispano land grants with similar eastern boundary calls—the mountain—that were surveyed to the crest. In Isleta's case, the pueblo owned the Hispano Lo de Padilla grant.[7]

Pablo Abeita's main motivation for his quest was to preserve the mountain for its traditional role in resource gathering, hunting, and ceremonial practices, and to prevent semi-legal encroachments on the land. Abeita began by consulting everyone he thought could help—lawyers, superintendents, and Father Ketcham. In December 1910 he contacted Special Attorney for the Pueblo Indians Francis Wilson about the issue. Wilson responded that after talking to Assistant Commissioner of Indian Affairs Abbott, he "has assured me that the matter of your eastern boundary will be pushed in their office."[8] Furthermore, in December 1913 Abeita complained to Father Ketcham, "I do hope before long we know for sure what land we have to our name . . . and not be moved on our lines from one place to another." He suggested that Will Tipton, translator for the Court of Private Land Claims, be sent to investigate and "settle all disputes as to lands, lines, etc., without the necessity of going to courts."[9] Although Tipton did not investigate, Ketcham's influence led to the beginnings of a resurvey when a party of government surveyors appeared at Isleta in May 1914 "to survey all our lands," according to

Figure 40. *Pablo Abeita in His Later Years, n.d.*, photographer unknown. Courtesy of the Albuquerque Museum, Negative no. PA 1992 005 166

Abeita.[10] When nothing happened, Abeita consulted Superintendent Lonergan, who had expressed frustration with Pueblo factionalism and its effect on projects like the eastern boundary survey. In December 1914, on the eve of elections in the village, Lonergan admonished Abeita to do all he could "in getting elected men who will work with me in harmony and good will for the good of the pueblo on issues like the survey of the eastern boundary."[11]

When nothing came of all these efforts, Pablo Abeita led another delegation to Washington in 1918 with his brother, Lieutenant Governor Marcelino Abeita, and Governor Bautista Zuni for the specific purpose of getting the patent to the Isleta mountain tract east of the pueblo. The delegation vowed not to leave Washington without the patent, but they had to accept a promise to send the patent rather than the patent itself.[12] Finally, in August 1919, Abeita was able to report to Ketcham, "the [Indian] office . . . has finally started to right the wrong that was done . . . in the long disputed Eastern boundary line of the Isleta Grant. A surveying party has finally reached Isleta to start the resurveying of the grant which will include the disputed [tract]. . . . The Pueblo in general is delighted over it," Abeita continued, "and wishes to thank you personally and . . . all our friends who have helped us in our fight."[13] Yet, this was not the end. Although the survey was completed to the crest, it would take fourteen more years of effort for Isleta to obtain the patent.[14]

Pablo Abeita continued his advocacy, but the General Land Office was dragging its feet and Isleta factionalism continued to hinder progress. Conservative governors like Jose Padilla were more interested in attacking Abeita, as Padilla did with the Dorrington investigation, than they were in pressuring Washington to issue the patent for the mountain tract. At one point during that investigation, Abeita told the gathering that they should be giving Colonel Dorrington "information on matters of importance . . . [such as] matters pertaining to our land rights," but that did not happen.[15]

Finally, in 1928, the Pueblo Lands Board considered the issue and decided that the Isleta mountain tract should be patented to the pueblo as it had been omitted by mistake from the original survey.[16] This was a huge victory. After almost three decades the government had admitted its error, and the Pueblo Lands Board ordered the patent to be issued. However, the homesteaders and small-holding claimants who had established claims on the land when it was public domain still had to be dealt with. Since their claims were made in good faith, the total claims of 324 acres were deducted from the total acreage. It still took four more years, until the 1933 hearings on the fairness of the Pueblo Lands Board, for Isleta to obtain the patent to the 21,090-acre Isleta mountain tract.

Now Isleta Pueblo could celebrate. Pablo Abeita's thirty-four-year quest for the crest was over. The mountain was theirs again; they could continue to hunt deer, antelope, and rabbits there, pray at their sacred shrines, and bring back resources, including spruce boughs used in their ceremonies.

Indian Agents and Superintendents in New Mexico

DATES OF SERVICE	NAME OF AGENT/ SUPERINTENDENT
1898–1900	Nimrod S. Walpole
1903–1906	James K. Allen
1906–1908	Burton B. Custer
1908–1911	Reuben Perry
1911–1919	Philip T. Lonergan
1920–1922	Leo Crane
1922–1924	Harmon P. Marble
1924	Chester E. Faris (temporary appointment)
1925	L. L. Odie
1926	Samuel A. M. Young
1926–1927	Thomas F. McCormick
1927	Chester E. Faris
1928–1935	Lemuel A. Towers
1935–1944	Sophie D. Aberle

Commissioners of Indian Affairs

NAME	DATES OF TERM SERVED
Orlando Brown	1849–1850
Luke Lea	1850–1853
George W. Mannypenny	1853–1857
James W. Denver	1857
Charles E. Mix	1858
James W. Denver (second term)	1858–1859
Alfred Burton Greenwood	1859–1861
William P. Dole	1861–1865
Dennis Nelson Cooley	1865–1866
Lewis Vital Bogy	1866–1867
Nathaniel Green Taylor	1867–1869
Ely Samuel Parker (Seneca)	1869–1871
Francis A. Walker	1871–1873
Edward Parmelee Smith	1873–1875
John Q. Smith	1875–1877
Ezra H. Hayt	1877–1880
Roland E. Trowbridge	1880–1881
Hiram Price	1881–1885
John D. C. Atkins	1885–1888
John H. Oberly	1888–1889
Thomas Jefferson Morgan	1889–1893
Daniel M. Browning	1893–1897
William A. Jones	1897–1904
Francis Ellington Leupp	1905–1909
Robert Grosvenor Valentine	1909–1912
Cato Sells	1913–1921
Charles Henry Burke	1921–1929
Charles James Rhoads	1929–1933
John Collier	1933–1945
William A. Brophy	1945–1948

Isleta Pueblo Governors

DATE	GOVERNOR	LT. GOVERNOR	2ND LT. GOVERNOR
1750	Juan Domingo Juancho	Juan Joseph	Domingo Sangre
1764	Augustine (n.s.)		
1783	Felipe Jojola		
1856	Ambrosio Abeita		
1868	Alejandro Padilla	Jose del Socorro Hixina	
1881	Bautista Lucero		
1882	Vicente Jiron		
1884	? Carpio		
1885	Juan Felipe Jojola	Jose Ignacio Abeita	
1886	Tomas Padilla		
1890	Simon Zuni	Jose Chiwiwi	Jose Fernando Lucero
1891	Bautista Lucero		
1894	Juan Felipe Jojola	Pablo Abeita	
1899	Vicente Jiron	Antonio Jojola	
1900	Jose Felipe Abeita	Pablo Abeita	
1901	Juan Felipe Jojola		
1902	Juan Domingo Abeita	Remijio Lucero	
1903	Domingo Abeita		
1904	Sito Jojola		
1905	Bautista Lucero		
1906	Domingo Jojola	Juan Trujillo	Bautista Zuni
1907	Jose Felipe Abeita		
1908	Juan P. Lente		
1909	Felipe Jiron		
1910	Bautista Zuni	Juan Felipe Jiron	Manuel Marruo
1911	Juan Domingo Lucero		
1912	Juan Domingo Lucero		
1913	Lalo Lucero		
1914	Juan P. Lente		
1915	J. Vicente Abeita	Francisco Jojola	Jose Padilla
1916	Juan P. Lente		
1917	Juan P. Lente		

DATE	GOVERNOR	LT. GOVERNOR	2ND LT. GOVERNOR
1918	Bautista Zuni	Marcelino Abeita	
1919	J. Felipe Abeita	Jose Jojola	Juan T. Abeita
1920	Juan Rey Juancho		
1921	Jose Padilla		
1922	Remijio Lucero		
1923	Jose Padilla		
1924	Lalo Lucero	Transito Abeita	Crescencio Anaya
1925	Juan Trinidad Abeita	Pablo Abeita	Antonio Montoya
1926	Juan Felipe Abeita	Jose Jaramillo	Pasqual Lucero
1927	Jose Padilla		
1928	Jose Padilla	Jose Jaramillo	
1929	Juan T. Abeita	Pablo Abeita	Frank Jiron
1930	Domingo Lujan	Frank Lucero	Jose Carpio
1931	Pasqual Abeita	Antonio Montoya	Juan Rey Abeita
1932	Jose Padilla	Crescencio Anzara	Tony Abeita
1933	Juan T. Abeita	Antonio Montoya	Pedro Lujan
1934	Pascual Abeita		
1935	Francisco Jiron	Pablo Abeita	Frank Lucero
1936	Bautista Zuni	Pedro Lujan	Domingo Jojola
1937	Juan Lente	Juan A. Montoya	John Jojola
1938	Pasqual Abeita	Solomon Lente	Domingo Jojola
1939	Jose F. Jojola	Frank Lucero	John Jojola
1940	Andres Romero Abeita	Juan Rey Lucero	Juan Domingo Jojola
1941	Bautista Padilla	Jose Lucero	Tony Abeita
1942	Frank Marrujo	Damacio Lujan	Carlos Jojola
1943	Andres Romero Abeita	Juan Rey Lucero	Frank Chiwiwi
1944	Domingo Jojola	Damasio Lujan	Patricio Olguin
1945	Andres Romero Abeita	Charley Jojola	Fernando Lucero
1946	Andres Romero Abeita	Charles F. Jojola	Fernando Lucero
1947	Andres Romero Abeita	Charles F. Jojola	Fernando Lucero
1948	Juan Jose Carpio	Joe Lucero	Felipe Lente
1949	Juan Jose Carpio	Joe Lucero	Felipe Lente
1950	Joe S. Abeita	Tom Abeita	Nick Lujan
1951	Juan Rey Abeita	Juan Rey Lucero	Isadore Abeita
1952	Elias Jiron	Mark Chavez	Jose Rey Chiwiwi
1953	Juan Rey Lucero	Esquipula Jojola	Bartolo Montoya
1954	Carlos (Charley) Jojola	Pat Olguin	Ambrosio (Buster) Abeita

DATE	GOVERNOR	LT. GOVERNOR	2ND LT. GOVERNOR
1955	Juan Rey Abeita	Abe Zuni	Richard Jojola
1956	Ramon Zuni	Joe L. Lucero	John D. Jojola
1957	Ramon Zuni	Joe L. Lucero	John D. Jojola
1958	Remijio Jojola	Bartolo Montoya	Juan B. (Abie) Jojola
1959	Joe L. Lucero	George Keryte	Juan Rey Jaramillo
1960	John D. Zuni	Damasio Lujan	Diego Abeita
1961	Esquipula Jojola	Joe S.C. Chirino	Juan B. Jiron
1962	Carlos Jojola	Felipe Sangre	Isadore Abeita
1963	Lawrence Jaramillo	Richard Padilla	Francisco L. Olguin
1964	Juan B. Jojola	Phillipe Jiron	Juan B. Abeita
1965	Andy Abeita	Louis Lente	Andy Lucero
1966	Andy Abeita	Louis Lente	Johnny Abeita
1967	John D. Zuni	Frank A. Jojola	Juan B. Abeita
1968	John D. Zuni	Juan B. Abeita	Pablo Abeita
1969	Pablo Abeita	Bartolo Lente	Joe D. Lucero
1970	Alvino Lucero	Frank Jojola	Seferino Lente
1971	Juan B. Abeita	Richard Padilla	Juan B. Jiron
1972	Juan B. Abeita	Richard Padilla	Juan B. Jiron
1973	Alvino Lucero	Frank Jojola	Eddy Jojola
1974	Alvino Lucero	Frank Jojola	Eddy Jojola
1975	Seferino Lente	Joe L. Jojola	Joe L. Jaramillo
1976	Seferino Lente	Joe L. Jojola	Joe L. Jaramillo
1977	John D. Jojola	Joe Jiron	Ernest Jaramillo
1978	John D. Jojola	Joe Jiron	Ernest Jaramillo
1979	Alvino Lucero	John Jaramillo	Joe D. Jiron
1980	Alvino Lucero	John Jaramillo	Joe D. Jiron
1981	Frank Jojola	Jose Lupe Jaramillo	Alex Lucero
1982	Frank Jojola	Jose Lupe Jaramillo	Alex Lucero
1983	Andy Lucero	John Hagen Jojola	August Lente
1984	Andy Lucero	Frank Montoya	Robert Lente
1985	Alvino Lucero	Richard Jojola	Al Sangre
1986	Alvino Lucero	Richard Jojola	Al Sangre
1987	Verna Williamson	Isadore Martin	Paul Shattuck
1988	Verna Williamson	Isadore Martin	Paul Shattuck
1989	Verna Williamson	Isadore Martin	Paul Shattuck
1990	Verna Williamson	Isadore Martin	Paul Shattuck

Pablo Abeita Marriage Record

A. ENGLISH

On 9 February 1889 after the customary proceedings, I married, with the waiver of two banns, the two related by second degree touching on third, Juan Pablo Abeyta, single, legitimate son of Jose P. Abeyta and Marcellina Lucero with Maria de los Dolores Abeyta, single, legitimate daughter of Juan Reyes Abeyta and Maria de los Reyes Zuñi.
Witnesses: Juan Domingo Abeyta and Guadalupe Lucero
Priest: A. Echallier

B. SPANISH

El dia 9 de Febrero de 1889 despues de las diligencias acostumbradas case con dispensa de dos banas y de parentesco tertii gradus secundum attengente a Juan Pablo Abeita solt[ero] hijo leg[itimo] de Jose P. Abeyta y Marcellina Lucero con Maria de los Dolores Abeyta solt[era] hija leg[itima] de Juan Reyes Abeyta y Maria de los Reyes Zuñi.
Testigos: Juan Domingo Abeyta y Guadalupe Lucero
Sacerdote: A. Echallier

Pablo Abeita Genealogy

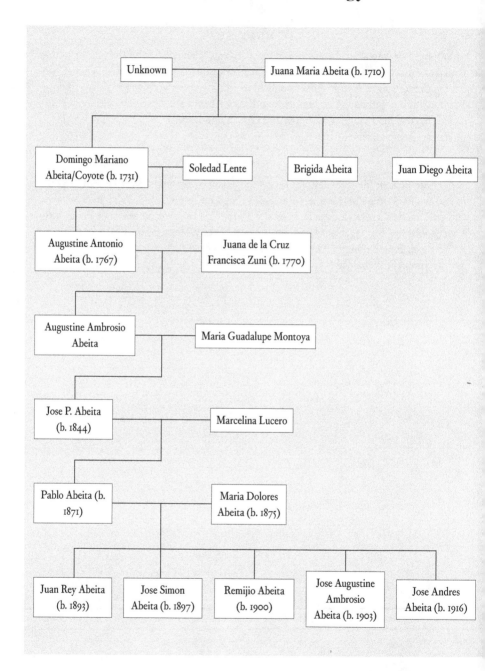

Pablo Abeita's Letters

Abeita's correspondence with Father Ketcham reveals a warm, personal relationship. His admiration for Father Anselm Weber, who served among the Navajos, is seen in a remembrance published in the *Sentinel*, the journal of the Bureau of Catholic Indian Missions, in 1921. "We, the Indians of the West, have lost a friend, a friend whom one and all liked and loved. It is a loss that will take years to fill, and if it is ever filled, it will be on our Lord's side, because it will never be filled on the Indian side."[1]

LETTER NO. 1

ISLETA, N.M.
MARCH 12, 1910
REV. WM. H. KETCHAM
Dear Father,
Your letter of March 3 on hand. Could not answer it sooner as I was in Santa Fe about <u>Land Matters</u>; have just come in, so will answer you at once.

In the matter of our disputed boundary line, would say that we want as many friends as we can to cooperate and work for the same good end.

While I was in Santa Fe I showed the U.S. Patent to our attorney (for Pueblos) with the field notes of the then surveyor, also the <u>original</u> old testimony taken by the Surveyor General at that time under which testimony the Grant or Patent was made; he finds that the Surveyor was ordered to survey to the top or <u>Backbone</u> of the mountains, but only went to the foot, which is about five and half miles from the foot to the Backbone of the mountains, thus making the survey shorter by about 5 ½ from west to east and about 6 miles north to south, thus depriving us of all the timber land that should be within the Grant of Patent. He promised me that he would also write to Our <u>Com. Of Ind. Affairs</u> about this matter, so I hope that between you all three, you will be able to do something for us in this matter.

As regards the Bridge matter, I can only say the same thing I said to you while you were here. Most all our cultivated lands are across the river; and the poor people have to cross the river every day to work their fields and also they have their horses and implements, sometimes their Wagons. At Harvest time also they have to cross what grain is raised—wheat, corn, alfalfa and vegetables. There is not a year that the river does not take a few poor mens' crops by upsetting the boat. Very nearly every year a poor woman of child is also drowned as they cannot swim; did not the men all know the art of swimming many and many a man would not be living today. Horses by the score have gone through the same old River.

Our wood supply for fuel purposes are also across the river and we have to cross it during winter and the Indians suffer a great deal through cold. We have no wood at any other place but across the river.

Of course there are a hundred and more reasons for why we ought to have a bridge here, but as our means are too slender, our only hope is the Great White Father of Washington.

We have some 120 to 50 stout young men that will furnish what labor they can perform with their hands taking turns as needed; this work will be free and will no cost to Uncle Sam anything.

As to what such a bridge would cost I have no idea, as I do not know the kind of material or the width of the bridge. The length may be from 400 to 600 feet. But should our Com. of Ind. Affair take the matter favorably, he can find out through our supt. Indian School Albuquerque and our Special Attorney for Pueblo Indians, Santa Fe, whether what I say is true or not. I leave it to them. I could fill pages with smaller reasons but I do not wish to tire you so I will close my letter hoping soon to hear favorably from you.

I enclose a clipping from a daily paper, will you please show this Gentleman from Minnesota and tell him that there are two Villages near Albuquerque, and neither has a single graduate nor even a Carlisle scholar; the few boys we have here can talk very little English but would not be afraid to talk to any Gentleman not excepting Mr. Tawney.

Very Respectfully
Pablo Abeita

LETTER NO. 2

PUEBLO OF ISLETA, N.M.
JAN. 3RD, 1911
Dear Father,

A merry Christmas and A Happy New Year to you Dear Father—and a thousand thanks for your nice card.

I cannot find words enough to express my sincere thanks for the great interest you have taken in our behalf.

I have your letter also the letter to you from Mr. Valentine Our coms. Which says that we have won our eastern boundary line of our Grant.

Now at present another question still just as important or more so is before us now—the matter of Indian Govt. among us; how are the Indians to Govern themselves without taking full Citizenship into ourselves, you know or saw by the short stay you had here that the Indians are not fit for full citizenship; as there are only about 10 per cent of the Indians who can talk a little English. We are at present making an effort to send a delegation to Washington to petition our Coms. of Ind. Affairs and find out from him what can be done or what need be done in order to obtain some kind of relief.

We do not intend to follow our old Customs, but at the same time we do not want to drop them entirely, as the majority of the people are ignorant and do not know a thing about Law. Another trouble is, we have no one who can explain the situation as it is now to the Coms. The present Gov. here being of the old type may not consult in sending an intelligent person to explain matters or do the interpreting.

These customs being of Indian origin none but an Indian can explain them in the right way. Writers of all nationalities write about Indian Customs, etc. I have read most all of them, no truth in their writing, none. Here at Isleta we have a few boys who can talk a little English, but none with enough nerve to talk of these matters to Mr. Valentine. I myself am not able enough to do it, although I have done so before Mr. Jones and Mr. Leupp; the last time I was there at Washington I had with me eleven of my tribe all from different Pueblos, three understood a little English, the rest nothing but Indian. Either of the three would talk this message to the first feller we met at the Indian Office. It showed they did not know enough. This years officers are a little worse off. But we have to do something, or will get lost.

I want your help all the help you can give—towards our cause. I do not care if I don't go to Washington, but I want someone to help the one that goes there. If I go so much the better for the Indian not for me (even if I do say it myself).

Dear Father, please let me know when would be the proper time for the Indians to go to Washington—is Congress in Session. How long will it be yet—etc.

I have a good many other matters in my mind to say to you yet, but time and space do not permit me to say all. If I get there will see you personally and talk matters over. Your address please?

I notified the Gov. here about our eastern boundary line through you to me about 2 weeks before he was notified by Our Attorney; They thanked God and then you for it. When the advice came from our attorney they simply said we knew about before from Father Ketcham.

I will close again thanking you in behalf of all my people.

Your Sincere Friend in Christ
Pablo Abeita

LETTER NO. 3

JANUARY 18, 1911
MR. PABLO ABEITA
ISLETA, N.M.

My dear Pablo,

Your letter of January 3rd pleased me very much indeed, I can assure you that my heart is with the Isleta people and my only regret is that I cannot do more for them than I have done. I do not know whether or not I told you that we have succeeded in getting the appropriation on the Indian Bill to build two bridges over the Rio Grande, one at Isleta and one at San Felipe. I believe that the bill will pass with this item on it, although we are never sure of these things until they are actually accomplished facts, of course, I shall do all that I can to try to secure these bridges and if I succeed, I feel that I shall have done a great work for your people.

I was talking with the Commissioner the other day about the question of a Delegation coming on to discuss Indian Government and Customs. He seems very much pleased with the idea. Congress is in session, and will continue in session, until May 4th. The Commissioner and I think that the best time for the delegation to come will be any time now while Congress is in session. I sincerely trust that you will be one of the Delegates. If you think it will be any good you may say to the Governor that I am very anxious for you to come along.

The question of Government and of customs for the Pueblos will be a very important one from now on, and I am glad that your people have seen fit to make the first move toward the discussion of these matters. You may rely upon me for all the help I can give you.

When the Delegation comes to Washington, be sure and have them come to see me just as soon as they get here. I will not only make it a point to have them see the sights of Washington, but I will be glad to be with them in all their councils with the authorities. I do not speak Spanish but I understand it and consequently can be of some assistance to the interpreter.

Give my love to all the Ysletas and wish them, in my name, a Happy New Year.

Very sincerely yours in Christ,

LETTER NO. 4

ISLETA, N.M.
JAN. 19TH, 1911
W.m H. Ketcham

Yours of the 12th came in yesterday and am very glad to hear from you.

Yes, Father you sent me some letters and also the Bill introduced from for the bridges, and can only say that the people here are delighted to hear about the bridges.

Now as regards the trip to Washington it may and may not make the trip, but if it does, I want your help, first in the way of using your influence so that these Pueblos would send me as one of the delegates.

Father, please do not think that because I want to go, its for the sake of going and having a good time—no Father not that; what I am anxious is that the matter may be presented in the right way and form and explain all the case point by point, explaining all the customs or <u>Govt.</u> by which we are <u>governed</u> and how we expect to live and be Governed and what then principal difficulties are at present and the future—there is a lot of explanation to do and I know hardly of any one at present who can do best for the best of our people.

I have been twice there and at both times I was elected <u>president</u> of the delegation. We had a speaker then that spoke for us, but after we got into Mr. Leupp office, the speaker could not speak and did not know what to say, so Mr. Leupp got a very bad idea of what the Pueblos are. And now I don't want another such thing to happen. It is only for that reason I would like to go.

Can you help me in any way, if you can Father I do not want the People here to know that I asked your help or that you are helping me because I asked you to. If I knew that there were better men than me I'd work for such a man but there is not even if I do say it myself. You ask an atty. Mr. F.C. Wilson of Santa Fe, our Agt. Mr. R. Perry Albuquerque.

I will give the governor and its officers your greetings just as soon as they come together. If I get to go to Washington I will sure hunt you up and you can rest assured that nothing will be done of those matters without consulting you or before we get your advice. Now Father this is personally; when I was in Santa Fe las I saw at Mr. Crandall office a book about Indians called Handbook of American Indians I asked Mr. Crandall about the book and he told me to write to the Bureau of American Ethnology or some one who I know in Washington. Now you can guess the rest why I write you this. Being an Indian myself I am interested in all books published about Indians and of course what I want is for you to see if you can get this or any book that concern

Indians especially of the Southwest. I have read a lot of these books and a good many of them are guess work no truth in them.

Again Father Thanking you from the bottom of my heart for what you have done and what will do in the future for us and me personally.

I am Your Sincere Son and J.C.
Pablo Abeita

LETTER NO. 5

DEPARTMENT OF THE INTERIOR
UNTITED STATES INDIAN SERVICE
U.S. INDIAN SCHOOL, ALBUQUERQUE, N.M.
JANUARY 30, 1911
Governor Isleta Pueblo
Isleta, New Mexico
Dear Sir:

I have incidentally learned that the Office is inclined to be favorable to a delegation visiting Washington to talk over their old customs, provided you send along with that delegation one or more of the brightest and best educated Indians, so the Commissioner can get a thorough understanding of all the matters pertaining to your affairs.

I consider Pablo Abeita the best posted of all the Pueblo Indians. He has been to Washington, could make the delegation feel at home and could get the Commissioner to understand what you wish to present to him better than any person among the Pueblos. Of course, it will be absolutely useless for a bunch of old Indians who do not understand English or understand only a little of it, to go by themselves. They must have the best interpreter and the best posted Indian they have so they will be able to answer promptly all questions put to them by the Commissioner or by the Congressmen. By taking a man like Pablo, as you go down on the train you can talk over the things you wish to present and the manner in which you will present them and be ready to talk to the Commissioner.

I would suggest that your delegation present everything to the Commissioner and everything to Congress. Tell them just exactly how you want to rule your pueblo, what authority you want the officers to have and in what way that authority has been limited, and all of the changes you desire to be made.

I shall be glad to hear from you and have some understanding of what you wish to do in the matter.

Very respectfully,
R.P. (SOS) Superintendent

Cases in Judge Abeita's Court
of Indian Offenses

Date/Type of Case	PARTIES	ISSUES	DECISION
1915 Nov. 1/1 Criminal	US vs. Juan P. Lente	Superintendent Philip T. Lonergan complains that Governor Juan P. Lente and his followers assaulted him on the pueblo feast day, Oct. 3, 1915.	Judge Abeita found Lente guilty and sentences him to forty days in the Isleta jail. Governor Lente appeals to the commissioner of Indian affairs who affirms the verdict and sentence.
1918 Mar. 2/2 Domestic	Alcario Remijio vs. Antonio Remijio	Alcario, the son, claims his father ejected him and his wife from father's house. Antonio says he gave the boy a piece of land to build his own house and offered to help him build.	Case dismissed.
1918 Mar. 2/3 Domestic	Felipe Sangre vs. Andres Olguin	Sangre claims Olguin will not live with and support his wife, who is Sangre's sister. On rehearing, it develops that wife has tuberculosis and is not able to take care of the baby and perform household tasks.	Judge orders Olguin to live with his wife. Case continued. On rehearing, wife and baby sent to Laguna Sanatorium.
1918 Mar. 9/5 Property	Francisco Martin vs. Louis Abeita	Martin claims Abeita took a plow he had purchased twelve years earlier. Abeita says he took it because it was his plough that he had lost two years before. He identified it by a specific washer he had used.	Case settled. Louis returns plow.
1919 Oct. 1/6 Criminal	Juanita Jaramillo	Charged with immoral conduct.	Fined $18 or twenty days in jail. Crane denies appeal.

Date/Type of Case	PARTIES	ISSUES	DECISION
1920 July 26/7 Community work	Ed Otero vs. Isleta Pueblo	Damage to ditch.	Judge decides that pueblo should do its share to repair damages.
1920 Sept. 1/8 Property/ inheritance	Bahe Guerro vs. Juan Guerro	Navajo pupil at AIS wants her inheritance of cattle, sheep, and horses currently in the possession of her stepfather, Juan Guerro, to be turned over to her uncle.	Case settled. Property turned over to uncle, but number of livestock reduced.
1920 Nov. 27/9 Domestic	Maria Lucero vs. Jose Seferino Abeita	Lucero claims that Abeita refused to keep his promise to marry her.	Abeita has agreed to marry Lucero by Christmas and "Officer [Louis] Abeita has been instructed to see that he does."
1921 Feb. 2/10 Criminal/ truancy	Isleta vs. Jose Chavez	Truancy/assault on police officer. Louis Abeita went to Chavez's home to find truant. Scuffle ensued. Each man claims he was assaulted by the other.	Judge Abeita sentences Chavez to fifteen days in jail.
1921 Nov. 3/11 Criminal	Isleta vs. Elon Riley	Re illegal possession of firearm by Riley.	Judge Abeita confiscates gun.
1921 Nov. 3/12 Truancy	Isleta vs. Jose D. Jojola, Juan D. Lucero, Felipe Padilla, and Cresencio Abeita	Truants from AIS.	Defendants ordered to be returned to school by the police; no excuses considered.

Date/Type of Case	PARTIES	ISSUES	DECISION
1921 Nov. 3/13 Domestic/ criminal	Isleta vs. Demasio Trujillo and Dominga Trujillo	Charged with cohabitation while Dominga is still married. Governor Padilla complained about this case at the Dorrington investigation, claiming that Pablo fined them "and allowed them to keep living together instead of making her get a divorce and get married [to Damasio]." Dorrington Investigation 14/112.	Sentenced to pay $10 fine each.
1922 Apr. 6/14 Criminal	Abeita vs. Shafer	Complaint by Pablo Abeita that Shafer ordered prisoners to work for him outside which contravenes Abeita's orders. He supports policeman Seferino who complains that the guilty are having a picnic at the jail.	Marble orders Shafer to respect court orders. Activities of the pueblo should be separated so Shafer has as little to do with the jail as possible.
1922 Apr. 13/15 Property	Pedro Lujan, et al. Complaint re fence	Property, right of way. Lujan and fourteen others complain about fence across public road.	Abeita orders removal of fence.
1922 Sept. 18/16 Community work	Isleta vs. Ten Parents	Ten parents failed to send sons to work on acequia, according to pueblo custom.	Governor Juan Rey Juancho fines them but two, former governor Juan P. Lente and Santos Chiwiwi, refuse to pay or take their boys to work on the ditch.
1922 Sept. 29/17 Property	Reyes Jiron	Complaint by Jiron that someone built a house on her land while she was in California.	Property cases to be decided by governor.

Date/Type of Case	PARTIES	ISSUES	DECISION
1922 Oct. 21/18 Criminal	Isleta vs. Emilia L. Carpio	Complaint against Abeita who she says in unjust. Carpio claims that as an interpreter, Abeita did not translate all of Mrs. Lucero's testimony. Mrs. Carpio complained that she did not get to testify. Marble assigned case to Judge Paisano of Laguna.	Paisano said he did not know who was telling the truth but fines Carpio $5 and Lucero $2.
1922 Oct. 30/19 Community work	Isleta vs. Thirteen Isletans	Governor Remijio Lucero complains that thirteen people (list provided) did not participate in community work. The governor excuses two.	Judge Abeita fines ten of them. Fines ranged from $1 to $2, totaling $15.
1922 Dec. 5/20 Domestic	Tomas Gerilla vs. Candelaria Gerilla	Marble asks policeman Cruz Abeita to assist Gerilla in his attempts to reconcile with his wife, Candelaria Gerilla. Candelaria refuses to reconcile, claiming Gerilla beat her while she was pregnant and caused her to miscarry.	Marble suggests that Judge Abeita can help with reconciliation.
1922 Dec. 20/21 Criminal	Isleta vs. Diego Abeita	Damage of crops by Abeita's goats. Abeita agreed to pay owner of corn but complains to Marble he does not want to pay.	Judge Abeita declares that the governor is backing Diego Abeita "as a spite against his enemies" (p. 198–99).
1922 Dec. 30/22 Truancy	Isleta vs. Three Isletans	Three fathers took children from the Loretto Indian School in Bernalillo without permission.	Judge Abeita will summon the fathers once they have completed the ditch work.
1923 Feb. 2/23 Property	Seferino Zuni vs. Gov. Jose Padilla	Zuni complains that the governor decreed that all stock be kept in herd. All obeyed except the governor himself whose cows have damaged Zuni's property.	

Date/Type of Case	PARTIES	ISSUES	DECISION
1923 May 11/24 Criminal/ property	Dominga Padilla vs. Domingo Lujan, Nicolas Lente, and Elias Jiron	Padilla and her daughter claim that the three men came into her home, took her trunk by force, and hit her.	Judge Paisano found no robbery and no assault but orders that the trunk be returned to Padilla.
1923 May 11/25 Criminal	Susie Lente Chirino vs. Candelaria G. Lucero	Chirino claims that Lucero stole shirts and $40.	Judge Abeita orders Lucero to pay $18 to Chirino to settle the matter. Lucero appeals to the governor.
1923 May/26 Criminal	Isleta vs. Bautista Lucero	Tomas Chaves complains of assault and battery.	Lucero found guilty, sentenced to five days in jail.
1923 ?/27 Criminal	Isleta vs. Domingo Chirino and San Juan Chirino	San Juan Chirino complains of "assault by words and fist."	Both found guilty of disorderly conduct. Domingo Chirino—ten days in jail; San Juan Chirino—five days in jail.
1923 May 24/28 Criminal	Domingo Lujan, Nicolas Lente, and Elias Jiron vs. Pablo Lente	Plaintiffs claim Lente made threatening remarks against Judge Paisano that he did not understand (language barrier). Men want Pablo Lente placed under bond.	Abeita asks for advice. Marble says to place Pablo Lente under bond to keep the peace.
1923 July 14/29 Personal property	Jose Jiron vs. Antonio Abeita	Sale of mower for $50, 2,000 torreones, and six days labor. Antonio claims Jose paid only $20, about 1,000 torreones, and three hours labor so he took the mower back. Jose wants his money back.	Marble asks Judge Abeita to settle the case.
1923 July 20/30 Inheritance and property	Candelaria Lucero vs. her husband, Tomas Cerrillos	Lucero claims Cerrillos sold a building on her property. Cerrillos claims building is his because he paid for the lumber.	Marble tells Agency Farmer Howard Smith that if the house is on wife's property it is hers no matter who paid for the lumber.

Date/Type of Case	PARTIES	ISSUES	DECISION
1923 Oct. 16/31 Domestic/ inheritance	Juana Abeita vs. Francisco Jojola	Abeita complains that Jojola abuses her, that she is sick and supports the family of two children and herself. Asks for separation.	Marble returns the case to field matron Leonore Shafer to effect a reconcil- iation. Shafer was not able to keep them together and asks how the property is to be divided. Marble says to let the governor decide re property if amicable, if not refer to Pablo Abeita and the Court of Indian Offenses.
1923 Nov. 3/32 Civil/ property rental	Remijo Lucero vs. Pablo Abeita	Abeita is renting two rooms to a Hispano working on the railroad. Lucero claims that Abeita owns only ¾ of one of the rooms and that Lucero's grandson owns the other ¼ and should receive a portion of the rent.	Marble asks Agency Farmer Smith to investigate. Smith says Lucero and his grandson do own ¼ of one room and should receive 1/5 of the rent. Marble agrees and admonishes Abeita against renting property to outsiders.
1923 Nov. 6/33 Inheritance	Jose Felipe Jiron vs. Jose Dolores Jojola	Re ownership of a barn/ corral and a peach tree.	After Judge Abeita hears the case and a second hearing, Burke tells Governor Padilla Jiron owns the barn/corral, and the peach trees is owned by whoever owns land on which the peach tree grows.
1923 Nov. 21/34 Criminal	Isleta vs. Simon Velasquez	Charged with drunk and disorderly; Velasquez pled guilty.	Abeita fines Velasques $20.
1923 Dec. 3/35 Civil/ property	Jose Jiron vs. Pascual Lucero	Jiron claims that Lucero owes him $17. Lucero says he repaid Jiron by letting him board with him.	Marble asks Agency Farmer Smith to try to get the parties to settle, otherwise send them to Indian Court. Smith looks at Abeita's [docket] book and finds notation that the parties settled.

Cases in Judge Abeita's Court of Indian Offenses   **147**

Date/Type of Case	PARTIES	ISSUES	DECISION
1924 Jan. 26/36 Civil/ property	Jose Lucero vs. Seferino Jaramillo and Jose T. Juancho	Lucero claims Jaramillo and Juancho killed his bull and asks for damages. Defendants claim the bull was impregnating their cows and was of inferior quality. The bull died when defendants castrated him according to the livestock laws.	Governor Lalo Lucero fines the two men $150, but they refuse to pay.
1924 Feb. 3/37 Community work	Isleta Pueblo vs. Several Individuals	The governor sends a list of individuals who did not show up to work on the ditch. The governor fined them, but they did not pay.	Marble says if individuals do not pay the fines they should appear before the Court of Indian Offenses.

Abbreviations

AMAW: Autry Museum of the American West, Los Angeles

BCIM: Bureau of Catholic Indian Missions Records, Marquette University Archives

FJCPA: Frank Jiron Collection of the Pablo Abeita Papers, Isleta Pueblo

IPCC: Isleta Correspondence, 1911–1922, Indian Pueblo Cultural Center, Albuquerque

NARA: National Archives and Records Administration

SG: Records of the Office of the Surveyor General

SRCA: State Records Center and Archives, Santa Fe

Glossary

acequia. An irrigation ditch; from the Arabic *as-saquiya.*

alcalde. A local governmental official with judicial, executive, and police powers.

Bureau of Catholic Indian Missions. A Roman Catholic institution established in 1874 to promote missionary efforts among Native Americans in the United States and to advocate on their behalf.

Bursum Bill. A bill proposed in 1922 that would have recognized the title to most non-Indian encroachers on Pueblo land without any compensation for the Pueblos.

cacique. An Indian religious leader.

Court of Private Land Claims. A judicial body established in 1891, comprised of five justices, responsible for adjudicating the validity of land grant claims in New Mexico. Its decisions were subject to appeal to the US Supreme Court.

Dawes Act. Also known as the General Allotment Act or the Dawes Severalty Act of 1887 (24 US Statutes 387), it provided for the allotment of formerly communal Indian lands to individual Indians and authorized the government to classify as "excess" those lands remaining after allotment and to sell those lands on the open market. It is estimated that the allotment of Indian land resulted in the loss of about seventy-two million acres formerly held by the tribes.

Enabling Act (1910). A Congressional act that authorized the qualified electors of the Territory of New Mexico to choose delegates to hold a constitutional convention to draft a constitution for the proposed State of New Mexico.

executive order reservations. Indian reservations established by presidential executive orders.

Joseph decision. The 1877 US Supreme Court decision, *United States v. Anthony (Antonio) Joseph* (94 US 614), which held that the 1834 Trade and Intercourse Act, making Indians wards of the federal government and guaranteeing them protection, did not apply to the Pueblo Indians. The 1834 act prohibited non-Indians from trading with Native Americans without a license, from selling them liquor, and from settling on their lands.

Joy surveys. A series of surveys conducted by Francis Joy in 1914 that the US government ordered to delineate the land non-Indians were occupying within the boundaries of pueblo grants.

mayordomo. The overseer of an acequia system; ditch boss. Also, the warden or caretaker of a church.

Meriam Report. A 1928 examination of conditions in Indian Country, *The Problem of Indian Administration*, found that the federal government was failing to protect the land and resources of Native peoples. It also highlighted the need for reform of the Indian education system. The report, authored by Lewis Meriam on commission from the Institute for Government Research, provided information used in the formation of the 1934 Indian Reorganization Act.

Pueblo Lands Board. A three-man board established in June 1924 that was responsible for reviewing the claims of non-Indians occupying Pueblo lands. The board issued a report describing non-Indian claims that were either rejected or upheld, then the United States filed quiet title suits on behalf of the pueblos. The Pueblo Lands Board also assessed monetary loss to both pueblos and non-Indians due to non-Indian claims and provided for their compensation.

Pueblo league. A square of land containing 17,400 acres to which a pueblo was entitled and which non-Indians could not (in theory) occupy. Established by Spanish colonial lawsuits, it was adopted in the Pueblo grants.

quiet title suit. A lawsuit that a claimant to a tract of land filed, naming as defendants all persons who might have a claim to that land and asking the court to confirm (or quiet) the title to the plaintiff. Usually, adjacent landowners and prior owners of the land were named as defendants.

Sandoval decision (Hispanic land grants). The 1897 US Supreme Court decision, *United States v. Sandoval* (167 US 268), involving the San Miguel de Bado community grant south of Santa Fe, held that only the private tracts, and not the common lands of a community grant, were entitled to confirmation. This was only about five percent of the total community land grant acreage in New Mexico. The common lands were considered public domain, which either the Bureau of Land Management or the US Forest Service now administers.

Sandoval decision (Indian lands). The 1913 US Supreme Court Sandoval decision (231 US 281), which reversed its earlier 1877 Joseph decision, now holding that the 1834 Trade and Intercourse Act did apply to the Pueblo Indians. This had the effect of reestablishing the federal government's trust status regarding Indians and potentially nullifying Pueblo land sales going back to 1848.

surveyor general of New Mexico. An administrative office created in July 1854 with the responsibility of holding hearings on land grant claims and making recommendations to Congress as to whether it should confirm or reject each grant.

Tewa. The linguistic group comprising the Ohkay Owingeh, San Ildefonso, Santa Clara, Tesuque, Nambé, and Pojoaque Pueblos.

Tiwa. The linguistic group, which in New Mexico comprises Taos, Picuris, Sandia, and Isleta Pueblos.

Notes

INTRODUCTION

1. Jojola, "Modernization and Pueblo Lifeways," 78–99.
2. Lummis, "Town of the Snake Girl."
3. Lummis, "Antelope Boy," 12–21.
4. Lummis; Parsons, *Pueblo of Isleta*, 386–90.
5. Marshall, "Isleta Pueblo Installation Project."
6. Jojola, "Modernization and Pueblo Lifeways," 81–82.
7. Ebright and Hendricks, *Pueblo Sovereignty*, 130–31.
8. Spicer, *Cycles of Conquest*, 163; Ebright and Hendricks, *Pueblo Sovereignty*, 132.
9. José Vega y Coca report, Embudo de Picurís, July 19, 1725, SG 91, roll 31, frames 287–88, SRCA; Ebright and Hendricks, *Pueblo Sovereignty*, 134.
10. Ebright and Hendricks, *Pueblo Sovereignty*, 134.
11. Ebright and Hendricks, 134–39.
12. Ebright and Hendricks, 138–42. The 37,229-acre Lo de Padilla grant was reduced in the amount of 14,710 acres by the Peralta purchase.
13. Ebright and Hendricks, 138–39.
14. Guggino, "Pablo Abeita," 13–14; telephone interview by Ebright with Randy Jiron, Jan. 12, 2022. Ambrosio Abeita finally received payment of his loan in 1874 and a thank you from President Ulysses S. Grant.
15. Jojola, "Modernization and Pueblo Lifeways," 89.
16. Ebright and Hendricks, *Pueblo Sovereignty*, 141–42.
17. Jojola, "Modernization and Pueblo Lifeways," 89–90.
18. Will de Chapparo, "Laguna Migration of 1879," 87–98; Dozier, "Factionalism at Santa Clara Pueblo," 172–85.
19. Jojola, "Modernization and Pueblo Lifeways," 90.
20. Jojola and Kushner, "Lummis and American Indian Policy," 13–14; Jojola, "On Revision and Revisionism," 41–47.
21. French, *Factionalism in Isleta Pueblo*, 1–12.
22. Guggino, "Pablo Abeita," 16.
23. Montgomery-McGovern, "General Survey of Isleta Pueblo," 130–31.
24. Trafzer, *Boarding School Blues*, 13. The slogan "Kill the Indian, save the man" was attributed to Richard H. Pratt, founder of the Carlisle boarding school.
25. Speech given at the US Indian Pueblo Council, Nov. 7, 1928. Minutes were entered into the records of US Senate Hearings on Senate Resolution 79 and 308 (70th Cong.) and Senate Resolution 263 and 416 (71st Cong.).
26. Guggino, "Pablo Abeita," 18.
27. Isleta v. Lente, Isleta, Nov. 1, 1915, FJCPA.
28. Ebright and Hendricks, *Pueblo Sovereignty*, 158–59.
29. Dozier, "Factionalism at Santa Clara Pueblo," 182, citing Kroeber, "Zuni Kin and Clan," 39–204, quote at 183.
30. Littlefield and Bal, "Factionalism and Argumentation," 87–101, quote at 88.

31. Interview by authors with Richard Luarkie by Zoom, Santa Fe, Dec. 10, 2021.
32. See chapter 8, "Pablo Abeita and the Court of Indian Offenses."
33. Sando, "Sotero Ortiz," 33–39, quote at 36; for Thomas B. Catron's anti-Pueblo activities, see Ebright and Hendricks, *Pueblo Sovereignty*, 17–18, and Ebright, *Advocates for the Oppressed*, 110. In one case Catron challenged a pasture grant to Zia, Santa Ana, and Jemez Pueblos and ended up with the land himself.
34. Sando, "José Alcario Montoya," 50–55.
35. Sando, "José Alcario Montoya," 53–54. The Cochiti tribal council resisted paying for Alcario Montoya's Washington delegation trips just as the Isleta council did for Pablo Abeita. The Cochiti council called them sightseeing trips, failing to see their importance in educating government officials and the public about the plight of New Mexico's Pueblos.
36. Isleta v. Lente, Isleta, Nov. 1, 1915, FJCPA.
37. Ebright and Hendricks, *Pueblo Sovereignty*, 25, 161–62.
38. Ebright and Montoya, "Twisting the Law," 148–51.
39. Crane, *Desert Drums*, 316–17.
40. Governor Bautista Lucero to Felipe Chávez, Isleta, Mar. 17, 1905, Felipe Chaves papers, SRCA, Santa Fe, citation courtesy Richard Melzer; Kelcher and Chant, *Padre of Isleta*, 24–37, 65.
41. "Belgian King is Greeted by Mob of Thousands on His Arrival Here," *Albuquerque Morning Journal*, Oct. 20, 1919.
42. Hagan, *Six Friends of the Indians*, 81.
43. Norcini, "Political Process of Factionalism," 561–70.
44. Wheeler Howard Act of 1934, commonly called the Indian Reorganization Act (IRA), 48 US Statutes 984; Norcini, "Political Process of Factionalism," 570–73.
45. Norcini, "Political Process of Factionalism," 571–73. Isleta was the second pueblo, after Santa Clara, to adopt an IRA constitution.
46. Sando, *Pueblo Indians*, 151.

CHAPTER ONE

1. Richard "Dikki" Garcia to Rick Hendricks, e-mail, Dec. 2, 2018. Garcia provided a "List of Isleta Governors and Lieutenant Governors," in the authors' possession.
2. Guggino, "Pablo Abeita"; Pueblo Cultural Center Records, roll 14, frame 8.
3. Isleta Baptisms LDS 007548706, image 165.
4. Bohme, "A History of the Italians," 54; Ambrosio Armijo was a prominent Albuquerque businessman and booster in the 1880s and owner of Albuquerque's first luxury hotel, The Armijo House. Bryan, *Albuquerque Remembered*, 129–30, 163; Simmons, *Albuquerque*, 206.
5. *Republican Review*, Dec. 17, 1872, and Nov. 8, 1873.
6. Pablo Abeita to Sister Josephine, Isleta, Mar. 19, 1925, roll 124, frame 1032, BCIM.
7. Although called a college, St. Michael's offered only a high school curriculum until 1945.
8. St. Michael's College, *Seventy-five Years of Service*, 75. The government did not support this venture, and all the expenses of board, tuition, washing, and so forth for twenty-two children for one year fell on the archbishop and the school.
9. Pablo Abeita to William H. Ketcham, Isleta Pueblo, April 24, 1916, roll 80, frames 1066–67, BCIM.
10. Pablo Abeita to Sister Josephine, Isleta, March 19, 1925, roll 124, frame 1032, BCIM. According

to Brother Emmet Sinitiere, archivist of the Archives of the District of San Francisco New Orleans in Napa, California, which houses the student records of St. Michael's College, there is nothing indicating that Pablo Abeita graduated from the school. Brother Emmet Sinitiere, FSC, to Rick Hendricks, Napa, CA, March 7, 2019; Marc Simmons, "Trail Dust: Abeita was One of NM's Most Memorable Leaders," *Santa Fe New Mexican*, Feb. 16, 2016. Simmons stated that St. Michael's awarded Pablo Abeita honorary degrees of master of ancient history and doctor of philosophy. Sinitiere indicated that St. Michael's did not award honorary degrees. Although he often said he was educated at St. Michael's, Abeita did not claim to have been a graduate of the school. "Says Indians First Devotees of Communism," *El Paso Herald Post*, Sept. 1, 1934. He did, however, refer to himself as a member of the class of 1888.

11. Guggino, "Pablo Abeita," 14–16. Eastern Keres is spoken at Cochiti, San Felipe, Santo Domingo, Zia, and Santa Ana. Western Keres is spoken at Acoma and Laguna. Isleta, Sandia, and Ysleta del Sur speak Southern Tiwa. Northern Tiwa is spoken at Taos and Picuris. Tewa is spoken at Nambe, Ohkay Owingeh, Pojoaque, San Ildefonso, Santa Clara, and Tesuque. Towa is spoken at Jemez. Shiwi'ma is the language of Zuni.

12. Almiral, "Tribesman of Isleta Pueblo," 15–16, quote at 150.

13. Curtis, *North American Indian*, 11–12. On one occasion, Abeita and a companion are said to have killed sixty antelope during a single hunt.

14. Marriage of Pablo Abeita and Maria de los Dolores Abeita, Isleta, Feb. 7, 1889, Isleta Marriages, LDS 007854350, image 85. A transcription and translation of the marriage record is found in appendix 4.

15. Baptism of Maria Dolores Abeita, Isleta, May 25, 1876, Isleta Baptisms, LDS 007548706, image 198.

16. Thanks to Dikki Garcia, Robert Martínez, and Felipe Mirabal for their assistance with the Abeita genealogy.

17. Permission for parish priests to grant dispensations for such close relationships had only been granted in the nineteenth century and clarified for priests in the Americas by Pope Pius IX in 1871. Another interesting aspect of the marriage record is that Father Echallier wrote "Reyes" between the lines so that Dolores's father appears as Juan Reyes Abeita. This error seems to derive from his wife's name.

18. Guggino, "Pablo Abeita," 16.

19. Pablo Abeita to William H. Ketcham, Isleta Pueblo, May 20, 1914, roll 71, frames 805–8, BCIM.

20. Ewen and Wollock, *Encyclopedia*, 3.

21. Guggino, "Pablo Abeita," 17. Pablo Abeita had five sons, at least two of whom entered the Indian Service: Remijio (in the Indian Service in Washington State) and Ambrosio (in the Indian Service in San Carlos, Arizona).

22. Crane, *Desert Drums*, 316–17; Simmons, "Pablo Abeita, a Leader," 49.

23. Pablo Abeita to William H. Ketcham, Isleta Pueblo, Jan. 3, 1911, roll, 56, frames 61–64, BCIM.

24. "Wise Indians Mock Chicago 'Wise Guys,'" *Ashland* (Illinois) *Tidings*, Feb. 17, 1913.

25. Lindstrom, "Not from the Land Side," 220.

26. Guggino, "Pablo Abeita," 23.

27. Simmons, "When the President Came to Call"; Simmons, "Pablo Abeita, a Leader."

28. Sando, *Pueblo Profiles*, 189–90; Weigle and White, *Lore of New Mexico*, 429.

29. "Pablo Abeita Is Buried with Simple Tribal Rites," *Albuquerque Journal*, Dec. 19, 1940.

30. Pablo Abeita to William Hughes, Isleta, October 23, 1922, roll 107, frame 833, BCIM.

31. Pablo Abeita to William H. Ketcham, Isleta, April 25, 1912, roll 62, frames 731–32, BCIM.

32. Pablo Abeita to William H. Ketcham, Isleta, May 20, 1914, roll 71, frames 805–8, BCIM.

33. Sando, *Pueblo Profiles*, 41–49, quote at 48.

34. Almiral, "Tribesman of Isleta Pueblo," 15–16, quote at 16.

35. Tiller, *Guide to Indian Country*, 722–24.

36. The US presidents serving during the fifty-year period that Pablo Abeita was politically active were Benjamin Harrison (1889–1893), Grover Cleveland (1893–1897), William McKinley (1897–1901), Theodore Roosevelt (1901–1909), William Howard Taft (1909–1913), Woodrow Wilson (1913–1921), Warren G. Harding (1921–1923), Calvin Coolidge (1923–1929), Herbert Hoover (1929–1933), and Franklin Delano Roosevelt (1933–1945).

37. Pablo Abeita's trunk in possession of Leonard Abeita, Isleta Pueblo.

38. Philp, "Albert B. Fall and the Protest from the Pueblos," 254.

CHAPTER TWO

1. Bingham, *Charles F. Lummis*, 14–18; French, "Inflation of Pueblo Culture," 9.

2. Lummis named his house El Alisal, using the Spanish word for alder grove because alders and syca-mores grew in Arroyo Seco, which is adjacent to the property on which the house was constructed.

3. Houlihan and Houlihan, *Lummis in the Pueblos*, 2–8; Thompson, *American Character*, 117–19.

4. Ted Jojola to authors, readers' report, Oct. 5, 2021.

5. Melzer, "Charles Lummis," 2.

6. Smith, *Reimagining Indians*, 129.

7. Starr, *Inventing the Dream*, 76.

8. Smith, *Reimagining Indians*, 131–32.

9. Bingham, *Charles F. Lummis*, 7.

10. Jojola and Kusher, "Charles F. Lummis and American Indian Policy," 7–8.

11. Lummis, "In the Lion's Den," *Land of Sunshine*, July 1900, 113–19; Lummis, *Letters from the Southwest*, xii; Hagan, *Six Friends of the Indians*, 54–5.

12. Thompson, *American Character*, 119–21. Lummis's income from his writing began to increase, depending on the number of publications that ran his dispatches. In 1888 he earned $218, and in 1890 his earnings were $1,044.

13. Fiske and Lummis, *Charles F. Lummis*, 49–51; Hagan, *Six Friends of the Indians*, 54–55.

14. Prucha, "Thomas Jefferson Morgan," 197.

15. Charles F. Lummis to Thomas Jefferson Morgan, Isleta Pueblo, July 16, 1891, Braun Research Library Collection, Lummis Letters on Albuquerque Indian School, AMAW.

16. Lummis promised Morgan to be responsible for Juan Rey Abeita's boys, describing himself as "a valid bondsman [as] an owner of the Los Angeles Times, sufficiently well known in literary circles," and the son of Henry Lummis, D.D.S. of Appleton, Wisconsin.

17. Thomas Jefferson Morgan to William Creager, Washington, DC, July 23, 1891, Braun Research Library Collection, Lummis Letters on Albuquerque Indian School, AMAW.

18. Collier and Marron, Attorneys, receipt for $45.00 attorneys' fee for habeas corpus proceedings, and Collier and Marron to Lummis, n.d., Albuquerque, Braun Research Library Collection, newspaper articles on the treatment of Indians, AMAW, MS 1, box 104. Thompson, *American Character*, 161–64.

19. Hagan, *Six Friends of the Indians*, 55.
20. Hagan, "Daniel M. Browning," 209.
21. Lummis continued to attack Creager, eventually forcing him to resign in 1894.
22. Fiske and Lummis, *Charles F. Lummis*, 51.
23. Thompson, *American Character*, 191–92; Bingham, *Charles F. Lummis*, 21.
24. Lummis Diary, Sept. 15, 1900, and Sept. 28, 1900, AMAW.
25. Frost, "Romantic Inflation of Pueblo Culture," 60. Frost notes only two genuine friendships between Anglos and Indians: Tony Lujan of Taos and John Collier and Juan Rey Abeita and Charles Lummis.
26. Lummis Diary, Sept. 17, 1900, AMAW.
27. Lummis Diary, Sept. 20, and Sept. 23, 1900, AMAW. Lummis spent a great deal of time at Simon Zuni's house, having his hair washed in amole (yucca root) by Marcelina, and leaving his own daughter, Turbesé, with them.
28. Lummis Diary, Sept. 21, 1900, AMAW.
29. Lummis Diary, Sept. 28, 1900, AMAW.
30. Lummis Diary, Sept. 28, 1900, AMAW.
31. Parsons, *Pueblo of Isleta*, 355.
32. Lummis Diary, Dec. 25, 1900, AMAW. Although Tuyo was outwardly obedient and content working for Lummis, he complained to his friend, Marcelino, that working for Lummis was hell. Antonio Abeita to Marcelino Abeita, Los Angeles, Apr. 9, 1901, Braun Research Library Collection, AMAW.
33. Antonio Abeita to Charles F. Lummis, Hampton, VA, Feb. 9, 1905, Braun Research Library Collection, AMAW.
34. Antonio Abeita to Charles F. Lummis, Isleta, Aug. 30, 1926; Antonio Abeita to Charles F. Lummis, Isleta, Oct. 30, 1922, Braun Research Library Collection, AMAW.
35. Antonio Abeita to Charles F. Lummis, Isleta, Oct. 17, 1922; for a biography of Collier and Lummis's connection to the Indian reform movement, see Philp, *John Collier's Crusade*, 60, 60n68.
36. Thompson, *American Character*, 175–76.
37. Charles F. Lummis to Pablo Abeita, Los Angeles, June 12, 1906, MS 1.1.15, Braun Research Library Collection, AMAW; Houlihan and Houlihan, *Lummis in the Pueblos*, 9–10.
38. For construction of El Alisal see, Gordon, "El Alisal," 19–28.
39. "In the Lion's Den"; Bingham, *Charles F. Lummis*, 115–16.
40. Bingham, *Editor of the Southwest*, 119; Hyer, *We Are Not Savages*, 107–10; The Cupeño homeland was in the backcountry near San Diego.
41. Bingham, *Charles F. Lummis*, 117–19; Warner Ranch v. the Cupeño Indians, 126 California Reports 262, Barker v. Harvey, 58 Pacific Reports 692, 181 US 481, 21 Supreme Court Reporter, 690–98; Hagan, *Six Friends of the Indians*, 120–21.
42. Hagan, *Six Friends of the Indians*, 120–22.
43. *Out West* 17, no. 2 (Aug. 1902): 215.
44. Hyer, *We Are Not Savages*, 107–28.
45. "Indians Bundled Away like Cattle to Pala," *Los Angeles Times*, May 13, 1903, Sec. 2, 1 as cited in Hagan, *Six Friends of the Indians*, 427; Hagan, *Six Friends of the Indians*, 127–28.
46. Jojola and Kushner, "Charles F. Lummis and American Indian Policy," 13–15.
47. Jojola and Kushner, 5–6; Bingham, *Charles F. Lummis*, 23. Lummis's son Jordon, named after

David Starr Jordan, president of Stanford University, was born Jan. 19, 1900, and given the Indian name Quimu by Abeita who later submitted it in a contest to name the refurbished theater in Albuquerque, now known as the Kimo Theater on Central Avenue.

48. Jojola and Kushner, "Charles F. Lummis and American Indian Policy," 21–23.

49. Smith, *Reimagining Indians*, 129–33.

50. Thompson, *American Character*, 275–76.

CHAPTER THREE

1. Parsons, *Pueblo of Isleta*, 245; Frost, 189–90, 192.

2. Frost, 193.

3. C. J. Crandall to Julius Seligman, July 13, 1908; Seligman to Crandall, July 19, 1908, Pueblo and Jicarilla Agency, Santa Fe Indian School, Miscellaneous Letters Sent, 1890–1913, Entry 32 Records of the Bureau of Indian Affairs, RG 75, NARA, Denver.

4. Lummis, *King of the Broncos*, 179–80.

5. Frost, "Photography and the Pueblo Indians," 202.

6. Benjamin M. Thomas to Richard H. Pratt, Sept. 15, 1880; Benjamin M. Thomas to John Menaul, Sept. 15, 1880; Benjamin M. Thomas to Richard H. Pratt, Sept. 15, 1880, Pueblo Agency, Miscellaneous Letters Sent by the Pueblo Indian Agency, 1874–1891, Letterbook vol. 6, roll 4, microfilm 941, Records of the Bureau of Indian Affairs, RG 75, NARA, Washington, DC; Thomas to Pratt, July 16, 1881; Thomas to Pratt, July 30, 1881, Pueblo Agency, Miscellaneous Letters Sent by the Pueblo Indian Agency, 1874–1891, Letterbook vol. 8, roll 4, microfilm 941, Records of the Bureau of Indian Affairs, RG 75, NARA, Washington, DC. Carlisle and Hampton were all-boys schools unlike St. Catherine's and the Santa Fe Indian School.

7. Benjamin M. Thomas to Richard H. Pratt, Pueblo Agency, Nov. 17, 1882, Letterbook vol. 10, roll 6, M941, RG 75, NARA, Washington, DC.

8. Philip T. Lonergan to Pablo Abeita, Sept. 6, 1912, FJCPA; Melzer, "Making of 'A Pueblo Legend,'" 7; "High School Junior Cultivates Silent Film Hobby," *Albuquerque Journal*, Nov. 22, 1972. Mary Pickford said that the movie crew was "run out of town . . . when the Indians thought we were making fun of them."

9. Melzer, "Making of 'A Pueblo Legend," 33–36.

10. "Biograph People Go Through to the Coast," *Albuquerque Morning Journal*, Jan. 2, 1911.

11. "Isleta Pueblo Is Seized Today by Photoplayers," *Albuquerque Evening Journal*, May 23, 1912, 2; "Biograph Advance Man Spends Day in This City," *Albuquerque Morning Journal*, April 24, 1912, 4; Melzer, "Making of 'A Pueblo Legend,'" 4.

12. "Biograph People in Albuquerque for Film Dramas," *Albuquerque Morning Journal*, May 30, 1912, 4; Melzer, 4.

13. "Indian Life Not Represented in True Manner," *Albuquerque Evening Herald*, Jan. 15, 1912, 3.

14. Governor Carlos Jojola, interview by Casey St. Charnez, introducing the New Mexico State Library's copy of *A Pueblo Legend*.

15. Melzer, "Making of 'A Pueblo Legend,'" 8; "History Reenacted at Isleta Yesterday," *Albuquerque Morning Journal*, June 1, 1912, 4; Lamadrid, "Ig/Noble Savages," 17.

16. "Isleta Pueblo is Seized Today by Photoplayers," *Albuquerque Evening Herald*, May 31, 1912, 2.

17. Governor Carlos Jojola, interview.

18. Mary Pickford, "My Own Story," *Ladies Home Journal*, Aug. 1923, 121; "Highschool Junior Cultivates Silent Film Hobby." *Albuquerque Journal*, Nov. 22, 1972.

19. "Indians Decline to be Photographed While Dancing," *Albuquerque Morning Journal*, Sept. 5, 1912, 4.

20. Philip T. Lonergan to Pablo Abeita, Albuquerque, Sept. 6, 1912, FJCPA.

21. Lonergan to Abeita, Sept. 6, 1912.

22. Barsh, "American Heart of Darkness," 111.

23. Barsh, 92.

24. Barsh, 93.

25. Barsh, 95. Dixon described the Indians in the council as "representing nearly every tribe in the nation," although only seven were represented and in even more exaggerated fashion "the very Indians who had slain Custer, although . . . only one of them, the Cheyenne Two Moons had actually fought Custer on that day."

26. "Indians See Taft Handle the Spade; They Help Him Break Ground . . . for a Memorial to the Red Man," *New York Times*, Feb. 23, 1913; "Visiting Chiefs on Sightseeing Trip; By Elevated and Subway They Journey to The American Museum and the Bronx Zoo; Not All of Them Taciturn; Oshkosh of the Menominees, a Carlisle Graduate Talks Eloquently," *New York Times*, Feb. 24, 1913.

27. Barsh, "American Heart of Darkness," 96–100.

28. Barsh, 106.

29. Transcript of proceedings at Isleta Pueblo, June 27, 1913, FJCPA; Barsh, "American Heart of Darkness," 107.

30. Barsh, 112.

31. Barsh, 101–2.

32. Barsh, 107; Transcript of proceedings at Isleta Pueblo, June 27, 1913, FJCPA.

33. Transcript of proceedings at Isleta Pueblo, June 27, 1913.

34. Barsh, "American Heart of Darkness," 108.

35. Wilson Irvine to Jose Abeita, Mercersburg, PA., July 7, 1914, FJCPA.

36. Wilson Irvine to Jose Abeita, Mercersburg, PA., Sept. 11, 1914, FJCPA; Reuben Perry to Pablo Abeita, Albuquerque, Apr. 5, 1915, FJCPA. Jose Abeita attended AIS, which Superintendent Ruben Perry ran, and was an honor student according to Perry. In April 1915 Perry wrote Pablo Abeita inviting him to attend a contest between the two literary societies (one for boys, one for girls); Jose Abeita was president of the boys' society.

37. Joseph K. Dixon to Reuben Perry, Philadelphia, Oct. 11, 1914, FJCPA.

38. Reuben Perry to Pablo Abeita, Albuquerque, Oct. 31, 1914, FJCPA.

39. Reuben Perry to Joseph K. Dixon, Albuquerque, Nov. 2, 1914, FJCPA.

40. Reuben Perry to Pablo Abeita, Albuquerque, Nov. 20, 1914, FJCPA.

41. Philip T. Lonergan to Pablo Abeita, Albuquerque, Nov. 18, 1914, FJCPA. Although the superintendent did not want Abeita to say anything to the commissioner about the removal petition, he was somewhat disgruntled in his job, noting that "sometimes I think that the [Indian] Office deliberately tries to make my work hard," and "I surely will welcome the time when I can get away from here." Lonergan was particularly concerned about the problems of taxation of the pueblos and the selling of liquor to Indians. Regarding the sale of liquor to Native Americans, Lonergan wrote, "we got two convictions in court today on cases of selling liquor to Isleta Indians," through the prosecution of lawyer Sumner Burkhart.

42. Pablo Abeita to William H. Ketcham, Isleta Pueblo, Dec. 1915, roll 75, frames 1093–101, BCIM.

43. Lindstrom, "Not from the Land Side," 209–27, 220.

Chapter Four

1. Frost, *Railroad and the Pueblo Indians*, 24, 44; Scurlock, *From Rio to Sierra*, 36–37.

2. Hagen, *Six Friends of the Indians*, 81. William H. Ketcham, a convert to Catholicism, trained as a missionary in the Ohio Indian Territory. The Sisters of Loretto's Indian Industrial School is discussed in chapter 7.

3. Prucha, *Churches and the Indian Schools*, 45.

4. William H. Ketcham to Pablo Abeita, Washington, DC, Feb. 6, 1910, FJCPA. Ketcham addresses Abeita, "My dear Friend."

5. Reuben Perry to Commissioner of Indian Affairs, Albuquerque, March 8, 1910, FJCPA; Senate Bill S. 7563, 61st Cong. 2nd Session.

6. William Henry Andrews to Pablo Abeita, Washington, DC, Feb. 1, 1911, FJCPA; Senate Bill S. 7563, 61st Cong. 2nd Session.

7. Marcus J. Patterson to Pablo Abeita, Denver, Dec. 1, 1911, Apr. 15, 1912, Apr. 15, 1912, and Apr. 24, 1912, FJCPA.

8. Pablo Abeita to William H. Ketcham, Isleta, Apr. 25, 1912, roll, 62, frames 731–32, BCIM.

9. William H. Ketcham to Pablo Abeita, Washington, DC, Apr. 10, 1912, FJCPA.

10. Philip T. Lonergan to Pablo Abeita, Albuquerque, Nov. 21, 1913, FJCPA.

11. Pablo Abeita to William H. Ketcham, Isleta, June 1913, Central files, 1907–1939, RG 75, NARA, Washington, DC, copy at IPCC. Abeita closed his letter, commenting on both federal and local Indian Office officials, asking for help "to retain Mr. F. C. Wilson as our atty. and Mr. P. T. Lonergan as Our Supt. or Agent." Pablo closed the letter "as ever your humble Indian son."

12. Edgar B. Merritt to Philip T. Lonergan, [Washington, DC], Dec. 18, 1913, Central files, 1907–1939, RG 75, NARA, Washington, DC, copy at IPCC.

13. Pablo Abeita to William H. Ketcham, Isleta, June 1913, roll 67, frames 64–67, BCIM.

14. Pablo Abeita to William H, Ketcham, Isleta, Feb. 7, 1923, roll 113, frame 12, BCIM.

15. Charles S. Lusk to Pablo Abeita, Washington, DC, Nov. 24, 1923, roll 113, frame 118, BCIM.

16. William H. Ketcham to Pablo Abeita, Washington, DC, Jan. 18, 1911, roll 56, frames 775–76, BCIM.

17. Pablo Abeita to William H. Ketcham, Isleta, Jan. 19, 1911, roll 56, frames 183–85, BCIM.

18. Reuben Perry to the Governor of Isleta Pueblo, Albuquerque, Jan. 30, 1911, roll 56, frames 806–7, BCIM.

19. Putney, "Robert Grosvenor Valentine," 233–42. Valentine served as commissioner of Indian affairs from 1909–1912. He was considered a progressive even though he supported the aims of the Dawes Allotment Act of 1887.

20. Pablo Abeita to William H Ketcham, Isleta, Feb. 8, 1911, roll 56, frame 808, BCIM.

21. Pablo Abeita to William H. Ketcham, Isleta, Apr. 15, 1911, roll 56, frames. 909–16, BCIM.

22. Pablo Abeita to William H. Ketcham, Isleta, May 20, 1914, roll 71, frames 805–8.

23. Pablo Abeita to William H. Ketcham, Isleta, Dec. 5, 1913, roll 67, frames 190–93.

24. Pablo Abeita to William H. Ketcham, Isleta, May 20, 1914, roll 71, frames 805–8.

25. Hodge, *Handbook of American Indians*, 622–24.

26. Pablo Abeita to William H. Ketcham, Isleta, Feb. 8, 1911, roll 56, frame 808, BCIM; Hodge, *Handbook of American Indians*, 624.

27. William H. Ketcham (by his secretary) to Pablo Abeita, Washington, DC, Jan 5, 1923, roll 113, frame 1, BCIM. In 1923 Father Hughes's secretary sent Abeita copies of the Bursum Bill and the Snyder Bill that replaced it, pointing out the differences between the two.

1. Governor Pasqual Abeita's reply to a circular from Commissioner of Indian Affairs Collins, 1934, roll 14, 920–24, IPCC.

2. Reuben Perry to Paul A. F. Walter, Supervisor of Census, Santa Fe, Aug. 24, 1909, FJCPA.

3. James Allen to Pablo Abeita, Santa Fe, July 24, 1905, FJCPA.

4. Paul A. F. Walter to Pablo Abeita, Santa Fe, Apr. 20, 1910, FJCPA.

5. Paul A. F. Walter to Pablo Abeita, Santa Fe, Dec. 6, 1909, FJCPA.

6. Paul A. F. Walter to Pablo Abeita, Santa Fe, Apr. 3, 1910, FJCPA.

7. Elmer W. Marsh to Pablo Abeita, Santa Fe, Apr. 6, 1910, FJCPA; Elmer W. Marsh to Pablo Abeita, Santa Fe, Apr. 21, 1910, FJCPA.

8. Paul A. F. Walter to Pablo Abeita, Santa Fe, Apr. 3, 1910, FJCPA.

9. Paul A. F. Walter to Pablo Abeita, Santa Fe, Apr. 18, 1910, FJCPA.

10. Elmer W. Marsh to Pablo Abeita, Santa Fe, Apr. 6, 1910, FJCPA.

11. *Annual Report of the Director of the Census to the Secretary of Commerce for the Fiscal Year Ended June 30, 1921* (Washington, DC: Government Printing Office, 1921), 25. No one considered microfilming these documents because Eastman Kodak did not fully develop the process until 1928. Had the documents survived, they could have been microfilmed later as were all the other censuses, https://www.microfilmworld.com/briefhistoryofmicrofilm.aspx (Brief History of Microfilm), Microfilmworld.com, accessed Aug. 27, 2022.

12. 1910 Federal Census of Isleta Pueblo, SRCA.

13. Elmer W. Marsh to Pablo Abeita, Santa Fe, Apr. 21, 1910, FJCPA.

14. Census of Laguna Pueblo, United States Bureau of Census, 1910 census schedules: New Mexico (Valencia County), roll 7.

15. Tiller, *Guide to Indian Country*, citing the year 2000 census, "Laguna," 734, "Isleta," 723.

16. For more information on Carlisle and Haskell, see Stout, *Native American Boarding Schools*, 27–45 and 47–59; St. Michael's College, *Seventy-five Years of Service*, 78–79.

17. Paul A. F. Walter to Pablo Abeita, Santa Fe, March 22, 1910; G. Malhorn, Assistant United States Treasurer, New Orleans, LA, Oct. 17, 1910, FJCPA.

18. Kimberly Powell, "Agricultural Schedules of the United States Census," ThoughtCo, https://www.thoughtco.com/agricultural-schedules-united-states-census-1422758, accessed March 18, 2018. The agricultural censuses prepared as part of the 1920 census were also destroyed.

19. 1920 Federal Census, New Mexico, Bernalillo, Chaves, and McKinley Counties, SRCA.

20. *Annual Report of the Department of the Interior for the Fiscal Year Ended June 30, 1905* (Washington, DC: GPO, 1906), 522.

21. Philip T. Lonergan to Pablo Abeita, Albuquerque, Aug. 16, 1912, FJCPA.

22. Philip T. Lonergan to Pablo Abeita, Albuquerque, June 13, 1912, FJCPA.

23. Philip T. Lonergan to Pablo Abeita, Albuquerque, July 7, 1914, FJCPA.

24. Pablo Abeita to William H. Ketcham, Isleta, May 20, 1916, roll 80, frame 1066–67, BCIM.

25. Philip T. Lonergan to Pablo Abeita, Albuquerque, Oct. 9, 1912, FJCPA.

26. Reuben Perry to Pablo Abeita, Albuquerque, Sept. 12, 1912, FJCPA.

27. Philip T. Lonergan to Pablo Abeita, Albuquerque, July 1, 1913, FJCPA.

28. Philip T. Lonergan to Pablo Abeita, Albuquerque, Nov. 15, 1912, FJCPA.

29. "Indians in Capital on Land Issue, Want to See Baseball," *Albuquerque Journal*, May 10, 1936;

"Boston Red Sox at Washington Senators Box Score, May 10, 1936," Baseball Reference, https://www.baseball-reference.com/boxes/WS1/WS119360510o.shtml; "Washington Nationals," Baseball Reference, https://www.baseball-reference.com/bullpen/Washington_Nationals_ (NA), accessed May 14, 2018. The Washington Senators, a charter member of the American League, were officially known as the Washington Nationals from 1905 to 1956. Grove pitched the game at Griffith Stadium on May 10, 1936, losing 4–0 to Bobo Newsom and the Nationals.

30. Sutter, *New Mexico Baseball*, 188. The material in the following pages is drawn from Sutter, 179–95.

31. Interview by authors with Randy Jiron, Santa Fe, Nov. 19, 2021.

32. Docher, "Quaint Indian Pueblo of Isleta," 30; Interview by authors with Randy Jiron, Santa Fe, Nov. 19, 2021.

CHAPTER SIX

1. Herald Square Jeweler, New York, to Pablo Abeita, Dec. 17, 1914, sending beads imported from Germany, FJCPA.

2. Frost, *Railroad and the Pueblo Indians*, 26–37.

3. Frost, 37.

4. Parsons, *Pueblo of Isleta*, 453; Frost, *Railroad and the Pueblo Indians*, 43–44.

5. US v. Joseph, 94 US 614 (1877); Frost, 44.

6. Frost, *Railroad and the Pueblo Indians*, 44–45.

7. Docher, "Quaint Indian Pueblo of Isleta." Anton Docher (1852–1928) served as priest for Isleta for thirty-four years. He had a progressive attitude toward Pueblo religion and incorporated Indigenous rituals into his church services.

8. "Isleta Indians Try to Cut Railroad," *Santa Fe New Mexican*, June 12, 1905.

9. *Santa Fe New Mexican*, Nov. 2, 1905, and April 28, 1906; Frost, *Railroad and the Pueblo Indians*, 44–45.

10. *Santa Fe New Mexican*, Jan. 11, 1899.

11. Nimrod S. Walpole to governor of Isleta, Jan. 12, 1899, Pueblo and Jicarilla Agency, Letter sent, 1874–1900 v. 35, NARA, Denver.

12. "Indian Boys Pinched: Stone Santa Fe Cars," *Santa Fe New Mexican*, Sept. 29, 1919.

13. Philip T. Lonergan to Pablo Abeita, July 28, 1914; Francis C. Wilson to Pablo Abeita, Sept. 9, 1914, FJCPA; Frost, *Railroad and the Pueblo Indians*, 33.

14. Robert Irwin to Francisco Jaramillo c/o C. E. Seis, Dec. 13, 1923, roll 14, frame 475, IPCC; Robert Irwin to Harmon P. Marble, Los Angeles, Dec. 24, 1923, roll 14, frame 477, IPCC; Harmon P. Marble to Robert Irwin, Albuquerque, Dec. 14, 1923, roll 14, frame 476, IPCC.

15. Harmon P. Marble to Robert Irwin, Albuquerque, Dec. 18, 1923, IPCC, roll 14.

16. Robert Irwin to Harmon P. Marble, Los Angeles, Dec. 29, 1923, roll 14, frame 479, IPCC; Harmon P. Marble to Robert Irwin, Albuquerque, Jan. 14, 1924, roll 14, frame 479, IPCC.

17. A. F. Morrissette to Harmon P. Marble, El Paso, May 21, 1923, roll 14, frame 609, IPCC.

18. John R. Abeita to A. F. Morrissette, Isleta, June 18, 1923, roll 14, frames 610–11, IPCC; Telling, "Ramah, New Mexico," 117–36. In 1876 Mormon missionaries established Ramah (named after a biblical city first mentioned in the Book of Joshua) in McKinley County between the Navajo and Zuni reservations.

19. Esquipula Jojola to Harmon P. Marble, Isleta, June 14, 1923, roll 14, frame 606, IPCC; Acoma Farmer to Harmon P. Marble, Acomita, June 20, 1923, roll 14, frame 607, IPCC.

20. Harmon P. Marble to A. F. Morrissette, Albuquerque, June 23, 1923, roll 14, frame 604, IPCC.

21. A. F. Morrissette to Harmon P. Marble, El Paso, Texas, July 11, 1923, roll 14, frame 603, IPCC.

22. Harmon P. Marble to A. F. Morrissette, Albuquerque, Aug. 14, 1923, roll 14, frame 600, IPCC.

23. Howard V. Smith to Harmon P. Marble, Isleta, Aug. 15, 1923, roll 14, frame 599, IPCC; "Origin of the Pecheron, Percheron Horse Association of America," https://igprescue.org/the-horses/origin-of-the-percheron/, accessed August 27, 2022. Percherons are a breed of draft horse originating in Southern France. They are well muscled and known for their intelligence and willingness to work.

24. Harmon P. Marble to A. F. Morrissette, Albuquerque, Sept. 16, 1923, roll 14, frame 598, IPCC; Harmon P. Marble to A. F. Morrissette, Albuquerque, Nov. 20, 1923, roll 14, frame 597, IPCC.

25. Harmon P. Marble to Howard V. Smith, Albuquerque, Feb. 8, 1924, roll 14, frame 595, IPCC; Howard V. Smith to Harmon P. Marble, Isleta, Feb. 14, 1924, roll 14, frame 594, IPCC.

26. Chester E. Faris to A. F. Morrissette, Albuquerque, April 2, 1924, roll 14, frame 593, IPCC.

27. Frost, *Railroad and the Pueblo Indians*, 35. New Mexico law (Compiled Laws of New Mexico, 1897, 156) required railroads to be fenced. The AT&SF did not fence its rights-of-way until 1909.

28. Frost, 208n42. In 1879 the AT&SF paid out a total of $33,524 for killing cattle all along its route.

29. Frost, 34, 38, quote at 38.

30. Frost, 34.

31. Frost, 32.

32. Frost, 33.

33. Victory et al., *Compiled Laws of New Mexico, 1897*, 156.

34. *Santa Fe New Mexican*, Dec. 18, 1901. For more on *Santa Fe New Mexican* editor Max Frost, see Dean, "King Maker," 317–37.

35. Frost, *Railroad and the Pueblo Indians*, 31–32; Interview by authors with Randy Jiron and William Abeita, June 14, 2019, Isleta Pueblo. A possible explanation for the pueblo tradition regarding free passes is that the railroad allowed Isletans to "ride the rails" by jumping onto freight cars.

36. Frost, *Railroad and the Pueblo Indians*, 32.

37. "Mashed Mutton," *Albuquerque Journal*, May 31, 1891, clipping in Charles F. Lummis Collection, AC 138, box 1, folder titled miscellaneous on Pueblo Indians, 1878–91, Fray Angélico Chávez History Library, Santa Fe.

38. Melzer, *Fred Harvey Houses of the Southwest*, 111–16; Weigle, *Alluring New Mexico*, 65–74.

39. Peters, "Continuing Identity," 187–98, quotes at 188.

40. "Belgium Special is Burnished Up for Last Journey," *Albuquerque Morning Journal*, Oct. 26, 1919.

41. Goemaere, *Across America*, 3, 8; Bryan, *Albuquerque Remembered*, 214; "King Albert and Labor," *Roswell Daily Record*, Oct. 22, 1919.

42. "Plaza of Isleta will be Arena of Sports for King," *Albuquerque Morning Journal*, Oct. 16, 1919.

43. "Belgian King is Greeted by Mob of Thousands on His Arrival Here," *Albuquerque Morning Journal*, Oct. 20, 1919.

44. "Indian Gifts to Belgian King," *Indian Sentinel* 2, no. 1 (Jan. 1920): 23–24.

45. "Belgian Special is Burnished for Last Journey," *Albuquerque Morning Journal*, Oct. 26, 1919.
46. "Indian Gifts to Belgian King," *Indian Sentinel* 2, no. 1 (Jan. 1920): 23–24.
47. Frost, "Romantic Inflation of Pueblo Culture," 61.

CHAPTER SEVEN

1. Horgan, *Lamy of Santa Fe*, 394–95. For a summary of Hiram Price's term as commissioner of Indian affairs, see O'Neil, "Hiram Price," 173–79. Archbishop Lamy set a precedent for Indian education at St. Michael's in 1878 when he sponsored a program to pay the expenses of twenty-two Pueblo Indian youth enrolled in a new department of the college, on the strength of a promise by the government to pay $100 each toward the expenses of each student. When the funds failed to arrive, Archbishop Lamy traveled to Washington to meet with Commissioner of Indian Affairs Price in hopes of gaining government support for the program. Price turned him down, so he scrapped the program.
2. Momaday, *Three Plays*, 176–77.
3. Child, "Indian Education," 161.
4. Gram, *Education at the Edge of Empire*, 100.
5. Adams, "Beyond Bleakness," 49.
6. Child, "Indian Education," 161.
7. Newland, "Indian Boarding School Initiative," 3–4. One of the findings of the initiative stated "that the United States directly targeted American Indian . . . children in the pursuit of a policy of cultural assimilation that coincided with Indian territorial dispossession." Bryan Newland to Debra Haaland, Washington, DC, April 1, 2022, letter attached to initiative report.
8. Trafzer, *Boarding School Blues*, 13.
9. Trafzer, 15.
10. Antonio Abeita to Charles Lummis, Hampton Institute, Feb. 4, 1905, folder MS 1.1.5A, AMAW.
11. Gram, *Education at the Edge of Empire*, 7.
12. Gram, 22.
13. Gram, 33.
14. Pablo Abeita to William H. Ketcham, Isleta, Aug. 6, 1919, roll 93, frames 563–64, BCIM.
15. 1889 Report of the Commissioner of Indian Affairs, House Executive Doc. No. 1, 51st Congress, 1st session, serial set 2725, 3.
16. Thompson, *American Character*, 156–57.
17. Ebright and Hendricks, *Pueblo Sovereignty*, 182.
18. Thompson, *American Character*, 159–61, quote at 159.
19. Prucha, "Thomas Jefferson Morgan," 202.
20. Svenningsen, *Preliminary Inventory of the Pueblo Records*, 14.
21. Hearings of the Subcommittee of the Committee on Indian Affairs, House of Representatives (Washington, DC: Government Printing Office, 1920), 686–87.
22. Indian Affairs Subcommittee Hearings, 675.
23. Reuben Perry to Pablo Abeita, Albuquerque, Sept. 20, 1910, FJCPA.
24. Reuben Perry to Pablo Abeita, Albuquerque, April 1, 1915, FJCPA.
25. Reuben Perry to Pablo Abeita, Albuquerque, July 24, 1914, FJCPA.
26. Reuben Perry to Pablo Abeita, Albuquerque, Jan. 12, 1914, FJCPA.
27. Reuben Perry to Pablo Abeita, Albuquerque, June 14, 1914, FJCPA.

28. Connell-Szasz, *Education and the American Indian*, 24.
29. Meriam, *Problem of Indian Administration*, 375.
30. Meriam, 392.
31. Connell-Szasz, *Education and the American Indian*, 20.
32. Meriam, *Problem of Indian Administration*, 360.
33. Meriam, 32.
34. Lomawaima, *They Called It Prairie Light*, 7.
35. Connell-Szasz, *Education and the American Indian*, 32.
36. Connell-Szasz, 67.
37. Bernstein and Rushing, *Modern by Tradition*, 70, drawing 57. Pablita Velarde was one of Dunn's best-known students.
38. Connell-Szasz, *Education and the American Indian*, 61.
39. Connell-Szasz, 64.
40. Sze, "Application for Registration," 12. Among the noted teachers at St. Catherine's were Joe F. Abeyta, who taught carpentry and coached for many years, and Jose D. Sena, who went on to become a state legislator and long-serving clerk of the New Mexico Supreme Court.
41. Owens, "Historical Sketch," 73–87. The Sisters of Loretto school operated until 1937.
42. 1910 Federal Census, Isleta Pueblo, SRCA.
43. Hyer, *One House, One Voice, One Heart*, 5.
44. Gram, *Education at the Edge of Empire*, 52.
45. Gram, 69.
46. Hyer, "Remembering Santa Fe Indian School," 126–27.
47. Gram, *Education at the Edge of Empire*, 69, 81, 127.
48. "Katherine Drexel, Catholic Educator Born," African American Registry, https://aaregistry.org/story/katherine-drexel-born, accessed August 27, 2022.
49. *Santa Fe New Mexican*, Dec. 26, 1993, and Oct. 2, 2000.
50. Sze, "Gone but Not Forgotten," 6–9.
51. Biddle, *Saint Katharine*, 150–55.
52. Sze, "Gone but Not Forgotten," 14–16.
53. Sze, 11–14.
54. Marriott, *Maria, the Potter of San Ildefonso*, 84–91. Maria Martinez (then Montoya) attended St. Catherine's with her sister, Desideria, for two years. This schooling was highly sought after by pueblo members, and each year the tribal council picked the children who would attend.
55. Sze, "Gone but Not Forgotten," 26–9.
56. *Albuquerque Journal North*, Oct. 14, 2001.
57. Sze, "Application for Registration," 18. Patrick's family was loyal to St. Catherine's; his father, brothers, sisters, wife, and two children attended. Patrick was the first Pueblo Indian to be ordained a deacon in the Catholic Church.
58. Sze, "Application for Registration," 9, 16–18; Sze, "St. Catherine's "School," 1–2.
59. Henry Kendall's response to Carlisle Survey, Former Student Survey Responses, 1890 (Part 3 of 5), 1890, NARA, Washington, DC, RG 75, Entry 91, box 637, 1890-#20195.
60. Some details of Kendall's life after he returned to Isleta are found in correspondence with Richard H. Pratt, superintendent of Carlisle; Rev. John H. Raven, Rutgers College to Richard

H. Pratt, Feb. 15, 1916, New Brunswick, NJ; and Richard H. Pratt to Rev. John H. Raven, Mar. 6, 1916, Washington, DC, Cumberland Historical Society.

61. Fear-Segal, *White Man's Club*, 284.
62. De Marco, "Education's Champion."
63. "Agnes Mary Shattuck Dill: Advocate Called Matriarch for Isleta Pueblo," *Albuquerque Journal*, March 24, 2012; Sando, *Pueblo Profiles*, 195.

CHAPTER EIGHT

1. Hagan, *Indian Police*, 107–10. Teller's bias against Native Americans "was reflected in his defense of the butchering of Cheyenne women and children by the Colorado militia in the infamous Sand Creek Massacre."
2. Hagan, *Indian Police*, 109–10; Hagan, "Rules for the Court of Indian Offenses," April 10, 1883.
3. Hagan, *Indian Police*, 109.
4. Crane, *Desert Drums*, 315.
5. Harring, *Crow Dog's Case*, 185–86; Deloria and Lytle, *American Indian*, 115–16. Although the Courts of Indian Offenses were informal and never sanctioned by federal statute, their legality was upheld by the Supreme Court in US v. Claypox, 34 federal reports 575 (1888).
6. Wenger, *We Have a Religion*, 99.
7. Wenger, 103; Speech given at the US Indian Pueblo Council, Nov. 7, 1928. Minutes were entered into the records of US Senate Hearings on Senate Resolution 79 and 308 (70th Cong. and Senate Resolution 263 and 416 (71st Cong.).
8. Hagan, *Indian Police*, 162–63.
9. Louis Abeita to Leo Crane, Isleta, roll 14, IPCC. In Juanita Jaramillo's defense, the policeman Louis Abeita told Superintendent Crane that Juanita's sister who filed the charges against her "had caused a great deal of trouble in the past," by filing charges before the justice of the peace against other women without sufficient proof.
10. Pablo Abeita to William H. Ketcham, Isleta Pueblo, Dec. 15, 1915, roll 75, frames 1093–101, BCIM; Hagan, *Indian Police*, 113–19, quote at 119.
11. Hagan, *Indian Police*, 42–43.
12. Pablo Abeita to Philip T. Lonergan, Nov. 1, 1911, and Philip T. Lonergan to Pablo Abeita, Albuquerque, Nov. 1, 1911, roll 14, frames 1, 10–11, 12, IPCC.
13. See appendix 3, "Isleta Pueblo Governors."
14. Leo Crane to Jose Seferino Abeita, Albuquerque, Nov. 20, 1920, roll 14, frame 58, IPCC; Leo Crane, memorandum, Albuquerque, Nov. 20, 1920, roll 14, frame 59, IPCC.
15. 1930 Federal Census of Isleta Pueblo, SRCA.
16. Guggino, "Pablo Abeita," 104n227.
17. For more on William Paisano, see Frost, *Railroad and the Pueblo Indians*, 113–14.
18. Case no. 36, Jose Jiron vs. Pascual Lucero, mentions Judge Abeita's docket book.
19. James R. Allen, letter of recommendation and good conduct, Sept. 9, 1905, FJCPA; Hagan, *Indian Police*, 134–35.
20. Ex Parte Crow Dog, 109 US 553 (1883), Deloria and Lytle, *American Indian*, American Justice, 168–73.
21. Owey and Getches, *Indian Courts and the Future*, 33–35.

22. Louis Abeita, complaint, Sept. 27, 1920, Isleta, and warrant for the arrest of Jose Chavez, roll 14, frames 12, 69–70, IPCC; Notes on trial of Jose Chavez for assault on Indian policeman, Nov. 27, 1920, roll 14, frames 3–7, IPCC.

23. Guggino, "Pablo Abeita," 102, citing Harmon P. Marble to Pablo Abeita, Dec. 17, 1923.

24. Isleta vs. Juan P. Lente, Nov. 1, 1915, FJCPA.

25. Pablo Abeita to Harmon P. Marble, Isleta, Nov. 8, 1923, roll 14, frames 448–49, IPCC.

26. Howard V. Smith to Harmon P. Marble, Isleta, Nov. 19, 1923, roll 14, frame 446, IPCC.

27. Harmon P. Marble to Pablo Abeita, Albuquerque, Nov. 7, 1923; Antonio Abeita for Governor Jose Padilla to Harmon P. Marble, Isleta, Nov. 3, 1923, roll 14, frames 450–52, IPCC.

28. Jose Jiron vs. Pascual Lucero, Dec. 3, 1923, roll 14, frame 465, IPCC.

29. Jose Jiron vs. Antonio Abeita, July 14, 1923, roll 14, frames 336–37, IPCC.

30. Remijio vs. Remijio, March 2, 1918, roll 14, frame 18, IPCC; 1930 Isleta census, household no. 169.

31. Felipe Sangre vs. Andres Olguin, cases heard before Pueblo officials at Isleta, March 2 and March 9, 1918, roll 14, frames 18–20, IPCC.

32. 1930 Isleta census, household no. 26.

33. Tomas Gerilla v. Candelaria Gerilla, Dec. 3, 1922, roll 14, frame 190, IPCC.

34. In case no. 12, Isleta vs. John D. Jojola et al., Judge Abeita ordered the truants returned to school and considered no excuses.

35. Wenger, *We Have a Religion*, 188–90.

36. Owens, "Historical Sketch," 77, 79. The Sisters of Loretto opened a school in Bernalillo with eight pupils from Isleta Pueblo on December 18, 1885. The school operated until 1937.

37. Harmon P. Marble to Pablo Abeita, Albuquerque, Dec. 30, 1922, roll 14, frame 210, IPCC.

38. Reuben Perry to Pablo Abeita, Albuquerque, Jan. 12, 1914; April 1, 1914; June 14, 1914; and July 24, 1914, FJCPA.

39. Isleta vs. Jose Chavez, Nov. 27, 1920, roll 14, frame 3–7, IPCC.

40. Wenger, *We Have a Religion*, 100.

41. Pablo Abeita to Harmon P. Marble, Oct. 30, 1922, roll 14, frames 163–65, IPCC.

42. Ebright, "Benjamin Thomas," 318; Hagan, *Indian Police*, 109–10.

43. Leo Crane to Pablo Abeita, Albuquerque, March 3, 1920, FJCPA.

44. Ebright and Hendricks, *Pueblo Sovereignty*, 161–62. Hanna was a leading advocate for reform in the 1931 hearings that led to additional compensation for Isleta due to unfair decisions, particularly in the Lo de Padilla grant overlap.

45. Richard Hanna to Pablo Abeita, Albuquerque, July 28, 1919, roll 14, frames 18–20, IPCC. In one case, Bautista Montoya requested an opinion regarding the disposition of the separate property of his deceased wife Placida Chiwiwi. Hanna told Judge Abeita that the statute provided that one-fourth of the wife's separate property passed to the surviving spouse and three-quarters to any surviving children, but since the couple had no children all her property would go to the husband, Bautista Montoya.

46. Charles F. Hanke to the superintendents, Washington, DC, July 26, 1912, FJCPA.

47. Philip T. Lonergan to Pablo Abeita, Albuquerque, Dec. 30, 1914, FJCPA. Lonergan urged Abeita to allow the Indian Office to establish a Court of Indian Offenses and to serve as judge.

48. Bahe Guerro to Leo Crane, Albuquerque, n.d., roll 14, frames 55–56, IPCC; Leo Crane,

statement concerning the property of Miss Bahe Guerro, roll 14, frame 57, IPCC; Leo Crane to Pablo Abeita, Albuquerque, Sept. 7, 1920, roll 14, frames 51–52, IPCC.

49. Pablo Abeita to Leo Crane, Isleta, Sept. 2, 1920, roll 14, IPCC.

50. Antonio Abeita for Governor Jose Padilla to Harmon P. Marble, Isleta Pueblo, Sept. 15, 1923, roll 14, frames 391–92, IPCC.

51. Pablo Abeita to Harmon P. Marble, Isleta Pueblo, Sept. 25, 1923, roll 14, frames 400–401, IPCC.

52. Teddy Lente to Harmon P. Marble, Isleta Pueblo, Sept. 28, 1923, roll 14, frames 396–98; Conference hearing at Isleta, Oct. 23, 1923, roll 14, frames 406–14, IPCC.

53. Harmon P. Marble to F. C. H. Livingston, Albuquerque, Oct. 30, 1923, roll 14, frame 418, IPCC.

54. F. C. H. Livingston to Harmon P. Marble, Belen, Nov. 6, 1923, roll 14, frames 420–21, IPCC.

55. Harmon P. Marble to Governor Jose Padilla, Albuquerque, Nov. 6, 1923 (with copies to F. C. H. Livingston, Teddy Lente, Pablo Abeita, and Howard V. Smith), roll 14, frame 426, IPCC.

56. Hagen, *Indian Police*, 111.

57. Guggino, "Pablo Abeita," 85, citing Pablo Abeita to Charles Burke, Dec. 14, 1922.

58. Guggino, 93–94.

59. Guggino, 91–92.

60. General meeting, Isleta Pueblo, Dec. 15, 1921, roll 14, frames 85, 107, IPCC.

61. At the end of the meeting, Frank Lucero brought up the fencing problem, which had not been addressed earlier because of the high cost of barbed wire; general meeting, roll 14, frames 85–86, 112, IPCC.

62. Statement of Governor Jose Padilla, general meeting, Dec. 15, 1921, roll 14, frames 85–86, IPCC. Governor Padilla asked Superintendent Crane about who had the greater authority in the pueblo; the superintendent told him the judge was under the governor, although Padilla complained that Crane held the judge higher than the governor.

63. General meeting, Dec. 15, 1921, roll 14, frame 86, IPCC.

64. General meeting, Dec. 15, 1921, roll 14, frames 86–87, IPCC.

65. General meeting, Dec. 15, 1921, roll 14, frames 85–87, 89, IPCC.

66. General meeting, Dec. 15, 1921, roll 14, frames 85–87, IPCC.

67. General meeting, Dec. 15, 1921, roll 14, frames 85–89, IPCC.

68. General meeting, Dec. 15, 1921, roll 14, frames 87–89, IPCC.

69. Statement of Superintendent Crane, general meeting, Dec. 15, 1921, roll 14, frame 94, IPCC.

70. General meeting, Dec. 15, 1921, roll 14, frame 91, IPCC. Jose Lucero also complained that Judge Abeita had sent his policeman Seferino Jojola to bring his daughter back to school and that Seferino had "dragged her out by the hair." However, when Jojola testified, he said he took her by the hand or arm but "she tried to pull away . . . when she heard her father say she did not have to go."

71. Statement of Pablo Abeita, general meeting, Dec. 15, 1921, roll 14, frame 111, IPCC.

72. Statement of Governor Jose Padilla, general meeting, Dec. 15, 1921, roll 14, frame 85, IPCC.

73. Statements of Bautista Zuni, Dec. 15, 1921, and Dec. 16, 1921, general meeting, Dec. 15, 1921, roll 14, frames 93, 107, IPCC.

74. Statements of Superintendent Crane, general meeting, Dec. 15, 1921, roll 14, frames 109, 111, IPCC.

75. Pablo Abeita to Leo Crane, Isleta Pueblo, Feb. 4, 1922, and Leo Crane to Pablo Abeita, Albuquerque, Feb. 10, 1922, general meeting, Dec. 15, 1921, roll 14, frames 116–17 and 113–14, IPCC.

76. Pablo Abeita to Leo Crane, Isleta Pueblo, April 4, 1922, general meeting, Dec. 15, 1921, roll 14, frames 125–28, IPCC. Judge Abeita had discounted the defendant's testimony, relying on a book of official decisions of former governors that, while referring to public roads, was determined to be a forgery. The entry in question was written by Pablo's deceased brother, Marcelino, and according to Judge Abeita was written years later "with the intent of helping the two defendants who are his brothers-in-law."

77. Leo Crane to Pablo Abeita, April 13, 1922, general meeting, Dec. 15, 1921, roll 14, frames 121–23, IPCC.

78. Crane to Abeita, Apr. 13, 1922.

79. Emily Carpio to Harmon P. Marble, Isleta, Nov. 23, 1922, 14, frames 18–20, IPCC.

80. William Paisano to Pablo Abeita, Casa Blanca, Dec. 1, 1922, roll 14, frame 187, IPCC.

81. Pablo Abeita to Leo Crane, Isleta, April 6, 1922, roll 14, frames 118–19, IPCC. Abeita complained that Shafer refused to give him lumber to construct bridges over an irrigation ditch but gave "lumber liberally to all those who would cuss me."

82. Pablo Abeita to Harmon P. Marble, Isleta Pueblo, May 18, 1923, roll 14, frames 301–2, IPCC.

83. Abeita to Marble, May 18, 1923.

84. "Case Against Pablo Abeita Thrown Out," *Santa Fe New Mexican*, May 7, 1923.

85. Antonio Abeita to Harmon P. Marble, Isleta Pueblo, Sept. 15, 1923, roll 14, frames 391–92, IPCC.

86. Pablo Abeita to Harmon P. Marble, Isleta Pueblo, n.d., roll 14, frames 394–95, IPCC.

87. Harmon P. Marble to Felipe Abeita et al., Albuquerque, Aug. 8, 1923, roll 14, frame 381, IPCC.

88. Harmon P. Marble to Howard V. Smith, Albuquerque, Sept. 14, 1923, roll 14, frame 388, IPCC.

89. Pablo Abeita to Charles Burke, Isleta, Dec. 14, 1923, cited in Guggino, "Pablo Abeita," 108.

90. Pablo Abeita to Harmon P. Marble, Isleta, Feb. 23, 1924, cited in Guggino, "Pablo Abeita," 109.

91. Harmon P. Marble to Pablo Abeita, Albuquerque, Feb. 28, 1924, NARA, Denver, RG 75, box 21, no. 066, copy at IPCC.

92. Pablo Abeita to Harmon P. Marble, Isleta, Jan. 24, 1924, roll 14, frames 518–22, IPCC.

93. Harmon P. Marble to Pablo Abeita, Albuquerque, Nov. 7, 1923, roll 14, frame 424, IPCC.

94. Harmon P. Marble to Howard V. Smith, Albuquerque, Nov. 18, 1923, roll 14, frame 441, IPCC.

95. Wenger, *We Have a Religion*, 100.

96. Harmon P. Marble to Pablo Abeita, Albuquerque, Feb. 28, 1924, NARA Denver, RG 75, box 21, no. 066; copy at IPCC.

97. Pablo Abeita to Harmon P. Marble, Isleta, Jan. 24, 1924, roll 14, frames 518–22, IPCC.

98. Pablo Abeita to Charles Burke, Isleta, March 28, 1925, IPCC.

99. Pablo Abeita to F. C. H. Livingston, Isleta, n.d., NARA Denver, S. Pueblo 169, 1911–1935, box 5; copy at IPCC.

100. Pablo Abeita to Chester E. Faris, Isleta, Jan. 21, 1925, roll 14, frames 636–37, IPCC.

101. Pablo Abeita to Lemuel Towers, Isleta, Nov. 12, 1927, roll 14, frames 755–56, IPCC.

102. Pablo Abeita to Lemuel Towers, Isleta, May 29, 1928, roll 14, frames 764–65, IPCC.

103. Pablo Abeita to Lemuel Towers, Isleta, May 18, 1932, roll 14, frame 862, IPCC.

104. The four pro-Abeita governors serving between 1914 and 1924 were Vicente Abeita (1915), Bautista Zuni (1918), Felipe Abeita (1919), and Remijio Lucero (1922). See appendix 3, "Isleta Pueblo Governors."

CHAPTER NINE

1. Guggino, "Pablo Abeita," 9–32. Abeita reminded his admirers that he was the only living Indian to have met all the presidents from Grover Cleveland in 1886 to F. D. R. in the 1930s.

2. Simmons, "Pablo Abeita, a Leader," 49.

3. Ebright and Hendricks, *Pueblo Sovereignty*, discusses Isleta's purchase of the Gutiérrez-Sedillo and Lo de Padilla grants at 134–36 and 136–38, respectively.

4. Crandall, *These People Have Always Been a Republic*, 202–3.

5. US v. Joseph, 94 US 614 (1876); Hall, *Four Leagues of Pecos*, 133–37; Ebright, Hendricks, and Hughes, *Four Square Leagues*, 253–54.

6. Crandall, *These People Have Always Been a Republic*, 206.

7. Antonio Jojola and Pablo Abeita to George H. Howard, Isleta, Nov. 27, 1899, Indian Affairs Collection, box 1, folder 7, Center for Southwest Research, University of New Mexico. Howard's response to the letter was to request a resurvey of the Lo de Padilla grant to run to the crest, but when he asked the Land Claims Court to establish a general rule requiring a surveyor to survey to the crest in all cases where a mountain was specified as a boundary, it refused to do so.

8. Elmer Veeder to Pablo Abeita, Las Vegas, Jan. 15, 1908, FJCPA.

9. Ebright and Hendricks, *Pueblo Sovereignty*, 145–47, 152–55.

10. Ebright, "Benjamin Thomas in New Mexico," 316–18.

11. Elmer Veeder to Pablo Abeita, Las Vegas, Sept. 25, 1909, FJCPA. Veeder posed questions regarding inheritance customs at the pueblo.

12. Elmer Veeder to Pablo Abeita, Las Vegas, July 31, 1907, FJCPA.

13. 1910 Federal Census of Isleta Pueblo, SRCA.

14. Elmer Veeder to Pablo Abeita, Las Vegas, July 14, 1909, FJCPA.

15. Elmer Veeder to Pablo Abeita, Las Vegas, Feb. 8, 1909, FJCPA.

16. Elmer Veeder to Pablo Abeita, Las Vegas, Jan. 23, 1908, Elmer Veeder to Pablo Abeita, Las Vegas, July 14, 1909, FJCPA.

17. Guggino, "Pablo Abeita," 13–14; Prince, *Spanish Mission Churches of New Mexico*, 200; Elmer Veeder to Pablo Abeita, Las Vegas, July 31, 1907, FJCPA. "We also want to get witnesses to show that Ambrosio Abeyta was wealthy and loaned the government troops . . . money."

18. Territory of New Mexico v. Delinquent Taxpayers, 12NM139 (1904).

19. Crandall, *These People Have Always Been a Republic*, 221–24.

20. Pablo Abeita to William H. Ketcham, Isleta, June 1913, roll 67, frames 64–67, BCIM.

21. US v. Sandoval, 198 Federal Supplement 539 (1912).

22. Frederick. H. Abbott to William Ketcham, Washington, DC, June 2, 1913, FJCPA.

23. William H. Ketcham to Pablo Abeita, Washington, DC, June 25, 1913, FJCPA.

24. Francis C. Wilson to Pablo Abeita, Santa Fe, Apr. 26, 1911, FJCPA. Wilson informed Abeita that he was leaving for Taos for two weeks.

25. Francis C. Wilson to Pablo Abeita, Santa Fe, Apr. 26, 1911, FJCPA.

26. Francis C. Wilson to Pablo Abeita, Santa Fe, May 20, 1910, FJCPA.

27. Francis C. Wilson to Pablo Abeita, Santa Fe, Jan. 18, 1911, FJCPA.

28. Francis C. Wilson to Pablo Abeita, Santa Fe, Dec. 2, 1910, FJCPA.

29. Francis C. Wilson to Pablo Abeita, Santa Fe, Nov. 18, 1910, FJCPA.

30. Francis C. Wilson to Pablo Abeita, Santa Fe, Sept. 9, 1914, FJCPA.

31. US v. Joseph, 94 US 614 (1876).

32. Hall, *Four Leagues of Pecos*, 202–5; US. v. Joseph, 94 US 614 (1876).

33. US v. Sandoval, 198 F, Supp. 539 (1912), federal court for the district of New Mexico.

34. William H. Pope to Pablo Abeita, Santa Fe, Sept. 23, 1912, FJCPA.

35. Francis C. Wilson to Pablo Abeita, Santa Fe, Sept. 2, 1913, FJCPA. Wilson promised to send a copy of a New Mexico Supreme Court decision to Abeita.

36. William H. Pope to Pablo Abeita, Santa Fe, Sept. 23, 1912, FJCPA.

37. The Dawes Act, US Statutes, vol. 29, 388–91.

38. Hall, *Four Leagues of Pecos*, 207–8; Hearings Before the Senate Committee on Indian Affairs, 62nd Congress, 3rd session, on S. 6085, A Bill to Authorize the Acceptance of Trusts from the Pueblo Indians of New Mexico, Testimony of Francis T. Wilson, 6.

39. Testimony of Francis C. Wilson, 6.

40. Testimony of Pablo Abeita, Washington, DC, Feb. 13, 1913, Senate Committee on Indian Affairs Hearings, 21–22.

41. The Peralta tract on the Lo de Padilla grant was determined by the Pueblo Lands Board to contain 14,710 acres, a gross exaggeration of the size of the tract; a later Act of Congress allocated funds to compensate Isleta for their loss of the overblown Peralta tract. Testimony of Pablo Abeita, Washington, DC, Feb. 13, 1913, Senate Committee on Indian Affairs Hearings, 23–24.

42. Testimony of Pablo Abeita, Washington, DC, Feb. 13, 1913, Senate Committee on Indian Affairs Hearings, 24–25; Brayer, Pueblo Indian Land Grants of the "Rio Abajo," 58–59.

43. Testimony of Pablo Abeita, 25, 27, 75.

44. Philip T. Lonergan to Pablo Abeita, Albuquerque, July 15, 1912, FJCPA.

45. Hall, *Four Leagues of Pecos*, 205; US v. Sandoval, 231 US 281 (1913).

46. Philip T. Lonergan to Pablo Abeita, Albuquerque, Dec. 26, 1913, FJCPA.

47. Ebright, Hendricks, and Hughes, *Four Square Leagues*, 167.

48. Ebright and Hendricks, *Pueblo Sovereignty*, 92–96.

49. Francis Joy to Pablo Abeita, Chamita, Apr. 11, 1915, FJCPA.

50. Ebright, Hendricks, and Hughes, *Four Square Leagues*, 269–70,

51. Ebright, Hendricks, and Hughes, 270–71.

52. Ebright, Hendricks, and Hughes, 268–72.

53. Pablo Abeita to William Hughes, Oct. 23, 1922, roll 107, frame 833, BCIM.

54. Downes, "Crusade for Indian Reform," 331–54; *New York Times*, Jan. 21, 1924; Feb. 2, 1924, Sec. II, 7.

55. Pablo Abeita to Charles S. Lusk, Nov. 19, 1923, Isleta, roll 113, frames 116–17, BCIM.

56. Philp, "Albert B. Fall and the Protest from the Pueblos," 254.

57. D. H. Lawrence, "Certain Americans and an Englishman," *New York Times*, Dec. 24, 1922. Lawrence continues his analysis of the Bursum Bill with the following assessment of American

society in the 1920s: "Finally, in some curious way, the pueblos still lie here at the core of American life. In some curious way, it is the Indians still who are American. This great welter of whites is not yet a nation, not yet a people."

58. Pablo Abeita to F. C. H. Livingston, Isleta, Feb. 8, 1925, roll 15, frame 48, IPCC.

59. Sando, *Pueblo Profiles*, 186.

60. Sando, 188.

61. United States, Survey of Conditions, 4347.

62. Statement of Lawrence Elkus, United States, 4434.

63. Statement of Pablo Abeita, United States, 4436–37.

64. United States, 4449.

65. Testimony of Richard Hanna, Jan. 30, 1931. United States, 4447 and May 2, 1931, 10729.

66. Ebright, Hendricks, and Hughes, *Four Square Leagues*, 285, 413n523.

67. Testimony of Pablo Abeita, Jan. 30, 1931. United States, Survey of Conditions, 4437.

68. Ebright, Hendricks, and Hughes, *Four Square Leagues*, 287–88; Pueblo Compensation Act of May 31, 1933, 48 US Statutes 108.

69. Taylor, *New Deal and American Indian Tribalism*, 18.

70. Testimony of Diego Abeita, Jan. 30, 1931. United States, Survey of Conditions, 10086

71. Philp, "John Collier," 278–80.

72. Philp, 277–78.

73. Taylor, New Deal, 28.

74. Philp, "John Collier," 277.

75. Joseph E. Abeita to Collier, Isleta Pueblo, Jan. 3, 1936, and Superintendent to Bautista Zuni, Washington, DC, May 5, 1934, roll 15, frames 17, 19, 41, IPCC.

76. Testimony of Antonio Abeita, May 14, 1936, United States, 17428.

77. Testimony of Pablo Abeita, May 14, 1936, United States, 17431.

78. Philp, "John Collier," 278. Collier replied to Merkel's accusations, defending the IRA and noting that, at the time of writing the article, only Santa Clara Pueblo had adopted a constitution. Collier, "Collier Replies to Merkel," 422–26.

79. Smith, "Wheeler-Howard Act," 524–34.

80. Taylor, *New Deal*, 119–21, 128–29. Collier later admitted that the Navajo stock-reduction program was mishandled, with the smallest stock owners faring the worst.

81. Ebright and Hendricks, *Pueblo Sovereignty*, 155–56; Brayer, *Pueblo Indian Land Grants*; Aberle, *Pueblo Indians*, 71; French, *Factionalism in Isleta Pueblo*, 17–18.

82. Pablo Abeita at All Pueblo Council meeting, Dec. 11, 1926, Survey of Conditions, 4418; Sando, *Pueblo Profiles*, 181.

CHAPTER TEN

1. Pueblo of Isleta, SG Report Q, roll 17, frame 233; Ebright, Hendricks, and Hughes, *Four Square Leagues*, 247; Ebright and Hendricks, *Pueblo Sovereignty*, 155–56.

2. Parsons, *Isleta Paintings*, 230. The participants in the *pinitu* (spruce) Kachina dance hike to a shrine on the mountain where they spend the night praying and fasting, bringing spruce trees back to the pueblo where they are used in the dances in the following days.

3. Antonio Jojola and Pablo Abeita to George H. Howard, Isleta, Nov. 27, 1899, Indian Affairs

Collection, box 1, folder 7, Center for Southwest Research, University of New Mexico. The other important challenge facing the pueblo was the encroachment of the Peralta tract on the Lo de Padilla grant.

4. Ebright and Hendricks, *Pueblo Sovereignty*, 153–56.

5. Pablo Abeita to William H. Ketcham, Isleta Pueblo, Aug. 6, 1919, roll 93, frames 563–64, BCIM.

6. Ebright, Hendricks, and Hughes, *Four Square Leagues*, 137–39.

7. For the Isleta grant, see Ebright and Hendricks, *Pueblo Sovereignty*, 151 (map), 155; for the Sandia grant, see Ebright, Hendricks, and Hughes, *Four Square Leagues*, 137–40.

8. Francis C. Wilson to Pablo Abeita, Albuquerque, Dec. 2, 1910, FJCPA.

9. Pablo Abeita to William H. Ketcham, Isleta, Dec. 5, 1913, roll 67, frames 190–93, BCIM.

10. Pablo Abeita to William H. Ketcham, Isleta, May 20, 1914, roll 71, frames 805–8, BCIM.

11. Philip T. Lonergan to Pablo Abeita, Albuquerque, Dec. 30, 1914, FJCPA.

12. Ebright and Hendricks, *Pueblo Sovereignty*, 155–56.

13. Pablo Abeita to William H. Ketcham, Aug. 6, 1919, roll 93, frames 563–64, BCIM.

14. Ebright and Hendricks, *Pueblo Sovereignty*, 159–62.

15. Statement of Pablo Abeita, general meeting, Isleta, Dec. 15, 1921, roll 14, frame 111, IPCC.

16. Aberle, *Pueblo Indians of New Mexico*, 71.

APPENDIX SIX

1. Abeita, "An Indians's Appreciation," 316.

Bibliography

ARCHIVAL MATERIAL

Archives of the Archdiocese of Santa Fe, Isleta Marriages
Autry Museum of the American West, Braun Research Library Collection
Bernalillo Collection, Loretto Indian School, New Mexico Photo Archives, New Mexico History Museum
Bureau of Catholic Indian Missions, Marquette University
Frank Jiron Collection of the Pablo Abeita Papers, Isleta Pueblo
Isleta Correspondence, 1911–1922, Indian Pueblo Cultural Center
National Archives and Records Administration, Washington, DC, and Denver, Record Group 75

GOVERNMENT DOCUMENTS

Annual Report of the Department of the Interior for the Fiscal Year ended June 30, 1905. Washington, DC: GPO, 1906.
Annual Report of the Director of the Census to the Secretary of Commerce for the Fiscal Year Ended June 30, 1921. Washington, DC: Government Printing Office, 1921.
Committee on Indian Affairs, House of Representatives. Hearings of the Subcommittee of the Committee on Indian Affairs, House of Representatives. Washington, DC: Government Printing Office, 1920.
Senate Committee on Indian Affairs. Hearings on the Bursum Bill. Washington, DC: Government Printing Office, 1923.
Senate Committee on Indian Affairs Hearings. Survey of the Conditions of the Indians of the United States. Washington, DC: Government Printing Office, 1936.

PUBLISHED SOURCES

Aberle, Sophie D. *The Pueblo Indians of New Mexico: Their Land, Economy and Civil Organization.* New York: American Anthropological Association; Kraus Reprint Co., 1969.
Abeita, Pablo. "An Indian's Appreciation." *The Indian Sentinel* 2, no. 7 (July 1919–1920): 316.
Adams, David Wallace. "Beyond Bleakness: The Brighter Side of Indian Boarding Schools, 1870–1940." In *Boarding School Blues: Revisiting American Education Experiences,* edited by Clifford E. Trafzer, Jean A. Keller, and Lorene Sisquoc. Lincoln, NB: University of Nebraska Press, 2006.
Almirall, Leon V. "Tribesman of Isleta Pueblo." *Desert Magazine* 3 (Oct. 1940): 15–16.
Barsh, Russel Lawrence. "The American Heart of Darkness: The 1913 Expedition for American Indian Citizenship." *Great Plains Quarterly* 13, no. 2 (Spring 1993): 91–115.
Bernstein, Bruce, and W. Jackson Rushing. *Modern by Tradition: American Indian Painting in the Studio Style.* Santa Fe: Museum of New Mexico Press, 1995.
Biddle, Cordelia Frances. *Saint Katharine: The Life of Katharine Drexel.* Yardley, PA: Westholme Publishing, 2014.
Bingham, Edwin R. *Charles F. Lummis: Editor of the Southwest.* San Marino, CA: The Huntington Library, 1955.

Bolger, Eileen. *Pamphlet Describing M1304: Records Created by BIA Field Agencies Having Jurisdiction over the Pueblo Indians, 1874–1900.* Washington, DC: National Archives and Records Administration, 1988.

Brayer, Herbert O. *Pueblo Indian Land Grants of the "Rio Abajo."* Albuquerque: University of New Mexico Press, 1939.

Bryan, Howard. *Albuquerque Remembered.* Albuquerque: University of New Mexico Press, 2006.

Child, Brenda J. "Indian Education, American Education." In *Native Universe: Voices of Indian America,* edited by Gerald McMaster and Clifford E. Trafzer, 161–73. Washington, DC: National Museum of the American Indian, Smithsonian Institution, 2004.

Collier, John. "Collier Replies to Merkel." *American Anthropology* 46 (July–Sept. 1944): 422–26.

Connell-Szasz, Margaret. *Education and the American Indian: The Road to Self-Determination Since 1928.* Albuquerque: University of New Mexico Press, 1999.

Crandall, Maurice. *These People Have Always Been a Republic: Indigenous Electorates in the US-Mexico Borderlands, 1598–1912.* Chapel Hill: University of North Carolina Press, 2019.

Crane, Leo. *Desert Drums: The Pueblo Indians of New Mexico.* Boston: Little, Brown and Co., 1928.

Curtis, Edward S. *The North American Indian Being a Series of Volumes Picturing and Describing the Indians of the United States, the Dominions of Canada, and Alaska.* Vol. 16, edited by Frederick Webb Hodge. Seattle, WA: E. S. Curtis, 1926.

Dailey, Martha LaCroix. "Symbolism and Significance of the Lincoln Canes for the Pueblos of New Mexico," *New Mexico Historical Review* 69, no. 2 (April 1994): 127–45.

De Marco, Marisa. "Education's Champion: Native American Elder Receives Top Honors at UNM." *Weekly Alibi,* May 20–26, 2010.

Deloria, Vine, Jr., and Clifford M. Lytle. *American Indian, American Justice.* Austin: University of Texas Press, 1983.

Dean, Robert K. "King Maker in the Back Room: Max Frost and Hardball Politics in the Late Territorial Period." In *All Trails Lead to Santa Fe,* 317–35. Santa Fe, NM: Sunstone Press, 2010.

Downes, Randolph C. "A Crusade for Indian Reform, 1922–1934." *Mississippi Valley Historical Review* 32, no. 3 (Dec 1945): 331–54.

Docher, Rev. Anton. "The Quaint Indian Pueblo of Isleta." *Santa Fe Magazine* 7, no. 7 (June 1913): 30.

Dozier, Edward P. "Factionalism at Santa Clara Pueblo." *Ethnology* 5, no. 2 (April 1966): 172–85.

Dublán, Manuel, and José María Lozano. *Legislación mexicana.* Mexico City: Imprenta del Comercio a cargo de Dublán y Lozano, 1876.

Ebright, Malcolm. *Advocates for the Oppressed: Hispanos, Indians, Genízaros, and Their Land in New Mexico.* Albuquerque: University of New Mexico Press, 2014.

———. "Benjamin Thomas in New Mexico, 1872–1883: Indian Agents as Advocates for Native Americans." *New Mexico Historical Review* 93, no. 3 (Summer 2018): 303–31.

Ebright, Malcolm, and Alfredo Montoya. "Twisting the Law on the Sebastian Martín Grant: Its Formation, Dismantling, and Revitalization." *New Mexico Historical Review* 96, no. 2 (2021): 131–79.

Ebright, Malcolm, and Rick Hendricks. *Pueblo Sovereignty: Indian Land in New Mexico and Texas.* Norman: University of Oklahoma Press, 2019.

Ebright, Malcolm, Rick Hendricks, and Richard Hughes. *Four Square Leagues: Pueblo Indian Land in New Mexico.* Albuquerque: University of New Mexico Press, 2014.

Ewen, Alexander, and Jeffrey Wollock. *Encyclopedia of the American Indian in the Twentieth Century*. New York, NY: Facts on File, 2014.

Fear-Segal, Jacqueline. *White Man's Club: School, Race, and the Struggle of Indian Acculturation*. Lincoln, NB: University of Nebraska Press, 2007.

Fiske, Turbesé Lummis, and Keith Lummis. *Charles F. Lummis: The Man and His West*. Norman: University of Oklahoma Press, 1975.

French, David H. *Factionalism in Isleta Pueblo*. New York: J. J. Augustin, 1948.

Frost, Richard H. "Photography and the Pueblo Indians of New Mexico, 1870-1930." *New Mexico Historical Review* 84, no. 2 (2009): 187-232.

———. "The Pueblo Indian Smallpox Epidemic in New Mexico, 1898-1899." *Bulletin of the History of Medicine*, 64, no. 3 (Fall 1990): 431-32.

———. *The Railroad and the Pueblo Indians: The Impact of the Atchison, Topeka, and Santa Fe on the Pueblos of the Rio Grande, 1880-1930*. Salt Lake City: University of Utah Press, 2015.

———. "The Romantic Inflation of Pueblo Culture." *American West* 17, no. 1 (Jan.-Feb. 1980): 5-9, 56-60.

Goemaere, Pierre. *Across America with the King of the Belgians*. New York: E.P. Dutton, 1921.

Gordon, Dudley. "El Alisal: The House that Lummis Built." *Historical Society of Southern California Quarterly* 35, no. 1 (March 1953): 19-28.

Gram, John R. *Education at the Edge of Empire: Negotiating Pueblo Identity in New Mexico's Indian Boarding Schools*. Seattle: University of Washington Press, 2015.

Hagan, William T. "Daniel M. Browning, 1893-97." In *The Commissioners of Indian Affairs, 1824-1977*, edited by Robert M. Kvasnicka and Herman J. Viola, 205-9. Lincoln: University of Nebraska Press, 1979.

———. *Indian Police and Judges: Experiments in Acculturation and Control*. Lincoln: University of Nebraska Press, 1966.

———. *Quanah Parker, Comanche Chief*. Norman: University of Oklahoma Press, 1995.

———. "Quanah Parker, Indian Judge." *El Palacio* 69, no. 1 (Spring 1962): 30-39.

———. *Theodore Roosevelt and Six Friends of the Indian*. Norman: University of Oklahoma Press, 1997.

Hall, G. Emlen. *Four Leagues of Pecos: A Legal History of the Pecos Grant, 1800-1933*. Albuquerque: University of New Mexico Press, 1984.

Harring, Sidney L. *Crow Dog's Case: American Indian Sovereignty, Tribal Law, and United States Law in the Nineteenth Century*. Cambridge, MA: Cambridge University Press, 1994.

Haskett, Robert S. "Living in Two Worlds: Cultural Continuity and Change among Cuernavaca's Colonial Indigenous Ruling Elite." *Ethnohistory* 35, no. 1 (Winter 1988): 131-50.

Hodge, Frederick Webb, ed. *Handbook of American Indians North of Mexico*. Towtowa, NJ: Rowman and Littlefield, 1975.

Horgan, Paul. *Lamy of Santa Fe*. New York: Farrar, Straus, and Giroux, 1975.

Houlihan, Patrick T., and Betsy E. Houlihan. *Lummis in the Pueblos*. Flagstaff, AZ: Northland Press, 1986.

Hyer, Joel R. *We Are Not Savages: Native Americans in Southern California and the Pala Reservation, 1840-1920*. East Lansing: Michigan State University Press, 2001.

Hyer, Sally. *One House, One Voice, One Heart: Native American Education at the Santa Fe Indian School*. Santa Fe: Museum of New Mexico Press, 1990.

"Indian Gifts to Belgian King." *Indian Sentinel* 2, no. 1 (Jan. 1920): 23-24.

Jojola, Theodore S. "Modernization and Pueblo Lifeways: Isleta Pueblo." In *Pueblo Style and Regional Architecture*, edited by Nicholas C. Markovich, Wolfgang F. E. Preiser, and Fred G. Strum, 78–99. New York: Von Nostrand Reinhold, 1990.

———. "On Revision and Revisionism: American Indian Representations in New Mexico." *American Indian Quarterly* 20, no. 1 (Winter 1996): 41–47.

Kelcher, Julia, and Elsie Ruth Chant. *The Padre of Isleta*. Santa Fe, NM: Sunstone Press, facsimile of 1940 edition, 2009.

Kroeber, Alfred L. "Zuni Kin and Clan." *Anthropological Papers of the American Museum of Natural History* 18, no. 2 (1917): 39–204.

Kvasnicka, Robert M., and Herman J. Viola, eds. *The Commissioners of Indian Affairs, 1824–1977*. Lincoln: University of Nebraska Press, 1979.

La Gaceta: El Boletín del Corral del Santa Fe Westerners. "St. Catherine's School." *La Gaceta: El Boletín del Corral del Santa Fe Westerners* 3 (Oct. 1965): 1–2.

Lamadrid, Enrique. "Ig/Noble Savages of New Mexico's Silent Cinema, 1912–1914." *Spectator* 13, no. 1 (Fall 1992): 13–23.

Lawrence, D. H. "Certain Americans and an Englishman." *New York Times*, Dec. 24, 1922.

Lindstrom, Richard. "'Not from the Land Side, but from the Flag Side,' Native American Responses to the Wanamaker Expedition of 1913." *Journal of Social History* 30, no. 1 (Autumn 1996): 209–27.

Littlefield, Robert S., and Jane A. Ball. "Factionalism and Argumentation: Case Study of the Indigenous Communication Practices of Jemez Pueblo." *Argumentation and Advocacy* 41 (Fall 2004): 87–101.

Lomawaima, K. Tsianina. *They Called It Prairie Light: The Story of Chilocco Indian School*. Lincoln: University of Nebraska Press, 1994.

Lummis, Charles F. "The Antelope Boy." In *The Man Who Married the Moon and Other Pueblo Indian Folk Stories*, edited by Charles F. Lummis, 12–21. New York: Century, 1894.

———. *The Man Who Married the Moon and Other Pueblo Indian Folk Stories*. New York: Century, 1894.

———. "In the Lion's Den." *The Land of Sunshine: The Magazine of California and the West* 13 (June–December 1900): 113-19.

———. *King of the Broncos and Other Stories of New Mexico*. Amsterdam, NL: Fredonia Books, 2004.

———. *Letters from the Southwest*. Tucson: University of Arizona Press, 1989.

———. "The Town of the Snake Girl." In *The Man Who Married the Moon and Other Pueblo Indian Folk Stories*, edited by Charles F. Lummis. New York: Century, 1894.

Lummis, Turbesé, and Keith Lummis. *Charles F. Lummis: The Man and His West*. Norman: University of Oklahoma Press, 1975.

Marriott, Alice. *Maria, the Potter of San Ildefonso*. Norman: University of Oklahoma Press, 1948.

Melzer, Richard. *Fred Harvey Houses of the Southwest*. Charleston, SC: Arcadia Publishing, 2008.

———, ed. *Sunshine and Shadow in New Mexico's Past*. Los Ranchos, NM: Rio Grande Press, 2011.

———. "When D.W. Griffith and Mary Pickford Invaded Isleta: The Making of 'A Pueblo Legend' in 1912." *New Mexico Historical Review* 95, no. 1 (Winter 2020): 33–66.

Meriam, Lewis. *The Problem of Indian Administration*. Baltimore, MD: Johns Hopkins University Press, 1928.

Momaday, N. Scott. *Three Plays: The Indolent Boys, Children of the Sun, The Moon in Two Windows*. Norman: University of Oklahoma Press, 2007.

Morgan, Thomas J. "Rules for Indian Courts." In *Americanizing the American Indians: Writings by the Friends of the Indian, 1880–1900*, edited by Francis Paul Prucha, 300–305. Cambridge, MA: Harvard University Press, 1973.

Murphy, Lawrence R., ed. *Indian Agent in New Mexico: The Journal of W. F. M. Arny, 1870*. Santa Fe, NM: Stagecoach Press, 1967.

"Necrology [Pablo Abeita]." *New Mexico Historical Review* 39, no. 1 (Jan. 1941): 120–22.

Nichols, David. *Lincoln and the Indians: Civil War Policy and Politics*. Saint Paul: Minnesota Historical Society Press, 2012.

Norcini, Marilyn. "The Political Process of Factionalism and Self-Governance at Santa Clara Pueblo, New Mexico." *Proceedings of the American Philosophical Society* 149, no. 4 (Dec. 2005): 544–90.

O'Neil, Colleen. *Working the Navajo Way: Labor and Culture in the Twentieth Century*. Lawrence: University Press of Kansas, 2005.

O'Neil, Floyd. "Hiram Price, 1881–1885." In *The Commissioners of Indian Affairs, 1824–1977*, edited by Robert M. Kvasnicka and Herman J. Viola, 173–79. Lincoln: University of Nebraska Press, 1979.

Out West 17, no. 2 (August 1902): 215.

Owens, Sister M. Lilliana. "Historical Sketch of Bernalillo Public High School, 1891–1945." *Records of the American Catholic Historical Society of Philadelphia* 57 (June 1946): 73–87.

Parsons, Elsie Clews. *The Pueblo of Isleta, New Mexico*. Albuquerque, NM: Calvin Horn Publisher, Inc., 1974.

———. *Isleta Paintings*. Washington, DC: Smithsonian Institution, 1962.

Peters, Kurt M. "Continuing Identity: Laguna Pueblo Railroaders in Richmond, California." *American Indian Culture and Research Journal* 22, no. 4 (1998): 187–98.

Philp, Kenneth R. "Albert B. Fall and the Protest from the Pueblos, 1921–23." *Arizona and the West* 12, no. 3 (Autumn 1970): 254.

———. "John Collier, 1933–1945." In *The Commissioners of Indian Affairs, 1824–1977*, edited by Robert M. Kvasnicka and Herman J. Viola, 273–82. Lincoln: University of Nebraska Press, 1979.

———. *John Collier's Crusade for Indian Reform, 1920–1954*. Tucson: University of Arizona Press, 1977.

Pickford, Mary. "My Own Story." Ladies Home Journal (Aug. 1923): 121.

Powell, Kimberly. "Agricultural Schedules of the United States Census." ThoughtCo. Accessed March 18, 2018. https://www.thoughtco.com/agricultural-schedules-united-states-census-1422758.

Prince, L. Bradford. *Spanish Mission Churches of New Mexico*. Cedar Rapids, IA: The Torch Press, 1915.

Putney, Diane T. "Robert Grosvenor Valentine, 1909–12." In *The Commissioners of Indian Affairs, 1824–1977*, edited by Robert M. Kvasnicka and Herman J. Viola, 233–42. Lincoln: University of Nebraska Press, 1979.

Pritzker, Barry. *A Native American Encyclopedia: History, Culture, and Peoples*. Oxford: Oxford University Press, 2000.

Prucha, Francis Paul. *American Indian Policy in Crisis: Christian Reformers and the Indians, 1865–1900*. Norman: University of Oklahoma Press, 1976.

———. *The Churches and the Indian Schools, 1888–1912*. Norman: University of Oklahoma Press, 1979.

———. "Thomas Jefferson Morgan, 1889–93." In *The Commissioners of Indian Affairs, 1824–1977*, edited by Robert M. Kvasnicka and Herman J. Viola, 193–203. Lincoln: University of Nebraska Press, 1979.

"Realm of the Retailer." *American Lumberman* (Aug. 2, 1924): 42–44.

Republican Review. Dec. 17, 1872, and Nov. 8, 1873.

Sando, Joe S. "José Alcario Montoya." In *Pueblo Profiles: Cultural Identity through Centuries of Change*, by Joe S. Sando, 50–55. Santa Fe, NM: Clear Light Publishers, 1998.

———. *Pueblo Profiles: Cultural Identity through Centuries of Change*. Santa Fe, NM: Clear Light Publishers, 1998.

———. "Sotero Ortiz." In *Pueblo Profiles: Cultural Identity through Centuries of Change*, by Joe S. Sando, 33–39. Santa Fe, NM: Clear Light Publishers, 1998.

Scurlock, Dan. *From Rio to Sierra: An Environmental History of the Middle Rio Grande Basin*. Fort Collins, CO: Rocky Mountain Research Station, 1998.

Simmons, Marc. *Albuquerque: A Narrative History*. Albuquerque: University of New Mexico Press, 1982.

Smith, Michael T. "The Wheeler-Howard Act of 1934: The Indian New Deal." *Journal of the West* (July 1971): 521–34.

Smith, Sherry. *Reimagining Indians: Native Americans Through Anglo Eyes: 1880–1940*. New York: Oxford University Press, 2002.

Spicer, Edward. *Cycles of Conquest: The Impact of Spain, Mexico, and the United States on the Indians of the Southwest, 1533–1960*. Tucson: University of Arizona Press, 1986.

Starr, Kevin. *Inventing the Dream: California through the Progressive Era*. New York: Oxford University Press, 1985.

St. Michael's College. *Seventy-five Years of Service, 1859–1934: An Historical Sketch of St. Michael's College*. Las Vegas, NM: Smith-Hursh Publishing Co., 1934.

Stout, Mary A. *Native American Boarding Schools*. Westport, CT: Greenwood Publishing, 2012.

Sutter, L. M. *New Mexico Baseball: Miners, Outlaws, Indians, and Isotopes, 1880 to the Present*. Jefferson, NC: McFarland and Co., 2010.

Svenningsen, Robert. *Preliminary Inventory of the Pueblo Records Created by Field Offices of the Bureau of Indian Affairs, Record Group 75*. Washington, DC: National Archives and Records Service, General Services Administration, 1980.

Sze, Corinne P. "Application for Registration [on] the New Mexico State Register of Cultural Properties for Saint Catherine's Industrial Indian School." Santa Fe, NM: Historic Preservation Division, 1993.

———. "Gone but Not Forgotten: St. Catherine's Industrial Indian School." *Bulletin of the Historic Santa Fe Foundation* 30, no. 1 (summer 2003): 6–9.

Taylor, Graham D. *The New Deal and American Indian Tribalism: The Administration of the Indian Reorganization Act, 1934–45*. Lincoln: University of Nebraska Press, 1980.

Teller, Henry M. "Courts of Indian Offenses." In *Americanizing the American Indians: Writings by the Friends of the Indian, 1880–1900*, edited by Francis Paul Prucha, 295–99. Cambridge, MA: Harvard University Press, 1973.

Telling, Irving. "Ramah, New Mexico, 1876–1900: An Historical Episode with Some Value Analysis." *Utah Historical Quarterly* 21, no. 2 (April 1953): 117–36.

Thompson, Mark. *American Character: The Curious Life of Charles Fletcher Lummis and the Rediscovery of the Southwest*. New York: Arcade Publishing, 2001.

Tiller, Veronica. *Tiller's Guide to Indian Country: Economic Profiles of American Indian Reservations*. Albuquerque: Bow Arrow Publishing, 2006.

Trafzer, Clifford E. *Boarding School Blues: Revisiting American Indian Educational Experiences*. Lincoln: University of Nebraska Press, 2006.

Treuer, David. *The Heartbeat of Wounded Knee: Native America from 1890 to the Present*. New York: Riverhead Books, 2019.

United States. *Survey of Conditions of the Indians in the United States, Hearings before the Subcommittee of the Committee on Indian Affairs*. Washington, DC: Government Printing Office, 1931.

Victory, John P., Edward L. Bartlett, Thomas N. Wilkerson, Jose D. Sena , and George A. Johnson. *Compiled Laws of New Mexico: In Accordance with an Act of the Legislature, Approved March 16th , 1897. Including the Constitution of the United States, The Treaty of Guadalupe Hidalgo, the Gadsden Treaty, the Original Act Organizing the Territory, the Organic Acts as Now in Force, the Original Kearny Code, and a List Of Laws Enacted since the Compilation of 1884 as well as those in that Work*. Santa Fe: New Mexican Printing Company, 1897.

Weigle, Marta. *Alluring New Mexico, Engineering New Mexico, 1821–2001*. Santa Fe: Museum of New Mexico Press, 2010.

Weigle, Marta, and Peter White. *The Lore of New Mexico*. Albuquerque: University of New Mexico Press, 1988.

Wenger, Tisa. *We Have a Religion: The 1920s Pueblo Indian Dance Controversy and American Religious Freedom*. Chapel Hill: University of North Carolina Press, 2009.

Will de Chaparro, Martina. "The Laguna Migration of 1879: Protestant, Catholic, and Native Visions." In *Sunshine and Shadow in New Mexico's Past: The U.S. Territorial Period, 1848–1912*, edited by Richard Melzer, 85–106. Los Ranchos, NM: Rio Grande Press, 2011.

UNPUBLISHED WORKS

Bohme, Frederick G. "A History of the Italians in New Mexico." PhD diss. University of New Mexico, 1958.

Guggino, Patricia Burke. "Pablo Abeita (1871–1940): Cultural Broker Between Isleta Pueblo in New Mexico and the United States Government." Master's thesis. University of New Mexico, 1995.

Hyer, Sally. "Remembering Santa Fe Indian School, 1890-1990." PhD diss. University of New Mexico, 1994.

Jojola, Theodore S. and Jayrm Kushner. "Charles F. Lummis and American Indian Policy." Article for Charles F. Lummis Centennial Symposium, Southwest Museum, Los Angeles, CA., 1985.

Lummis, Suzanne. "The Good, the Bold, and the Ornery." In "Charles F. Lummis, 'As I Remember,'" edited by Richard Melzer. Unpublished manuscript in authors' possession.

Marshall, Mike. "Isleta Pueblo Installation Project Reveals New Information About Early Isleta Pueblo History." Unpublished manuscript in authors' possession.

Newland, Bryan. "Federal Indian Boarding School Initiative: Investigative Report, May 2022." SRCA.

McKinney, Lillie G. "History of the Albuquerque Indian School." Master's thesis. University of New Mexico, 1934.

Montgomery-McGovern, Janet Blair. "General Survey of Isleta Pueblo with Especial Reference to Acute Transitional Conditions." Master's thesis. University of New Mexico, 1932.

Owey, Orville N., and David H. Getches. *Indian Courts and the Future*. Report of the National American Indian Judges Association, 1978. Manuscript in authors' possession.

INTERVIEWS BY AUTHORS

Abeita, James, June 14, 2019, Isleta Pueblo

Abeita, William, June 14, 2019, Isleta Pueblo

Jaramillo, Ernest, May 24, 2019, Isleta Pueblo

Jiron, Randy, May 24, 2019, Isleta Pueblo; June 18, 2019, Isleta Pueblo

Jojola, Theodore "Ted," May 3, 2019, Albuquerque

Lucero, Ben, May 3, 2019, Isleta Pueblo

Zuni, Max, May 24, 2019, Isleta Pueblo

Index

Page numbers in italic text indicate illustrations.

Ryan, Raymond R. (New Mexico judge), 103, 105
Ryan, W. Carson (coauthor of Meriam Report), 79

Salpointe, Jean-Baptiste (Santa Fe archbishop, 1884–1894), 77, 81
Sanchez, Blaine (Isleta Pueblo lieutenant governor, 2021–2022), viii
Sandia Pueblo (Tiwa), 11, 18, 43, 54, 77
Sando, Joe (Jemez Pueblo historian), 15, 22
Sandoval case, 9, 113–18; defined, 151; Pueblo delegation to Washington, DC, and, 110
San Felipe Pueblo (Keres), 4, 19, 31, 53–54; bridge at, 14, 47, 48, 49, 139; education and, 38, 77; railroad and, 64
Sangre, Felipe, 91, 142
San Juan (Ohkay Owingeh) Pueblo (Tewa), 10; education and, 77; Sandoval case and, 113–14
Santa Ana Pueblo (Keres), 19; education and, 77; land issues and, 111, 113, 153n33
Santa Clara Pueblo (Tewa), 14; education and, 77, 84; Indian Reorganization Act and, 153n45, 171n78
Santa Fe Indian School, 57, 67, 75, 80, 82, 84; composition of student body of, 81, 157n6
Santo Domingo Pueblo (Keres), 11, 19; ban on photography and, 37; flood at, 47; meeting of All Pueblo Council at, 31, 118–19, 120; railroad accidents and, 70
Sells, Cato (Commissioner of Indian Affairs, 1913–1921), 45, 131
Senate Committee on Indian Affairs, 1, 47, 51, 64, 86, 121–22, 123, 125
Seonia, Charles, 11
Shafer, John (Isleta agency farmer), 103, 106, 144, 147, 168n81
Shattuck, Paul (Agnes Shattuck Dill's father), 58, 59, 75, 85
shinny, 58, 62–63
Sisters of Loretto: schools staffed by, 47, 55, 57, 80, 81, 82, 92, 164n41, 166n36. See also Indian Industrial School
Smith, Edward Parmelee (Commissioner of Indian Affairs, 1873–1875), 131
Smith, Howard V. (Isleta Pueblo agency farmer), 69, 91, 105, 106, 146, 147
Smith, John Q. (Commissioner of Indian Affairs, 1875–1877), 131
Snyder, Homer Peter (Congressional representative from New York, 1915–1925), 118, 159n27
Sockalexis, Louis (Penobscot baseball player), 58

Solignac, Gustave Louis (attorney for Isleta), 110. See also Court of Private Land Claims
St. Catherine's Indian School, 55, 56, 57, 74, 80, 83, 157n6, 164n40, n54, n57; founding of, 82; Katharine Drexel and, 82; Mary Ruth Aquino and, 84; Patrick Toya and, 84, 164n57
Stevenson, James D. (United States Geological Survey officer), 37
Stevenson, Matilda Coxe (ethnologist), 37
St. Michael's College, 17, 19, 55, 74, 153n7, n8, 154n10, 163n1

Tafoya, Teofilo, 82
Taft, William Howard, 41, 43, 44, 155n36
Taos Pueblo (Tiwa), 71; education and, 80, 92; Isleta Pueblo and, 1, 2; Sandoval case and, 115
Taylor, Nathaniel Greene (Commissioner of Indian Affairs, 1867–1869), 131
Teller, Henry Moore (Secretary of the Interior, 1882–1885), 86, 165n1
Teller, Verna Williamson (Isleta Pueblo governor, 1987–1990), viii
Tesuque Pueblo (Tewa): Fence War at, 118
Thomas, Benjamin (Indian agent, 1872–1882), 38, 65, 71, 93
Tipton, Will (Court of Private Land Claims translator), 127
Towers, Lemuel (superintendent), 107, 130
Toya, Patrick, 84
Trowbridge, Roland E. (Commissioner of Indian Affairs, 1880–1881), 131
Trujillo, Damasio, 144
Trujillo, Dominga, 144
Trujillo, Juan, 70
Twitchell, Ralph Emerson (New Mexico attorney, historian, and politician), 37, 118, 119

United States Indian Pueblo Council, 121. See also All Indian Pueblo Council

Valentine, Robert Grosvenor (Commissioner of Indian Affairs, 1909–1912), 49, 131, 138, 159n19
Van Devanter, Willis (associate justice of the United States Supreme Court, 1911–1937), 117
Vargas, Diego de (New Mexico governor, 1688–1697, 1703–1704): resettlement of Isleta and, 2
Vázquez de Coronado, Francisco, 20–21
Veeder, Elmer (attorney for Isleta Pueblo), 108; claims for livestock losses to Navajos by, 108–12, 169n11, n17
Velarde, Pablita (Santa Clara Pueblo artist), 83–84, 164n37